A Birder's Guide

to the

Texas Coast

A BIRDER'S GUIDE

TO THE

TEXAS COAST

by
Harold R. Holt
1993

Revised from original text by
James A. Lane

American Birding Association, Inc.

Library of Congress Catalog Card Number: 93-70809

ISBN Number: 1-878788-03-5

Fourth Edition
2   3   4   5   6   7   8   9
Printed in the United States of America

Publisher
American Birding Association, Inc.
William J. Graber, III, Chair, Publications Committee

Series Editor
Paul J. Baicich

Associate Editors
Cindy Lippincott and Bob Berman

Copy Editor
Hugh Willoughby

Layout and Typography
Bob Berman; produced using Ventura Publisher, Windows Ver. 4.1

Maps
Cindy Lippincott; produced using CorelDRAW version 3

Cover Photography
front cover: Whooping Cranes; Bradley Steiner
back cover: White-tailed Hawk; Brian K. Wheeler

Illustrations
F.P. Bennett; Shawneen E. Finnegan; Charles H. Gambill; Gail Diane Luckner

Distributed by
American Birding Association Sales
PO Box 6599
Colorado Springs, Colorado 80934-6599 USA
Tel: (800) 634-7736 (USA & Canada) or (719) 578-0607
Fax: (800) 247-3329 (USA & Canada) or (719) 471-4722
abasales@abasales.com

Distributed by
Subbuteo Natural History Books, Ltd.
Pistyll Farm, Nercwys, Nr Mold, Flintshire, CH7 4EW
United Kingdom
Tel: +1352-756551; Fax: +1352-756004
sales@subbooks.demon.co.uk

This book is dedicated
to those tireless workers
in non-governmental organizations
who strive to preserve valuable
wildlife habitats on the Texas Coast.
Among their organizations are
the Texas Ornithological Society,
the National Audubon Society,
The Nature Conservancy,
and, especially,
the Houston Audubon Society.

ACKNOWLEDGEMENTS

The Texas Coast is such a huge area that I would have been completely lost in trying to write about it without the help of the many local birders. I am sure that most of them could have done a better job, but instead they spent many days showing me their favorite areas and many hours checking my manuscript. I shall always treasure the memory of those precious days spent afield with such friendly and wonderful people.

So wrote James A. Lane in the very first edition of this book, written in 1973. Later he was assisted by John L. Tveten in two other editions.

By 1982, I began to relieve Jim Lane in doing revisions of his many helpful birdfinding guides. I wrote the revisions for this guide for the Texas Coast in 1984 and 1988, a task that has been continually rewarding. As written above, the job has always been made easier through the help of others. Those who have helped Jim Lane, John Tveten and me in past editions are listed below:

Richard Albert, Margaret Anderson, Tess Barry, Gene Blacklock, Russ Clapper, Fred Collins, Bessie Cornelius, Marilyn Crane, Larry Ditto, Victor Emanuel, Christine Enright, Ted Eubanks, Jr., Ben Feltner, Orlyn Gaddis, Sarah Gordon, William Graber, Sharon Hackleman, Eric Hall, Dan Hardy, Wes Hetrick, Ned Hudson, Ed Jackson, Horace Jeter, Margaret Jones, Katrina Ladwig, Violetta Lane, Ray and Terry Little, Kay McCracken, Ernest McDaniels, Elric McHenry, Robert Moore, Norma Oates, Andy O'Neill, Ernest Ortiz, Dennis Shepler, Jerry Smith, Larry Smith, Linda Snyder, Jerry and Nancy Strickling, George Unland, George Venatta, Doris Winship, and Fern Zimmerman.

I would like to thank everyone who has submitted records and suggested changes for this new edition. It is only with their help that I can hope to keep the book current and meaningful. I particularly want to recognize the following: Ken Able, Lynne Aldrich, Mike Austin, Betty Baker, Sharon Bartels, Jim Bell, Alan H. Chaney, Charlie Clark, Jenny Kate Collins, Arlie and Mel Cooksey, Bessie Cornelius, Arch Dillard, Kim Eckert, Mark A. Elwonger, Ted Eubanks, Jr., Craig Faanes, Mike and Rose Farmer, Peter Gottschling, William Graber, Jesse Grantham, Brent Giezentanner, Marcella Jenkins, Jane Kittleman, Greg W. Lasley, Jon and Glenda Llast, Ray Little, Gail Diane Luckner, Martha Micks, Jim Morgan, Allan Mueller, Paul C. Palmer, R. H. Payne, Dwight Peake, Fr. Tom Pincelli, Kirby Stafford, Ro Wauer, Doris Wyman, and Phyllis Yochem.

Artwork by F.P. Bennett, Shawneen Finnegan, Charles H. Gambill, and Gail Diane Luckner graces these pages. The fine cover photographs by Bradley Steiner and Brian K. Wheeler are much appreciated, as are the black-and-white photos by others. I am especially grateful to Cindy Lippincott, who drew the maps and assisted in editing, to Bob Berman for his technical skills, and to Hugh Willoughby for his invaluable copy-editing. Paul J. Baicich, the ABA Birdfinding Guide series editor, performed his tasks with both speed and care.

Of course, I want to keep this book current. Toward this goal, I wish to ask for corrections and additions from anyone who uses this book.

Harold Holt
Denver, Colorado
January 1993

Scissor-tailed Flycatcher
Charles H. Gambill

American Birding Association Code of Ethics

We, the Membership of the American Birding Association, believe that all birders have an obligation at all times to protect wildlife, the natural environment, and the rights of others. We therefore pledge ourselves to provide leadership in meeting this obligation by adhering to the following general guidelines of good birding behavior.

I. Birders must always act in ways that do not endanger the welfare of birds or other wildlife.

In keeping with this principle, we will

- Observe and photograph birds without knowingly disturbing them in any significant way.
- Avoid chasing or repeatedly flushing birds.
- Only sparingly use recordings and similar methods of attracting birds and not use these methods in heavily birded areas.
- Keep an appropriate distance from nests and nesting colonies so as not to disturb them or expose them to danger.
- Refrain from handling birds or eggs unless engaged in recognized research activities.

II. Birders must always act in ways that do not harm the natural environment.

In keeping with this principle, we will

- Stay on existing roads, trails, and pathways whenever possible to avoid trampling or otherwise disturbing fragile habitat.
- Leave all habitat as we found it.

III. Birders must always respect the rights of others.

In keeping with this principle, we will

- Respect the privacy and property of others by observing "No Trespassing" signs and by asking permission to enter private or posted lands.
- Observe all laws and the rules and regulations which govern public use of birding areas.
- Practice common courtesy in our contacts with others. For example, we will limit our requests for information, and we will make them at reasonable hours of the day.
- Always behave in a manner that will enhance the image of the birding community in the eyes of the public.

IV. Birders in groups should assume special responsibilities.

As group members, we will

- Take special care to alleviate the problems and disturbances that are multiplied when more people are present.
- Act in consideration of the group's interest, as well as our own.
- Support by our actions the responsibility of the group leader(s) for the conduct of the group.

As group leaders, we will

- Assume responsibility for the conduct of the group.
- Learn and inform the group of any special rules, regulations, or conduct applicable to the area or habitat being visited.
- Limit groups to a size that does not threaten the environment or the peace and tranquility of others.
- Teach others birding ethics by our words and example.

TABLE OF CONTENTS

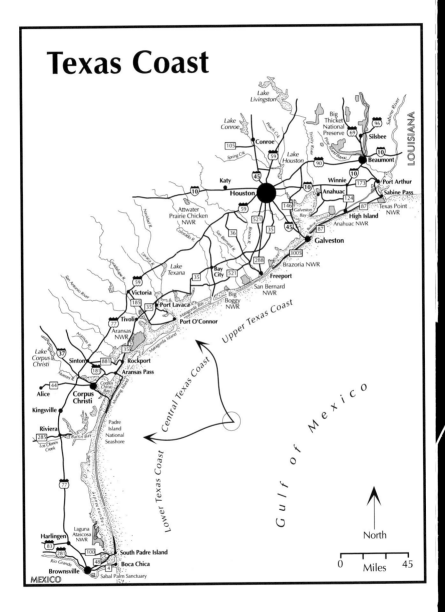

Texas Coast

INTRODUCTION

One of the greatest thrills of birding is to be on the Gulf coast in spring when a "norther" blows in and it rains birds! The fields, bushes, and trees may be "dripping" with tanagers, orioles, buntings, kingbirds, thrushes, flycatchers, vireos, and warblers, warblers, warblers. On these spectacular occasions, it is possible to see more birds in an hour than in a couple of years of normal birding. However, the ingredients that make up this phenomenon have to be just right.

Most trans-Gulf migrants are nocturnal, and will launch themselves from the Yucatan and points south after sunset. After a night's flight these long-distance migrants find themselves at dawn over water, and reach the coast by mid-morning at the earliest. (This means that early-morning birding along the immediate coast cannot be the best time for finding trans-Gulf migrant landbirds. Most ironically, as Ken Able has pointed out in a recent article in Birding, good weather for migrating birds—from the bird's point of view—is the poorest for finding migrants in the field.) But the weather is not always "ideal." Birds en route to the Texas Gulf coast may encounter a cold-front over water. Encountering such a front with its showers and opposing winds can increase the difficulty of the crossing. This kind of front will produce weary birds struggling in from the Gulf and landing on the first perch available. If the front lingers, then the birds will stack up. When the weather clears, and the birds resupply their fat reserves, they will resume their migration. The migrant in a relatively favorable energetic condition will depart the Texas coast for points north on the same day as its arrival. Contrariwise, fat-depleted birds will remain longer on the Texas Coast than birds in a stronger condition.

Another element in the drama of spring migration is the appropriate habitat in which to stop. Though birds will grasp on to the coast at "the first perch available," they must find shelter (from predators and the elements), and they must seek food and water. We are just beginning to understand the importance of "stopover sites" during migration that can provide both these necessities, and not simply view the sites as "magnets" which will attract migration-weary passerines. High Island, for example, is seen as both an important stopover site in Texas as well as a traditional magnet for migrants. There are other—less famous—spots along the coast, and you may witness trans-Gulf migrants at a number of them. The loss of coastal habitat

1

appropriate for trans-Gulf migrants that are forest-dwellers is of concern to most birders. And the degradation of stopover sites increases the hazards of migration for the long-distance migrant.

Lest we forget, besides the weather component and the habitat component there is the essential element of the birds themselves. In recent years, students of bird life have found evidence that many of our North American migratory songbirds have been in a serious decline. This decline seems to be related to land-use changes—habitat destruction in the neotropics and habitat fragmentation in the north. The "river of birds" that flows twice yearly across the Americas is clearly under stress; migrations seem to be less dramatic than they used to be. Nevertheless, when the "river" intersects the Texas Coast it is still possible to experience the spring fallout phenomenon.

But, where on the long Texas Coast does one look for spring landbird migrants? Along the Texas Coast most of the cold-fronts are strong enough to reach only the Upper Coast, so your chances of finding waves of migrants are far better there. However, on the Central and Lower Coasts, you may encounter migrants that in response to encountering a front over the Gulf, actually may have turned westward. When you do find great numbers of birds on the lower coasts, the phenomenon can even be more impressive, because there is less vegetation and the birds are concentrated in fewer bushes. It is also good to remember that most of the inland wooded areas can be very productive during a migrant wave, and may have birds even when the coastal areas are bare.

The spring cold-front phenomenon is not the only birding thrill on the Texas Coast. April shorebirding on the Upper Texas Coast, and watching for Broad-winged Hawks, Swainson's Hawks, kites, and other raptors in March and April flesh out the spring opportunities.

In summer there are great rookeries of gulls, terns, cormorants, herons, egrets, and spoonbills. Miles of beaches, estuaries, and islands beg for exploration by birders.

Fall passerines will peak about early September; shorebirds will attract your attention in August and September; raptor flights will pass through from late August through October. And the possibility of fall vagrants on the Upper Texas Coast can spice up any birding trip at that season too.

In winter, the mild climate will hold thousands of waterfowl; it is a wonderful time to study the ducks and geese. Small landbirds will winter, making the Christmas Bird Counts exciting. And even some of the larger species, such as the Whooping Crane, will spend the winter.

Even in the "off-seasons," a birder can seek out unusual residents such as the Red-cockaded Woodpecker, Greater Prairie-Chicken, or the Mexican specialties of the Lower Rio Grande Valley. There is always something to see along the Texas Coast.

TOPOGRAPHY

The Texas coast is a large, flat plain that barely rises above the Gulf of Mexico, which it borders for 367 miles. The outer shoreline is a string of long, narrow barrier islands and peninsulas that run parallel to the mainland. Behind these is a series of long, shallow lagoons with bays at the mouths of the larger rivers. The lagoons, in turn, are bordered by salt marshes that extend well inland and blend with the grasslands of the Coastal Prairie. Only occasionally is there an island of land high enough to support a motte (an isolated grove) of Virginia Live Oak or Hackberry. Extensive stands of trees are encountered only along the streams, and only after one has traveled inland for some 20 miles or more.

Man has greatly altered the natural landscape. He has organized coastal cities, built houses, and planted trees. He has dredged the lagoons in some places and filled them in others. In fact, he is well on the way to changing the entire area. The great undeveloper, the hurricane, is the only force that prevents man's complete alteration of the coast.

For reference purposes most Texas birders will divide the coast into three parts: Upper Coast, Central Coast, and Lower Coast. The *Upper Coast* extends from the Sabine River to Port O'Connor. It receives considerable rainfall and is very humid. Its coastal regions are covered with rice fields and great sections of *Spartina*-grass salt-marsh. The inland areas have large rivers with heavily wooded bottoms. Many eastern species reach the southwestern limits of their range in this sector. The *Central Coast* (also known as the Texas Coastal Bend) from Port O'Connor to Baffin Bay is a transition zone with many features of both the Upper and Lower Coasts. Its inland areas are mostly prairie grasslands with scattered mottes of scrub oak. However, in some areas, such as Aransas National Wildlife Refuge and around Rockport, there are extensive oak groves. The *Lower Coast* from Baffin Bay south is largely arid. Its coastal areas have fewer marshes and more brushlands, where western species are not uncommon and where several Mexican species reach their northern limits.

There are at least two other bio-geographic areas which overlap regions covered in this text—one each at each end of the book's routing. The *East Texas* pine woods characterize areas at the northeastern beginning of the tour; the *Lower Rio Grande Valley* with its richer vegetation and near-Mexican character is described in the final chapters of the book.

For your information, a helpful map of the entire Texas Coast, including birding points-of-interest and routes, is included at the beginning of this Introduction and on the back inside cover of the book.

WHERE TO STAY

Most of the towns along the coast are resort areas, so motels are plentiful. Reservations are usually not needed except during the summer. There are improved public campgrounds, and overnight camping is permitted on most ocean beaches in unincorporated areas. Just drive your car onto the **wet** sand and pitch your tent. (Watch out for the arrival of high tide!) Private campgrounds have been developed in many areas, and most of them offer laundries, grocery stores, and other facilities.

PUBLIC CAMPGROUNDS

Below are listed most of the public campgrounds on the Texas coast, from north to south:

Port Arthur Pleasure Island—tables only
Sabine Pass Sea Rim State Park—beach, all facilities, fee
Anahuac National Wildlife Refuge Double Bayou Park—no facilities
Fort Anahuac Park—restrooms and tables
Turtle Bay Park (Anahuac)—restrooms
Fort Travis Seashore Park—tables, restrooms
White Memorial Park—tables, restrooms, cold showers
Baytown McCollum Park—tables, restrooms
Houston Alexander Deussen Park—tables, restrooms, fee
Brazos Bend State Park—all facilities, fee
Bear Creek Park—tables, restrooms, hot showers
Galveston East Beach Campground—bathhouse
Galveston State Park—all facilities fee
Texas City Texas City Dike—tables, restrooms
Freeport Quintana Beach County Park
Matagorda—beach, no facilities
Port Lavaca Port Lavaca Lighthouse State Park—tables, restrooms
Indianola—tables only
Rockport Goose Island State Park—tables, restrooms, hot showers, fee
Port Aransas Port Aransas Beach Park—bathhouse, fee
Mustang Island State Park—fee
Corpus Christi Padre Island National Seashore—bathhouse, fee
Nueces River City Park—tables only
Hazel Bazemore County Park—tables only
Fort Lipantitlan State Park—tables only
Lake Corpus Christi State Park—tables, hot showers, fee
Port Isabel South Padre Island—hot showers, fee
Boca Chica Boca Chica State Park—beach, no facilities

PARK FEES

Two special permits are available for Texas State Parks. The *State Parklands Passport* exempts those 65 years of age or older, or veterans with a 60 percent or greater Veteran's Administration disability, from park entrance fees. The passport is available at most state parks; those eligible must apply in person with the proper identification or proof of disability. You will get a sticker for your car.

The *Texas Conservation Passport* is an annual state park entrance permit, and also allows the holder entry into some generally restricted Wildlife Management Areas and State Natural Areas. The cost is $25 per year, from date of purchase. It is available at most state parks or by mail from: Texas Parks and Wildlife Department, 4200 Smith School Road, Austin, Texas 78744 (send name and address, driver's license number, and $25). You will receive a wallet identification card. The Passport is a bargain for birders living in the state and for those visiting and planning multiple entries into the state parks.

For more information on either of these Passports write to the address above or call 800/792-1112 or 512/389-4800.

WHEN TO COME

Birding is always exciting along the Texas Coast, but most out-of-state birders visit during spring migration, which starts early here.

Purple Martins return about the end of January and are soon followed by Tree Swallows. By the end of February, the ducks and geese begin to thin out, but the shorebirds are more numerous and the trees begin to leaf out. The first real wave of migrants arrives late in March.

It is difficult to say just when to come in the spring, because it depends a good deal on what birds you wish to see. Hawks will pass through in March and April. Passerines nesting in the southern states normally pass through earlier than those nesting farther north. So to see birds such as Prothonotary and Swainson's Warblers or Louisiana Waterthrush, you should come before April 15.

However, the bulk of the migrants pass through during the last two weeks in April and the first week in May. If this is your first trip to the area, it may be wise to come after April 15. Spring shorebirding can also be attractive. No matter when you come, you will probably hear that old lament, "You should have been here last week!"

Don't discount fall birding. Shorebirds will arrive in numbers starting in the late summer and early fall. The fall landbird migration will start about the end of July (with Black-and-white Warblers), peak about early September, and continue into November. Raptors observed in places like Smith Point will start in September and go through October.

Many birds winter along the coast. After September you can find numerous ducks, geese, sparrows, and other northern species that will spend the winter.

However, the bulk of these do not arrive until the cold weather starts near the end of October. Whooping Cranes arrive in late October and stay until early April.

A fun way to bird in winter is to take part in one or more of the Christmas Bird Counts. The tallies for most counts in this area exceed 150 species, and the Freeport count has reached a record-breaking 226. The Corpus Christi count is usually not far behind, and can break 200 species. Not only will you be helping with a worthwhile project, but you will also enjoy the companionship of many friendly and helpful local birders. For details, write to the compilers listed in the Christmas Count edition of *American Birds*.

SOME INFORMATION SOURCES

Some of the books that are particularly useful in this area are: **A Field Guide to the Birds of Texas** by Roger Tory Peterson, **Flora of the Coastal Bend** by E. B. Austin Jones, **Texas Mammals East of the Balcones Fault Zone** by D. J. Schmidly, **Roadside Flowers of Texas** by Howard S. Irwin, and **Wild Flowers of the Big Thicket** by Geyata Ajilvsgi. Other books that will enhance your visit are listed in the "References" at the end of this book.

A good map of Texas and maps of several sight-seeing trails can be obtained by writing to the Texas Highway Department, Austin TX 78763, or you can pick them up at one of the welcome-stations at the Texas boundary. The Texas Highway Department also has detailed county maps for sale at any of their regional offices. Another source is an atlas of Texas entitled **The Roads of Texas** put out by the Shearer Publishing Company ($12.95), and available in many stores throughout the state. The local bird clubs, Audubon Society chapters, nature clubs, and chambers of commerce may also be able to provide you with much useful information, from maps to checklists. They are listed below geographically, from north to south along the coast.

Texas Ornithological Society—statewide
Sabine Audubon Society—Orange
East Texas Nature Club—Beaumont
Houston Audubon Society—Houston
Outdoor Nature Club—Houston
Piney Woods Wildlife Society—North Harris County
Brazosport Birders—Freeport area
Golden Crescent Bird Club—Victoria
The Main Group Bird Club—Sinton
Audubon Outdoor Club of Corpus Christi—Corpus Christi
Coastal Bend Audubon Society—Corpus Christi
Alice Audubon Society—Alice
Kingsville Bird and Wildlife Club—Kingsville
Lower Rio Grande Valley Audubon Society—McAllen

RARE BIRD ALERTS

A few of the organizations listed above sponsor "Rare Bird Alerts" or "Birding Hotlines" as a service to the birding community. These recordings are exceedingly helpful and informative to all birders, resident and visitor alike. The current numbers for areas in this book are as follows:

Statewide: 713/992-2757
Coastal Bend: 512/364-3634
Rio Grande Valley: 210/565-6773

PESTS

While birding in Texas, be prepared to defend yourself against mosquitos, ticks, chiggers, and other insect nuisances. One of the things you will certainly need to buy for your Texas birding is insect repellent. Of course, Texans would never admit that the bugs are bad, but they do sell repellents in nearly every store. The important thing to remember, according to entomologist Kirby Stafford, is that bug bites should not stop you from enjoying some top-notch birding.

During most of the year the mosquitoes are numerous, to say the least. They are a nuisance that most birders—from Florida to Alaska—are familiar with. A healthy dose of insect spray can keep mosquitos at bay. Other insects may not be so easily discouraged.

American Dog Ticks and Lone Star Ticks are the ones most likely to be found feasting on Texas birders. Ticks particularly like the woods, brushy areas, underbrush along riverbottoms, and thickets, but are often encountered along trails, roads, and in recreation areas. Check for these little "freckles with legs" every day. If you find one of these blood-suckers on you, remove it with tweezers or protected fingers. Don't crush it, but pull with slow, steady pressure—which usually will get the "head" of the tick, too. Ticks can transmit disease, such as Rocky Mountain spotted fever, tularemia and Lyme disease. Lyme disease reports have come in from parts of East Texas. The overall incidence is low, and it is still not clear which tick is responsible.

Chigger larvae are almost invisible red mites. (They are less than 1/150th of an inch long.) You won't notice them until it is too late—the intense itching begins the day after chiggers have left your body. Contrary to popular myth, chiggers do not burrow into the skin. They inject a digestive fluid that dissolves skin cells, forming a feeding tube. The tube may surround the chigger, giving the appearance that it burrowed into the skin. A hot, soapy bath after exposure to chigger-infested areas will help to kill and remove the chigger larvae. You will probably feel better taking a bath after a day's hot birding anyway! A commercial anesthetic may also be used to relieve the continual itch.

Of course, a little prevention can go a long way. For ticks and chiggers, try tucking the pants legs into your socks and spray them with repellent before walking through grass or brush. Better yet, spray your birding outfit with Duranon Tick Repellent before leaving home and use a 30-50% DEET repellent on exposed skin when you are in the field.

If you don't look where you are standing while watching a bird, you may also be attacked by a swarm of many, many imported fire ants. Fire ant mounds are usually obvious, as they may be 1½ feet high and 1 to 2 feet wide. However, mounds may also be hidden by tall grass or be under logs. To sting, a fire ant grabs the skin with its mouth and then pushes in the stinger. The fiery sting forms pustules which itch and can become infected. In very sensitive people, fire ant stings, especially multiple stings, can even be life-threatening.

A relatively recent addition to Texas wildlife is the Africanized honey bee. Labels like "killer bees" in the news create scary images, but the bees pose no great threat to the general public. Having arrived in Texas in 1990, these bees look like the European honey bees and their sting is reportedly no worse. However, Africanized honey bees are more aggressive in defending their hives and will pursue intruders farther than other bees. Noise and vibration of tractors and lawnmowers have incited attacks. Birders should avoid nests of Africanized honey bees just the way one would avoid wasp nests. If you find a nest, just walk away. If attacked, run for cover in a zig-zag pattern and keep running until you are clear of bees. (Spraying an insect repellent containing DEET over the head may also help disperse attacking bees.)

One would hope that the multitudes of biting and stinging bugs along the Texas Coast haven't scared you unduly. Most birders don't encounter all these threats, and a few precautions, such as looking down once in a while and using a repellent, will help to keep Texas coastal birding a pleasure.

Then there is the issue of Texas snakes. Snakes may be encountered at any time of the year if it is warm, but they become most active after the first hot spell in March. Most of the poisonous kinds that are found in the United States occur in Texas. (See the list of reptiles at the end of this book.) You will probably not be lucky enough to see a single one on your entire trip, but it is best to use caution. More people are killed in the United States by the Diamond-backed Rattlesnake than by any other kind, and this snake is common in the grasslands and brushlands of Texas. It even occurs on the coastal sand dunes wherever there is a little grass.

HOW TO USE THIS BOOK

This book is designed for use on a trip by car from Beaumont to Brownsville. Most of the suggested routes follow the roads closest to the coast. Each chapter covers a specific area, and most chapters are short. Side trips to inland areas of interest are also described. The main purpose of the book is to help you find the best birding spots, particularly those areas where uncommon or hard-to-find species occur.

The more outstanding spots are shown in **bold-face type**. If you are in a hurry, stop only at these places. Many spots mentioned are followed by a number, thus: (11.9). This system indicates the mileage from the last spot so listed.

The bird names used in this book, for the most part, follow the **American Ornithologists' Union Check-list,** 6th edition (1983), with supplements in 1985, 1987, 1989, and 1991. The reader can also use the American Birding Association's **ABA Checklist: Birds of the Continental United States and Canada**, 4th Edition (1990) for a basically up-to-date nomenclature.

BIRDING BEHAVIOR

Today, birders have responsibilities that many didn't consider years ago. Of course, we have the responsibility to support the broad issue of bird conservation. But we have also personal, individual responsibilities in the field.

This leads us to the applicability of the "American Birding Association Code of Ethics" while birding along the Texas coast. Opposite the table of contents of this book is a copy of the code. I suggest that birders using this book familiarize themselves with this Code of Ethics. Generally, the code indicates that birders should:

1. Always act in ways that do not endanger the welfare of birds or other wildlife;
2. Always act in ways that do not harm the natural environment;
3. Always respect the rights of others;
4. Assume special responsibilities when birding in groups.

Here I would like to stress two aspects of the code. First, birders should always, but especially in Texas, respect the private property of others. Uninvited trespassing in Texas is a major offense to many Texans, and birders should be especially sensitive to this fact. Though most of the sites in this book are public ones, there are some exceptions. These exceptions are well-marked. Secondly, the first rule in the ABA Code of Ethics—on the welfare of the birds themselves—needs some special emphasis. Today there are increasing concerns over possible harassment of nesting and rare birds, as well as excessive tape use in the field. Nesting birds can be easily disturbed. If adult birds are frightened off the nest by you, unattended nestlings can succumb to predators or exposure. Always use special care around nest sites. A similar warning goes for tape-recorder use. Any excessive use of tapes that results in the agitation of owls, of secretive species, and, especially, of endangered species is certainly inappropriate.

Adhering to the ABA Code of Ethics will make birding better for you, for your companions, for other birders in the field, and most importantly, for the birds.

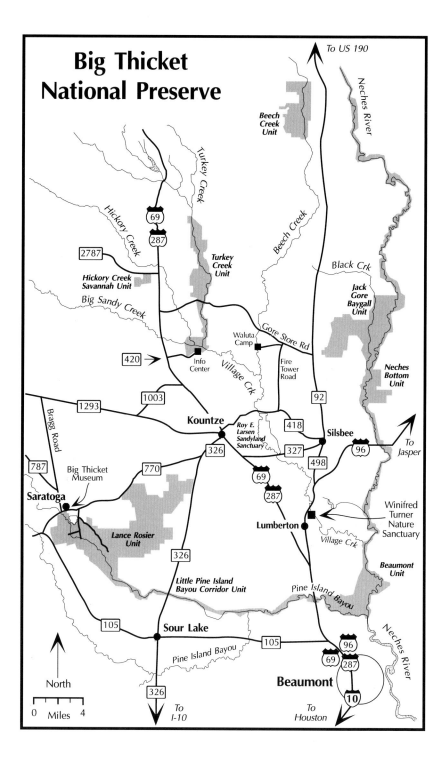

CHAPTER 1:
BEAUMONT AND
BIG THICKET

The starting-point for your trip down the Texas Coast is in from the coast, in Beaumont, at the intersection of Highway 69/96/287 coming from the north and Interstate 10. From this location you can easily reach many of the good birding spots inland in East Texas, and you may want to explore some of them before heading south. This chapter will start in Beaumont, guide you through the Big Thicket area of Hardin County and, bring you back to Beaumont for local birding.

HARDIN COUNTY

When Texans say "East Texas," they are normally referring to the area covered by pine forest in the northeastern corner of the state. In fact, they usually call this area the "piney woods". These pines grow on a belt of well-drained, sandy soil extending westward from the Louisiana border to a line running unevenly northward from Houston. Pines, however, are not the only vegetation in this area of heavy rainfall. Groves of oak, beech, hickory, magnolia, Sweetgum, and other hardwoods grow in the bottomlands, and there are Bald Cypress/Tupelo swamps with their impenetrable tangles. This is the heart of "The Big Thicket" which achieved the status of a National Preserve in 1974. Today, what was once a vast combination of virgin pine and cypress forest, hardwood forest, meadow, and blackwater swamp has been reduced to a handful of fragmented tracts. These remnants, totaling 84,500 acres, are now managed by the **Big Thicket National Preserve**. The preserve consists of eight land units and four river- or stream-corridor units. Seven of the units and three of the corridors lie within Hardin County.

The Big Thicket National Preserve provides literature, trail information, and organized programs. Information can be obtained at the National Park Service headquarters located at 3785 Milam in Beaumont (telephone: 409/839-2689). Other information about the preserve may be requested by writing to the privately operated Big Thicket Museum (PO Box 198, Saratoga,

Texas 77585; telephone: 409/274-5000). The Big Thicket Association that runs the museum is credited with organizing the drive to create the Big Thicket National Preserve.

A favored area of local birders for finding Bachman's Sparrow, Brown-headed Nuthatch, and Red-cockaded Woodpecker is some 25 miles north of Beaumont near Silsbee in Hardin County. To reach it go north on Highway 69/96/287. At the northern city limits of Beaumont you will cross Pine Island Bayou (6.6). This is the Beaumont Unit of the Big Thicket National Preserve. Here you can put in a canoe and drift down to the Neches River. Several of the reported but unconfirmed sightings of Ivory-billed Woodpecker in the late 1960s were made along this bayou. It is a fascinating creek to explore by boat; if you do not have a boat, you can rent one by calling Village Creek Canoe Rental (PO Box 1921, Kountze, Texas 77625; telephone: 409/246-4607).

Multiple pairs of Ivory-billed Woodpeckers were reported in the Big Thicket area during the late 1960s, and the sightings raised much controversy. Historically, Ivory-bills were to be found in mature river-bottom forests of Sweetgums, oaks, and elms. (The remnant Cuban population has been observed in 30-year-old pines, however.) The call of the Ivory-billed Woodpecker is distinctive, single or double tooting as if from a toy horn. And if you were wondering, yes, there are Pileated Woodpeckers in the Big Thicket area. But give them all a second look.

Brown-headed Nuthatch
Charles H. Gambill

This tract of virgin woodland and Bald Cypress/Tupelo swamp is a typical example of the river-bottom forests of the Southeast. You will find fine specimens of Loblolly and Shortleaf Pines, American Hornbeam, American Beech, Southern Magnolia, and Sweetgum. Most of the birds here are also typical of southeastern woodlands. Look for Wood Duck, Barred Owl, Red-bellied and Pileated Woodpeckers, Blue Jay, Carolina Chickadee, Tufted Titmouse, Carolina Wren, Pine Warbler, and Northern Cardinal. In summer there are also Great Crested and Acadian Flycatchers, Eastern Wood-Pewee, White-eyed and Red-eyed Vireos, and such warblers as Black-and-white, Northern Parula, Yellow-throated, Hooded, Prothonotary, Swainson's, and Louisiana Waterthrush.

Continuing north from Pine Island Bayou, take the right fork (2.7) and follow Highway 96 through Lumberton to the Village Creek crossing. Just before the Village Creek bridge, on the right, is the Winifred Turner Nature Sanctuary. This is an undeveloped tract of land open to the public which provides access to Village Creek. It contains mixed pines and deciduous trees at upper levels and typical riparian vegetation near the creek. Many of the birds listed for the Beaumont Unit of the Big Thicket National Preserve can be found here, and found more easily.

From this point follow Highway 96 north. When the main highway veers left, go right; drive through the underpass below the highway onto Business Route 498. Follow the road into Silsbee. When this road makes a right sharp turn in the middle of town (3.0), continue straight ahead on Farm Road 92. At the north edge of Silsbee, Route 418 takes off to the left. Continue from this intersection 7.0 miles on FM 92 to Gore Store Road. (At this point the R & B Grocery will be on the right and Gore Store Road on the left.)

Turn left onto Gore Store Road, which traverses an area of open pine savannah woodlands. Birds to watch for here include Yellow-billed Cuckoo, Chuck-will's-widow (which will be singing until just before first light), Red-headed Woodpecker, Northern Flicker, Eastern Bluebird, Brown Thrasher, Pine Warbler, Summer Tanager, Indigo Bunting, Orchard Oriole, and even Greater Roadrunner.

The four specialties of this area are Red-cockaded Woodpecker, Brown-headed Nuthatch, Prairie Warbler, and Bachman's Sparrow. A good spot to find all but the woodpecker is along the road to the Waluta Campfire Girls Camp. To reach it, turn left onto Fire Tower Road (2.7), go a block, and turn right. The nuthatch, warbler, and sparrow may be found anyplace where there are open stands of Longleaf Pines. Bachman's Sparrows prefer open pine-woods that have a good ground-cover of grass with occasional clumps of brush—grass that is rather thick and from 9 to 12 inches high. These birds can be hard to find unless they are singing, which they usually do from a perch on a horizontal dead branch situated 10 to 15 feet above the ground. Once you have located a sparrow, however, you will most likely be able to watch it sing from the same perch for many minutes at a time. Early morning and evening, from about March 15 through May 15, are the best times to see one well. At other seasons you sometimes can walk them out, but they usually just fly up and quickly disappear into another clump.

Where pines are regenerating in clear-cuts, listen for the buzzy, upslurred notes of the Prairie Warbler, a very local nester in Texas. The sites for the warbler may change from year to year, depending on the height of vegetation. Check likely places along the roads here.

Brown-headed Nuthatches are usually found feeding about the tops of tall pines, more frequently at the tip of the branches than along the trunk. Nuthatches are noisy birds, and, since they travel in small flocks, they normally are not hard to find. Red-cockaded Woodpecker is rather sociable for a woodpecker and nests in loose colonies. However, its distribution is limited by its need for mature pines that are infected with red-heart disease. The woodpeckers dig holes in a living but infected tree. They then peck the bark around the hole until a large shield of oozing sap is formed, which hinders predation from ants, snakes, and flying squirrels. Trees that have been used for several years may be almost covered with pitch, making them fairly easy to spot.

There is a good location along Fire Tower Road worth checking for Red-cockaded Woodpecker. Return to this road and turn right (south). A couple of pairs of woodpeckers nest in a pine a few yards down a dirt track on the east (left) side (1.3). The nest tree, with its several holes surrounded by sap, is visible 60 yards up the track on the right. The birds are most likely to be seen at dawn and dusk because they forage widely at other times of the day. They usually leave the nest or roost holes by 7am. Please remember that *any* type of harassment is completely inappropriate.

Other spots for finding the four specialties can be reached by continuing south on Fire Tower Road and watching for unlogged areas of pine.

If it has not rained recently, continue down the road and stop at the two small bridges. In summer the thickets here may harbor Yellow-crowned Night-Heron, Wood Thrush, Swainson's, Northern Parula, Kentucky, and Hooded Warblers, and perhaps a Louisiana Waterthrush. The latter prefers areas near small streams with gravelly bottoms. At Farm Road 418 (3.0) turn around and return north to Gore Store Road. Turn left (west); the first half-mile on your left is great habitat for more Bachman's Sparrows. Obey any *No Trespassing* signs.

Another interesting and productive site in this area is the **Turkey Creek Unit** (7.7) of Big Thicket National Preserve. This stand of mature timber along Turkey Creek contrasts sharply with the nearby clear-cuts and pine plantations. There are two access-points, both on the north side of Gore Store Road: a short trail on the east side of Turkey Creek which leads to a fine stand of Bald Cypress, and the Turkey Creek Trail, which starts at an ample parking lot and follows the west bank of the creek. A few hundred yards along the Turkey Creek Trail you will cross a boardwalk, and a mile or so farther north you will cross another. The little tannin-filled stream, its banks choked with Yaupon, is Swainson's Warbler country. The bird's loud, ringing song can be heard from mid-April through May. The songster uses a variety of perches, from ground-level to about 8 feet up. It prefers the densest cover, and, because it usually cohabits with the Cottonmouth and a variety of thorned bushes, commando-type excursions to view it are not recommended. Here, Mike Austin recommends "judicious use of a tape recorder. I emphasize *judicious*," Mike writes, "because almost no bird on territory responds better to a tape of its song than this species. Play a few recorded verses; the Swainson's will often stop singing, emit a short series of chips, and suddenly materialize, often at eye-level. It will then usually resume singing close at hand, often in an exposed situation, for extended periods of viewing."

Other interesting species present in spring are Barred Owl, Acadian Flycatcher, and Prothonotary and Yellow-throated Warblers.

Continue west to Highway 69/287 (3.4), and turn right to the Hickory Creek Savannah Unit (3.0) of the Big Thicket National Preserve, which consists of 660 acres of Longleaf Pine/savannah forest and acid bog/baygall wetlands. The entrance is 0.5 mile to the left on FM 2827. A one-mile-long loop trail leads through the savannah plant community. Another, shorter, quarter-mile loop is hard-surfaced for wheelchair visitors. Red-cockaded Woodpecker and Brown-headed Nuthatch have been reported in this unit.

To continue the tour, go south on Highway 69/287 to Farm Road 420 (6.5), and turn left (east) to the **Big Thicket Visitor Information Center** at the southern tip of the **Turkey Creek Unit**. Here, also, is the Kirby Nature Trail, located behind the Information Station where a ranger is on duty from 9am to 5pm daily. The nature trail has an inner loop of 1.7 miles and an outer loop of 2.4 miles; both pass through hardwoods and pines. Where the trail follows sections of Village Creek, there are Bald Cypress sloughs and floodplains. A guide booklet, available at the trailhead, interprets the plant communities and identifies many of the plants along the trails. Nesting birds include Pied-billed Grebe, Anhinga, Yellow-crowned Night-Heron, Wood Duck, Sharp-shinned and Red-shouldered Hawks, Inca Dove, Yellow-billed Cuckoo, Greater Roadrunner, Eastern Screech-Owl, Barred Owl, Chimney Swift, Ruby-throated Hummingbird, Belted Kingfisher, Red-headed, Red-bellied, Downy, and Pileated Woodpeckers, Northern Flicker, Acadian and Great Crested Flycatchers, Eastern Wood-Pewee, Purple Martin, Carolina Chickadee, Tufted Titmouse, Brown-headed Nuthatch, Carolina Wren, Eastern Bluebird, Blue-gray Gnatcatcher, White-eyed, Yellow-throated, and Red-eyed Vireos, Northern Parula, Yellow-throated, Pine, Black-and-white, Prothonotary, Swainson's, and Hooded Warblers, Louisiana Waterthrush, Summer Tanager, Northern Cardinal, and Indigo Bunting. Many migrant and wintering species are also found in season. A total of some 200 species have been recorded in all the units of Big Thicket National Preserve.

From the Big Thicket Visitor Information Center, proceed to Saratoga. Return to Highway 69/287, go left to Kountze, and right on 326. Southwest of Kountze turn right onto Farm Road 770 (2.5) into Saratoga. Near the center of town you will see the Big Thicket Museum on your right. Highlights of the museum include historical and cultural rooms containing farming

Anhinga
Gail Diane Luckner

implements, lumbering and oil-field tools, kitchen utensils, and articles of clothing worn by early settlers of East Texas. The Big Thicket is as rich in cultural history as it is in natural history. Although early Indians hunted in the area (which once encompassed over 3.5 million acres), they did not typically penetrate deep into the thicket. In the 1850s early settlers tended to avoid the "impenetrable woods", preferring to settle on its perimeter. The area eventually gained a reputation for lawlessness, becoming the lair of murderers, thieves, gamblers, and desperados of all sorts. During the Civil War some area residents hid out in the woods to avoid conscription. The flavor of the old Big Thicket life-style persists today in legends and lore.

On the south side of Farm Road 770, south and east of Saratoga, lies the **Lance Rosier Unit** of Big Thicket National Preserve. The unit's palmetto flats and hardwoods are excellent for warblers, especially in spring and fall migrations. Prairie Warblers nest here in small numbers. Several roads providing access to the area start here in Saratoga. A half-mile east of town (measured from the Fire Department Building) on 770 you will find a gravel road leading south. At a fork (0.7) you can drive either direction for up to four miles into the Unit. Although there are no new birds to be found here, these two roads take you into the heart of the "real" Big Thicket.

To continue the tour, take Farm Road 770 and then 326 back to Kountze. Turn right onto Highway 69/287 by the north end of town. Go left onto 327 (2.8) to the entrance on the left (north) side of the road to The Nature Conservancy's Roy E. Larsen Sandyland Sanctuary (2.5). This preserve of several thousand acres occupies the east bank of Village Creek between Farm Roads 327 and 418. A trail from the parking lot leads several miles through a variety of habitats.

To get back to Beaumont, either return to Kountze and then to Beaumont, or continue east on 327 to Silsbee (3.3) and then back south to Beaumont.

Food and accommodations are available in Silsbee and Beaumont. Especially recommended is the Pinewood Inn in Silsbee (telephone: 409/385-5592).

BEAUMONT

This city of 118,000 people is situated along the zone where the vast woodlands of East Texas merge with the coastal marshes that stretch from the Mississippi River to Galveston Bay. The city streets are lined with huge Magnolias, Virginia Live Oaks, Loblolly Pines, and other trees that attract numerous birds. There are also beautiful parks, where birds that are typical of southeastern woodlands can be found.

The best of these parks is close to the business and motel area. **Wuthering Heights** (also called Delaware Street Park) has been set aside as a sanctuary for birds and other wildlife. It has a good assortment of trees such as Loblolly

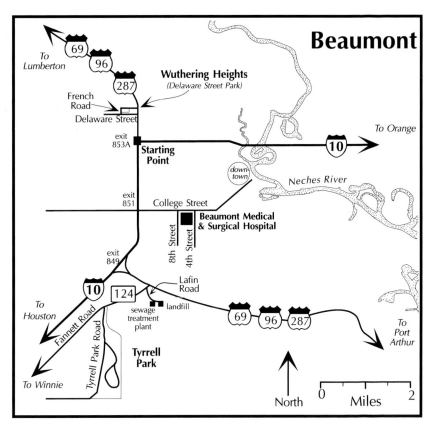

and Shortleaf Pines, Water Oak, Sweetgum, Hackberry, Cherry Laurel, much Wax Myrtle and Persimmon, and many others. There are good trails around the perimeter of this 22-acre park in which over 100 bird species have been observed since the East Texas Nature Club saved this pristine woodland from developers in 1985. This passive park is open seven days a week. To reach it, drive north on Highway 69 from exit 853A where Interstate 10 turns east. Turn left at the first exit (Delaware Street) and drive 0.3 mile to French Road. Turn right for one long block and then right again onto the blacktop road to the well-marked parking area (1/2 block) on your right. There is no charge for birding here.

Thirty species are resident, including numerous woodpeckers and various songbirds. The Fish Crow, a specialty of this area, may sometimes be found here. (It may be more easily found on the grounds of the Beaumont Medical and Surgical Hospital, located east of Interstate 10 on College Street—exit 851—between 4th and 8th streets.)

Perhaps the best spot for Fish Crow is the Beaumont Sanitary Landfill on the way to Tyrrell Park, another spot worth visiting. To reach these locations go south on Interstate 10, turn left at exit 849 onto Highway 69/96/287 (2.9) toward Port Arthur, and then take the Route 124 off-ramp (1.0). Directly opposite the bottom of this off-ramp is Lafin Road. This short road leads past the sewage-treatment plant (which can be very good for migrating shorebirds) and then to the landfill on the left. The Fish Crow is almost guaranteed here. (Both the sewage treatment plant and the landfill are closed on Sundays.)

To reach **Tyrrell Park** return to Route 124, and turn left to Tyrrell Park Road (1.0). Turn left into the wooded park.

On the left just past the entrance is the Garden Center, a good birding spot for landbirds. Also check the woods both north and south of the fence. In winter the latter woods usually has a few American Woodcocks.

Continue on the park road to just past the golf course clubhouse where the road makes a wide circle. On the back side of the circle is a poorly marked trail leading into the woods. The birds which you will find here are typical of southeastern woodlands. Some of the resident birds are Eastern Screech-Owl, Barred Owl, Red-bellied, Downy, and Pileated Woodpeckers, Blue Jay, Carolina Chickadee, Tufted Titmouse, Carolina Wren, Pine Warbler, Great-tailed and Common Grackles, and Northern Cardinal. In summer you should be able to find Great Crested and Acadian Flycatchers, Eastern Wood-Pewee, Yellow-throated, White-eyed, and Red-eyed Vireos, Black-and-white, Yellow-throated, Kentucky, and Hooded Warblers, Northern Parula, and Northern and Orchard Orioles. In winter look for Northern Flicker, Brown Thrasher, Eastern Phoebe, Rusty Blackbird, Yellow-rumped and Orange-crowned Warblers, and White-throated Sparrow. In migration you may find numerous other warblers, vireos, and small landbirds.

Red-headed Woodpeckers can usually be found in summer in the more open areas. Most reference literature for this area shows them as permanent residents, but they are hard to find in winter. Just where they go is a mystery. They do not migrate southward, but they do leave the coast, perhaps dispersing westward. They have been reported in winter in good numbers from the Cleveland/Livingston area (northwest of Beaumont), in the wooded areas north of Beaumont, and east in the Orange area.

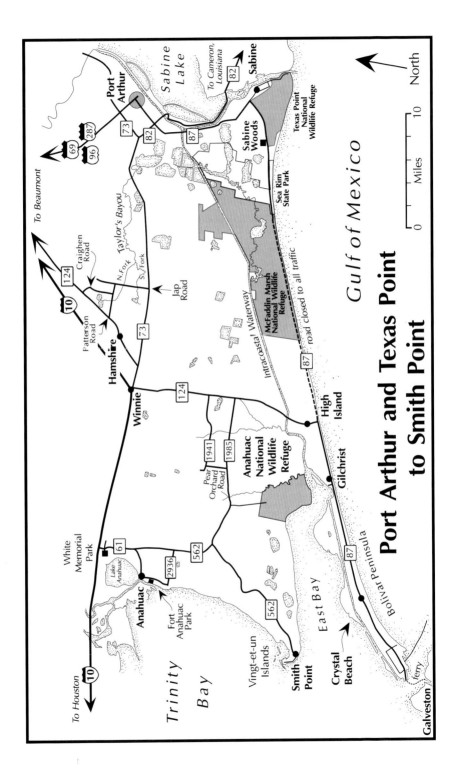

Port Arthur and Texas Point to Smith Point

CHAPTER 2:
PORT ARTHUR AND TEXAS POINT TO SMITH POINT

To start your trip on the Upper Texas Coast, go south on Highway 69/96/287 from Beaumont to Port Arthur. At the western edge of town the freeway ends, and you will soon come to Highway 87 (17.2). Turn right and continue to State Highway 82 (3.0) in the heart of the oil and chemical refinery area. Here you will be surrounded by huge storage tanks, cracking-towers, and smokestacks. The best thing about this spot is that regardless of where you go from here, things are bound to get better!

Turn left onto Texaco Gulf Highway 82 to Pleasure Island via the high arch of the Martin Luther King Memorial Bridge over the Intracoastal Waterway. (See map on following page.) Highway 82 comes to a T and turns left (2.3), where you should turn right (unmarked) onto Pleasure Island on the shores of Sabine Lake.

The main attractions for birders on Pleasure Island are along the jetty road (1.3) that loops far out into the lake and provides a good viewing point for wintering ducks and shorebirds. Past the marina, the main road veers to the right and then left (1.4), following the shore for 5.2 miles before it ends at a wooded wildlife refuge where migrant landbirds can be plentiful.

SABINE

To continue the tour, go south on Highway 87. When the road makes a right turn in Sabine Pass (11.0), go straight toward Sabine on South Gulfway (FM 3322). The road's name changes to Dowling Road past the intersection. The small fishing village overlooks the channel between Sabine Pass and the Gulf. It is a good place to study cormorants, gulls, and terns, and, in winter, grebes and diving ducks. Along the way (1.3 miles on your left) you can turn into **Sabine Pass Battleground State Historical Park** (56 acres). This attractive place has picnic facilities and restrooms. The site is where Dick Dowling and

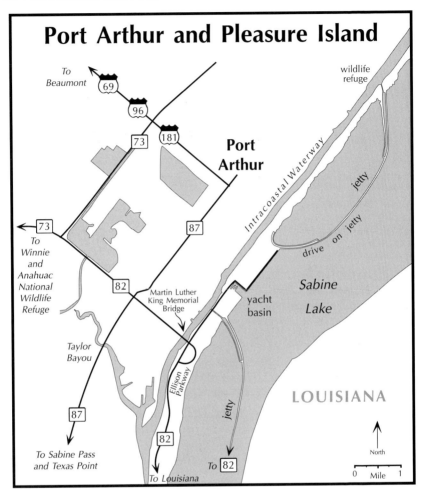

Port Arthur and Pleasure Island

To Beaumont — 69

96

73   181

Port Arthur

73

To Winnie and Anahuac National Wildlife Refuge

82

Martin Luther King Memorial Bridge

Taylor Bayou

87

82

To Sabine Pass and Texas Point

82

To Louisiana

Ellison Parkway

87

yacht basin

jetty

wildlife refuge

Intracoastal Waterway

jetty

drive on jetty

Sabine Lake

LOUISIANA

North

0   Mile   1

To 82

47 men of the Confederate Army won a decisive Civil War victory in 1863 against the forces of Union General William Franklin. From a mud fort the defenders repulsed an attack by four warships and 1,200 men of the Union Navy. Two of the ships and 350 of the men were captured, preserving southeast Texas from invasion. A small woods located just north of the park is a great spot for seeing migrating vireos, warblers, orioles, grosbeaks, and Indigo and Painted Buntings in spring.

Upon leaving the park continue left on Dowling Road to South 1st Avenue (0.1); turn right. Soon you will pass the Coast Guard Station, where in 1959 Robert Selander and Donald Giller first studied the two species of large-tailed grackles (Boat-tailed and Great-tailed) nesting together without interbreeding. Shortly the road runs through an extensive *Spartina*-grass marsh, part of **Texas**

Point National Wildlife Refuge. Walk along the road, checking for Clapper Rail, Mottled Duck, Seaside Sparrow, and other marsh-birds. Glossy Ibis, although rare in Texas, has been found regularly in this corner of the state. Look for the adult Glossy's dark legs and eyes and, in breeding season, the bluish facial skin with a narrow white border *absent* over the eye. In summer Least Bitterns are common, and in winter Sharp-tailed Sparrows can be plentiful. Even Black Rails might be encountered, if you are living right, especially during high spring tides.

So called "spring tides" have nothing to do with the seasons of the year. This term is used to describe the tides that occur when the moon and sun are in a line with the earth. This happens twice a month, when the moon is either full or new. During spring tides, you will encounter the highest high tides and the lowest low tides. The opposite condition is called a "neap tide", and

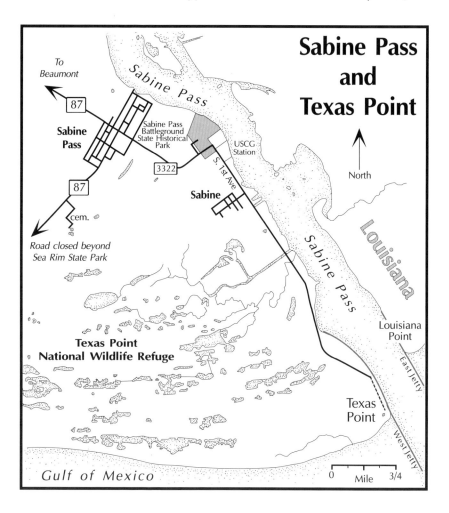

it occurs when the moon and sun are at right angles to the earth. This happens when the moon is in the first or last quarter. During neap tides, you will find the tidal changes less extreme. The time of the high or low tide advances about an hour each day.

The Tamarisks (often called Salt-cedars) which line the roadway near the end (5.0) are often attractive to migrant passerines including, in the spring of 1991, a vagrant Hermit Warbler.

Return to Sabine Pass and continue down Highway 87. The road borders the new Texas Point National Wildlife Refuge, but access to the marshy terrain is limited. Sabine Woods, a 32-acre oak motte (an isolated grove of trees) owned by the Texas Ornithological Society, is located 4.0 miles on the right (north) side of the road. Enter at the first metal gate on the right, just past the Petroleum Helicopters property. The gate will be closed; you will have to open and close it yourself. Park in the open area immediately inside the gate, not in front of the gate. This is a great spring migrant-trap, and all the regular Upper Texas Coast migrant passerines can be expected.

Sea Rim State Park (6.0), covering 15,094 acres on both sides of the road, is worth a stop (PO Box 1066, Sabine Pass, Texas 77655; telephone: 409/971-2559). A bird checklist with 289 species recorded in the park, including 29 species of waterfowl and 37 species of warblers, is available at the Visitor Center. The marshes on the inland side of the road are great for botanizing and for finding alligators, mosquitoes, and marsh birds such as Least Bittern in spring and summer. Look for American Bitterns and Sharp-tailed Sparrows in fall and throughout the winter. Seaside Sparrows are resident. Perhaps the best way to study them is by canoe (rentals available). In recent years, Cave Swallows have been nesting with Cliffs and Barns in the boat stall along the first paved road to the right. Camping is permitted in a limited area near the headquarters on the beach side by the Gambusia Nature Trail (a 3,640-foot boardwalk built two feet above the marsh) and on portions of the beach itself.

Beyond the park, Highway 87 follows the Gulf closely for many miles. This stretch of highway leading to the town of High Island is now *closed*, however, due to serious storm damage and unsafe driving conditions. *Do not attempt to drive any distance on this road.* Much of the area on the inland side of the road is part of the McFaddin Marsh National Wildlife Refuge (2.2). You may enter at the marked gate, which is open from 6am to dusk on weekdays. You can drive back a couple of miles here until the road ends.

To continue the tour, return via Highway 87 to Port Arthur, turn left onto Highway 82, and continue straight at the junction with Highway 73. The next seventeen miles are fairly flat and boring except in spring, when there may be an occasional flooded rice field full of shorebirds and waders. Turn north at the well-marked Jap Road. Soon you will cross the South Fork of Taylor's Bayou.

One mile beyond the North Fork bridge, turn left onto Patterson Road (unmarked). In 1.2 miles, Craighen Road (various local spellings) is intersected. Continue straight for 0.8 mile to a bridge over the **North Fork of Taylor's Bayou**. Park just beyond the bridge. On the south side of the road, just west of the bridge, is a Spanish-Moss-festooned cypress swamp with Wood Duck, Fish Crow, nesting Prothonotary Warblers and Northern Parulas, and a very curious pair of Barred Owls which will investigate hoots, even at midday. East of the bridge is a woods with a palmetto understory where Swainson's Warblers nest. This area was most famous, however, for a pair of American Swallow-tailed Kites which summered nearby for several years. There was some evidence that they nested, though not for the last two years. They might just reappear here. Also, watch overhead for flocks of migrating raptors, including Mississippi Kite. Check the area for Anhingas and several species of waders. Keep a sharp eye out in this area for Red-headed Woodpecker and Fish Crow.

Two miles west of its intersection with Craighen Road, Patterson Road ends at Highway 124. Turn south, through Hamshire, and drive 6.0 miles to rejoin Highway 73. Proceed west for two miles to Interstate 10's exit 828 at Winnie and get onto the freeway.

Drive west on Interstate 10 to exit 813 (14.7). Turn south onto Highway 61 toward Anahuac and Hankamer. Immediately on the right is the entrance to **White Memorial Park** on Turtle Bayou. Although the mosquitoes can be as big as the birds, this 73-acre park is a beautiful place to camp. There is even a cold-water shower here which can feel great after a hot day of birding.

In this oak/magnolia/pine forest one can find many of the birds that are typical of the eastern woodlands. Look for Red-bellied and Pileated Woodpeckers, Carolina Chickadee, Tufted Titmouse, Brown Creeper, Carolina Wren, Pine Warbler, and Common Grackle. Occasionally, Red-headed Woodpecker, Brown-headed Nuthatch, Purple Finch, or Dark-eyed Junco visits. In summer you should find Great Crested Flycatcher, Northern Parula and Yellow-throated Warblers, White-eyed and Yellow-throated Vireos, and Orchard Oriole. Winter brings Northern Flicker, Brown Thrasher, flocks of Yellow-rumped Warblers with Solitary Vireos tagging along, and White-throated Sparrow. Barred Owls hunt the park by night. Migrants are occasionally abundant here.

Before leaving, check Pinchback Road, which is straight across Highway 61 from the south entrance to White Memorial Park. In spring the south side of this road and the Chambers County Golf Course to which it leads have many of the species listed above. In addition, Red-headed Woodpecker is more common here. Each spring there are always two or three pairs of nesting Swainson's Warblers.

Return to Highway 61 and turn left (south), watching the dead pines on the east side of the road for Red-headed Woodpeckers and, rarely,

Brown-headed Nuthatches. Pileated Woodpeckers often fly back and forth across the road along this stretch. Turn west with the highway (3.2) to the small settlement of Anahuac. Turn left at the blinking light onto Main Street (2.8). Historians do not agree on the origin of the name Anahuac (AN-a-wack), but some residents say that the Mexicans, who established a fort just south of town, called it by the Aztec name for the central plateau of Mexico. Anyway, it is a nice little town with two main streets. Washington Street is one block west of Main Street where the town's only cafe and the Anahuac National Wildlife Refuge headquarters are located.

Continue south on Main Street to **Fort Anahuac Park** (0.7), on the right. In spite of the limited facilities, this is a nice place to camp or picnic, and you should be able to find a few migrants in the live oaks. There is usually a flock of Common Grackles here, and sometimes Boat-tailed and Great-tailed Grackles as well. Down the cliff past the boat ramp you will find a dirt road that follows the levee of the barge canal for a couple of miles. (If it has recently rained, do not try to drive this road.) At the very end, there are always a few shorebirds.

When leaving the park, continue south on South Main Street and turn left onto Farm Road 2936 (1.9). Take this road to its end at Farm Road 562 (3.5) and turn right (south). In spring watch the flooded rice fields along this road for shorebirds, including Whimbrel, and for Gull-billed Terns in migration. Check the utility wires along 562 for Couch's/Tropical Kingbirds. Almost every year, sometime from September to December, this "species" will appear. The problem is, that without vocalization local birders can't differentiate the two birds, and the individuals here simply refuse to call at all.

At the junction with Farm Road 1985 (5.0), FM 562 bears to the right to **Smith Point/Candy Abshire Wildlife Management Area** (14.0), off Plummer Road on the left. Because of its geographical location, the Abshire Wildlife Management Area (236 acres), a tract of oak motte and prairie on Smith Point, is a prime spot for viewing raptors during fall migration. Smith Point juts into Galveston Bay, and migrating raptors, passerines, and other birds which follow the coastline ultimately concentrate at this location before heading south over the Gulf of Mexico. In August Mississippi Kites pass over the area in hundreds, and by late September Broad-winged Hawks stream over by the thousands. Merlins and Peregrines are regular, and American Swallow-tailed Kite is seen occasionally. It is also an excellent place to study accipiters, since nearly a hundred each of Sharp-shinned and Cooper's Hawks can fly over in a single morning. From about mid-September through late October, the Smith Point Hawk Count is conducted from this site. Volunteers are stationed here every fall morning.

In early September, passerine migration peaks at Smith Point. Thousands of swallows head out over the Gulf of Mexico from this location daily, and the oak mottes attract warblers, flycatchers, buntings, orioles, and many others before they depart for points south. The spring migration can also make the mottes here exciting, especially with "fallouts," but this is basically a fall birding-spot.

A little farther on Farm Road 562 on your right is Hawkins Camp Road with Robbin's Park at the end (1.7). Here you can put in a boat and visit the famous rookery on the Vignt-et-un Islands (also spelled Vingt-un and pronounced locally as Van-TUNE). Lacking a boat, you can still climb the low observation tower to see Roseate Spoonbills and egrets nesting on the small islands to the west. Black Skimmers, American Oystercatchers, terns, and gulls loaf on the sand bars; waders, shorebirds, rails, gallinules, and cormorants can be seen in the surrounding marshes.

Return to the intersection of Farm Road 562 and Farm Road 1985.

Merlin
Gail Diane Luckner

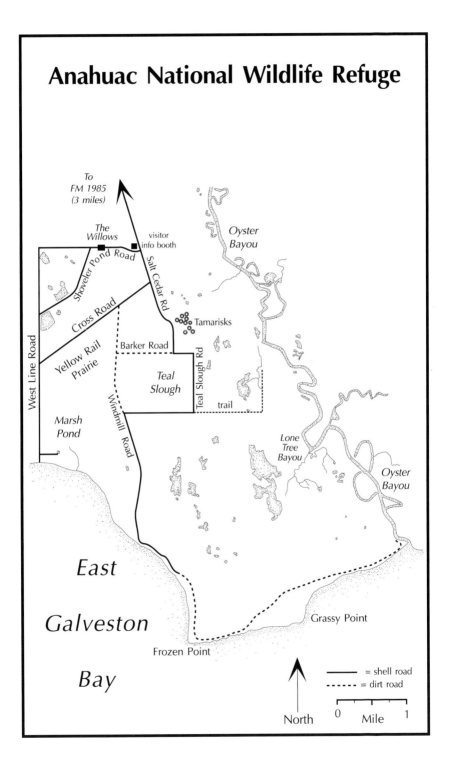

Anahuac National Wildlife Refuge

To
FM 1985
(3 miles)

The
Willows

visitor
info booth

Oyster
Bayou

Shoveler Pond Road

Salt Cedar Rd

Cross Road

Tamarisks

West Line Road

Yellow Rail
Prairie

Barker Road

Teal Slough Rd

Teal
Slough

trail

Windmill Road

Marsh
Pond

Lone
Tree
Bayou

Oyster
Bayou

East

Galveston

Grassy Point

Bay

Frozen Point

North

0   Mile   1

————— = shell road
- - - - - = dirt road

CHAPTER 3:
ANAHUAC NATIONAL WILDLIFE REFUGE

The best birding spot in the coastal marsh of the Upper Texas Coast is the 27,506-acre **Anahuac National Wildlife Refuge** (PO Box 278, Anahuac, Texas 77514; telephone 409/267-3337). To reach it from where we left off at the last chapter, turn right (east) onto Farm Road 1985 to the refuge entrance road (4.2), then go right to the check-station (3.0). Stop to register and to pick up a map, checklist of the birds, and information on road conditions. Parts of the refuge may be closed during the hunting season or in wet weather. This sign-in area is great at night for numerous (up to twenty) Barn Owls which hunt around the lights.

This refuge is situated in the coastal marsh adjacent to East Galveston Bay. Much of the land is low, poorly-drained, and covered by wet expanses of *Spartina* grasses. However, there are also cultivated fields, ponds, bayous, marshes, and a section of beach. During extremely wet weather, the refuge may be almost inundated, but a system of elevated roads allows vehicle access to much of the area. It does not take long to drive all the open roads, and you should do so. (Be warned, however, that the clay roads in the area can be extremely slippery when wet.)

Birding is good all year, and, although the refuge is managed primarily as a wintering area for ducks (20 species) and geese (4 species), some 250 other species of birds have been recorded here. There are also some interesting mammals, reptiles, and amphibians. Some of the birds to be found at any season are Great Blue, Little Blue, and Tricolored Herons, Cattle, Great, and Snowy Egrets, Black-crowned and Yellow-crowned Night-Herons, Mottled Duck, Blue-winged Teal, King and Clapper Rails, Purple Gallinule (nests), Common Moorhen, and Seaside Sparrow. In spring migration Black Terns and numerous shorebirds pass through, including Lesser Golden-Plover, Black-bellied Plover, American Avocet, and even such rarities as Hudsonian Godwit and Upland, White-rumped, Baird's, and Buff-breasted Sandpipers. If the weather is foul, you may find flycatchers, warblers, sparrows, and other landbirds in the Tamarisks. Many of the same species occur as fall migrants.

Numerically, birds are most abundant in late fall and winter when the ducks and geese arrive. Some 30 species have been recorded, of which 25 can be regularly expected. The early arrivals begin to gather in late August, and by November there are huge concentrations. The thousands of geese put on the most spectacular show, but the birder may be more interested in looking for Ross's Goose, Cinnamon Teal, the rare Masked Duck, or the Bald and Golden Eagles which follow the geese down from the north.

Ducks and geese are not the only interesting winter visitors. This is the time of year to look for loons, grebes, American White Pelican, Wilson's Phalarope, Short-eared Owl, Sedge Wren, Sprague's Pipit, Le Conte's and Sharp-tailed Sparrows, and the elusive Yellow Rail. The rail is rather common in the wet areas of *Spartina*, but very difficult to see. (The "Rail Buggy" excursions at the refuge that used to produce Yellow Rails—and sometimes Black Rails—were discontinued about ten years ago.)

While birds are the most conspicuous wildlife, there are other things as well. Some of the mammals to watch for are Otter, Mink, Muskrat, Gray Fox, Bobcat, Opossum, Swamp Rabbit, and Eastern Cottontail. The animal most frequently seen is the introduced Nutria (or Coypu). These large beaverlike

Buff-breasted Sandpiper
Gail Diane Luckner

mammals can be seen swimming or walking along most of the canals. They are larger than Muskrats; look for their yellow-orange front teeth.

The most impressive reptile here is the American Alligator. Its numbers are increasing; they may be seen about most of the ponds. The easiest place to find one is along the north side of Shoveler Pond; look on the grassy ridge about 30 feet offshore. You may also see Red-eared Slider, Western Cottonmouth, Gulf Salt Marsh Water Snake, and several species of frogs and toads.

The first place that local birders used to head for at Anahuac National Wildlife Refuge was Shoveler Pond, but according to Mike Austin, this generalization is no longer true. He claims that **The Willows** (a shallow pond surrounded by willows located one-half mile west of the sign-in station along the road to Shoveler Pond) has become a migrant trap of some repute. Sometimes in early fall, according to Mike, it will have migrants when High Island doesn't. At that season it is famous for flycatchers, particularly empids. In spring, warblers of three to five species, particularly Palms, will stop here. Mike says that he has not yet figured out why this one stand of willows is attractive to migrants while the other isolated groves of Hackberries and willows on the refuge are not. Occasionally, too, Barn Owls will roost in the grove.

At Shoveler Pond, you will find a big, shallow tract of fresh water attractive to ducks, grebes, coots, and gallinules, although you will need a scope to see most of them. The more interesting ones always seem to be out in the middle. In summer, beautiful Purple Gallinules almost outnumber Common Moorhens, and Roseate Spoonbills will be hard to miss. There are usually cormorants perched on the pilings—in summer they will be Neotropic and in winter, Double-crested. In the fall both species occur side by side, making comparisons easy. Fall is also the time to see the hundreds of Fulvous Whistling-Ducks which gather here before moving south in November.

In 1967, a local birder discovered a pair of Masked Ducks on the northeast corner of Shoveler Pond, and this species has been found here a number of times since then. They have even nested here. Normally they arrive in late July and disappear by November. However, nesting pairs in South Texas have lingered until February, so Masked Ducks found at Anahuac might stay longer. They may just become lost in the thousands of other ducks which are almost indistinguishable in their eclipse plumages. Look for Masked Ducks hidden in the vegetation, either on the bank or in the water. They are very shy and prefer to stay concealed. Another difficulty is that they may be in eclipse plumage. Both birds of the pair that nested here resembled females, but obviously not both of them were.

After searching Shoveler Pond, drive down West Line Road. In spring Seaside Sparrows sing from the fence line and Least Bitterns may be seen flying across the canal. In winter check the grassy fields on the other side of the fence for Sprague's Pipits and Le Conte's Sparrows, and the brackish ditches near the bay for Sharp-tailed Sparrows. If you sit quietly by the side of a slough, the sparrows will often come out and run along the open spaces between the water's edge and the vegetation. At the bay, scope the water for Magnificent Frigatebirds, which move northward in late summer. They often sit on the poles marking the oyster beds. At the spot where Oyster Bayou meets the bay, look for American Avocets.

In migration shorebirds are plentiful at many places on the refuge, depending on the water level. Marsh Pond and Teal Slough are usually good spots. Other migrants, such as Eastern and Western Kingbirds, Scissor-tailed Flycatcher, and Barn, Tree, Northern Rough-winged, and Bank Swallows, may be abundant. In bad weather check the Tamarisks (commonly called Salt-cedars) to the east of Salt Cedar Road for warblers, even if you have to walk in. These century-old trees, planted as windbreaks, serve as fine havens for weary birds. The best thing about these trees is that they are in rows, making birding easy. By getting someone to walk down each side, you can flush the birds ahead of you toward the end of the row, then watch them as they fly back past you.

After touring the refuge, return to Farm Road 1985 and turn right (east) to Highway 124 (10.4). (Refer to the map at the beginning of previous chapter.) In spring, this section of road traverses excellent rice field shorebird habitat. Another good road for shorebird-filled rice fields is Farm Road 1941, which parallels Farm Road 1985 and can be reached via Pear Orchard Road (unmarked at present, and an excellent place for Short-eared Owls in winter), a dirt road that runs north from Farm Road 1985 3.6 miles east of the Anahuac refuge entrance road. Good birds to look for here include Lesser Golden-Plover, Hudsonian Godwit, and Upland, White-rumped, and Buff-breasted Sandpipers. Some local birders regard these rice fields and other wet areas that you have just gone through as the finest freshwater shorebird habitat on the Upper Texas Coast. In summer look for Wood Storks here, also.

At Highway 124 turn right (south) toward High Island. Keep checking the fields for waders and shorebirds. In winter Snow and Greater White-fronted Geese are abundant. Try to pick out a few Ross's among the Snow Geese. Check the marshes on each side of the Intracoastal Waterway (6.0 miles from Farm Road 1985), where you may usually find the brown-eyed Boat-tailed Grackle. The area is also good for Pectoral and Solitary Sandpipers at the right season. From here you can begin to see High Island ahead (2.2), sitting as it does on a salt-dome.

Ross's Goose
Snow Goose
Blue morph Snow Goose
Gail Diane Luckner

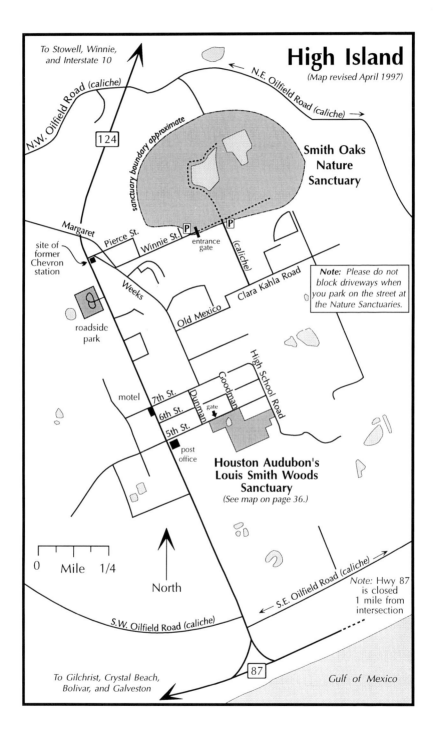

High Island
(Map revised April 1997)

To Stowell, Winnie, and Interstate 10

N.E. Oilfield Road *(caliche)* →

N.W. Oilfield Road *(caliche)*

124

sanctuary boundary approximate

**Smith Oaks
Nature
Sanctuary**

Margaret

Pierce St.

Winnie St.

site of former Chevron station

entrance gate

P P

(caliche)

Clara Kahla Road

Note: Please do not block driveways when you park on the street at the Nature Sanctuaries.

Weeks

Old Mexico

roadside park

High School Road

motel

7th St.

Goodman

Dunman

6th St.

gate

5th St.

post office

**Houston Audubon's
Louis Smith Woods
Sanctuary**
(See map on page 36.)

0   Mile   1/4

North

S.E. Oilfield Road *(caliche)* →

Note: Hwy 87 is closed 1 mile from intersection

S.W. Oilfield Road *(caliche)*

87

To Gilchrist, Crystal Beach, Bolivar, and Galveston

Gulf of Mexico

CHAPTER 4:
HIGH ISLAND

The land along the Gulf coast here is flat, low, and marshy with a very high water-table. Only occasionally is there a bit of ground high enough to support trees. Such islands are locally called "hummocks." They often have fine mottes of Virginia Live-Oak, Hackberry, or Chinese Tallow trees. An excellent example is **High Island**, a place that has become famous for birds during migration. Its dark green motte of oaks can easily be seen for miles across the flat marshes. To a migrating bird caught in a norther, it offers just about the only haven for miles. It is no wonder that High Island is one of the best birding spots along the coast during migration, especially in spring (mid-April to mid-May). But fall migration (mid-August through October) at High Island can sometimes be good, too.

As you enter town on Highway 124, proceed past Pierce Street on the left; you will notice a Chevron station at the intersection. From here continue to a small roadside park on the right (0.2), marked by a sign that says *Picnic Area* on the left of the road. This can be a fine place in spring for warblers and for Bobolinks.

During stormy weather any patch of trees in High Island, however, can be alive with vireos, up to thirty species a day of warblers, flycatchers, thrushes, Scarlet Tanagers, Rose-breasted Grosbeaks, Indigo Buntings, and orioles. Still, the best spots in town are two fine groves on the eastern side of town. At either of these two places one can often stand or sit in one spot and watch the bird species change by the minute. Both have large trees and fine tangles of underbrush. Both are now either fully or partially owned by the Houston Audubon Society. A small fee is required to visit. (The fees go for the maintenance of the sanctuaries and acquisition of more bird habitat.)

The **Houston Audubon's Louis Smith Woods Sanctuary**, commonly known as Boy Scout Woods (fee) is excellent for migrants that have just struggled across the Gulf. To reach the Sanctuary, continue to 5th Street (0.5), where you will see the Post Office on the corner, and turn left. Immediately you should see the huge trees down the road on the right. Drive to the Sanctuary entrance (0.2). You can park on the right side of 5th Street, but birders should be careful about blocking driveways. At the Sanctuary there are clean restrooms, boardwalks to birdy spots, attractive ponds, and benches

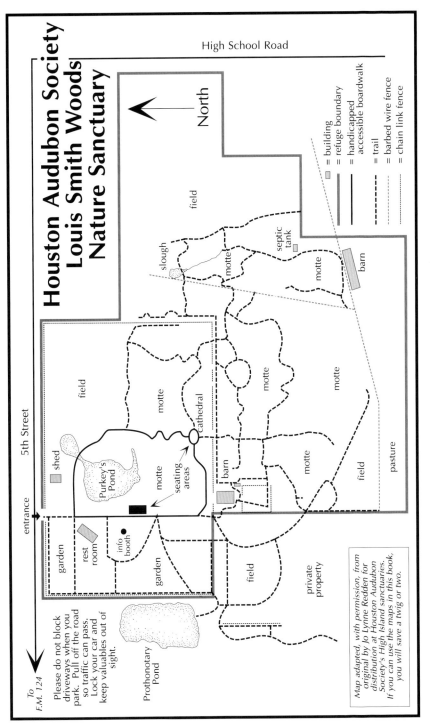

Houston Audubon Society
Louis Smith Woods
Nature Sanctuary

High School Road

North

= building

= refuge boundary

= handicapped
accessible boardwalk

= trail

= barbed wire fence

= chain link fence

5th Street

entrance

garden

shed

rest
room

info
booth

garden

Purkey's Pond

motte

seating
areas

Cathedral

motte

barn

motte

motte

field

field

private
property

Prothonotary
Pond

field

slough

motte

septic
tank

motte

barn

field

motte

field

pasture

To
F.M. 124

Please do not block
driveways when you
park. Pull off the road
so traffic can pass.
Lock your car and
keep valuables out of
sight.

Map adapted, with permission, from
original by Jo Lynne Redden for
distribution at Houston Audubon
Society's High Island sanctuaries.
If you can use the maps in this book,
you will save a twig or two.

Entrance station and gallery, Louis Smith Woods

Michael J. Austin

for viewing. Sanctuary volunteers are on duty during spring migration to help make your visit more enjoyable. They will give you information, answer your questions, pass out maps, take your entrance fees, and sell you checklists. They keep a daily list of reported birds, and also post all rarities seen in the High Island area—including down the Bolivar Peninsula and Galveston. Please stay on the boardwalks and on the deck at the Cathedral area so that the vegetation and underbrush may recuperate. The boardwalks are intended to restore areas of the sanctuary for such birds as Ovenbird, both waterthrushes, and Hooded, Worm-eating, Swainson's, and Kentucky

Swainson's Warbler
Gail Diane Luckner

Warblers. Check out the two large ponds and the small bathing-pond. In front of the pond is a tier of benches where birders may sit and watch the show. Other benches are scattered about in secluded areas where some birders may wish to sit and listen or quietly watch. The trees may yield a wonderful variety of landbirds, and sometimes a Barn Owl or a Yellow-crowned Night-Heron is located.

To reach **Smith Oaks Sanctuary** (fee) return on Highway 124 toward the north edge of town. Go past the roadside park (0.7) on the left and turn right at Pierce Street by the Chevron Station (0.2). Go one-half block and turn right onto Weeks Avenue. Go one block and turn left onto Winnie Street just before reaching a building with a radio transmitter. Follow this road as it gets narrower and narrower and finally ends at the entrance gate. You will pay a fee here and receive parking instructions. Some parking is also available just outside the gate. Do not block the drive when parking. Walk the numerous trails that have been cleared among the huge trees on this old estate. This is still partially private property and might be posted at some future date if birders abuse the privilege of being in this delightful spot.

The large trees and other vegetation here are similar to those found farther inland along the river-bottoms, so there is a resident population of typical eastern-woodland birds. However, the birding is at its best following a foul, rainy day during migration. At such times the trees lure vireos, warblers, orioles, tanagers, grosbeaks, thrushes, and buntings. The heavy underbrush attracts even such shy birds as Gray Catbird, Wood, Swainson's, and Gray-cheeked Thrushes, Veery, Swainson's, Worm-eating, Kentucky, and Hooded Warblers, Northern and Louisiana Waterthrushes, and Ovenbird. Other warblers that are difficult to find elsewhere in Texas, but may be found more easily here, include Black-throated Blue, Cape May, and Cerulean.

High Island   Michael J. Austin

Another spot worth checking at High Island is a pond excellent for migrating shorebirds. Go north on Highway 124 to Northeast Oilfield Road on the north end of town (1.1). Turn to the right, where you will soon find a pond on the left (0.3).

Migration time at High Island can truly be exciting. Westerly winds in the spring have brought in Western Tanager, Black-headed Grosbeak, and Townsend's Warbler. American Swallow-tailed Kites have been spotted flying over town. In late May 1984 a Greenish Elaenia from Mexico appeared at Louis Smith Woods Sanctuary and stayed around for lucky observers for four days. Almost anything is possible at High Island.

Accommodations at High Island, though, are at a premium. If you plan to stay in High Island during the peak of spring migration, it is wise to make reservations well in advance since tours and individual birders quickly fill the few motel rooms. Try the Gulfway Motel, the only motel in town (telephone: 409/286-5217). Jon and Glenda Llast have opened a Bed and Breakfast right near the Smith Oaks Sanctuary that can accommodate eight (telephone: 409/286-5362). Inquire at the Gulfway for other rooms in town. Overnight parking is allowed at the roadside park, but there are no restrooms or hook-ups there.

Outside of High Island there are some other possibilities. A Best Western Motel on Interstate 10 (exit 829) just north of Winnie is available (telephone: 409/296-9292). By the town of Crystal Beach on the shore there is the Crystal Palace Resort Motel (telephone: 409/684-6554). The small shoreline village of Gilchrist also has several RV facilities.

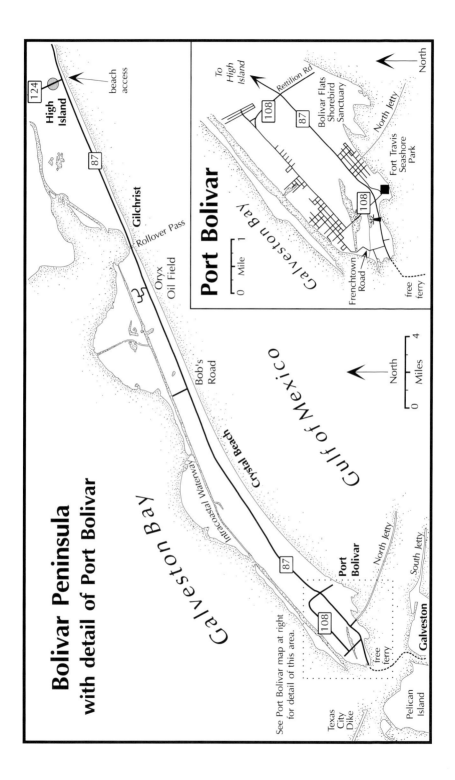

Bolivar Peninsula
with detail of Port Bolivar

124

High Island

beach access

87

Gilchrist

Rollover Pass

Oryx Oil Field

Bob's Road

Galveston Bay

Intracoastal Waterway

Crystal Beach

87

See Port Bolivar map at right for detail of this area.

108

Port Bolivar

North Jetty

free ferry

South Jetty

Gulf of Mexico

Galveston

Texas City Dike

Pelican Island

North

0   Miles   4

Port Bolivar

To High Island

Rettilion Rd

108

87

Bolivar Flats Shorebird Sanctuary

North Jetty

Fort Travis Seashore Park

108

Frenchtown Road

free ferry

Galveston Bay

North

0   Mile   1

CHAPTER 5:
BOLIVAR PENINSULA

To continue the tour down the coast, go south on Highway 124 from High Island to Highway 87 (0.5). This road will extend the length of the Bolivar (BAL-i-ver) Peninsula. The Peninsula is 27 miles long and varies in width from 3½ miles at Crystal Beach to ¼ mile at Rollover Pass.

There is a break at the beach at the intersection of Highways 124 and 87. You can simply observe at this opening, or you take a more adventurous route down the beach. Turn right at the beach. The sand is usually firm here for a few miles, and driving along the shore is permitted. Take into consideration the tides, weather, and vehicle capabilities. This stretch is a good bet for Snowy, Piping, and Semipalmated Plovers during the winter. There is an exit about two miles down this beach at Meacom's Pier. For those not wishing to chance getting stuck in the sand, stay on 87.

Highway 87 borders the beach, and houses become more common as you start down Bolivar Peninsula. The first town is Gilchrist (7.3) at Rollover Pass, where a canal has been cut between the ocean and the bay. The pass gets its name from the days when early ship captains could import merchandise from the Gulf over to East Bay and from there to the mainland without the bothersome contact with officials at Galveston. Reportedly, supplies were rolled across the peninsula. Today the canal allows easy passage, is a much-used fishing spot, and is a good place to bird.

Before crossing the canal, investigate both sides. On the right, just offshore, is a long sandbar, where gulls, terns, skimmers, shorebirds, and sometimes American Oystercatchers rest. Farther out you will see several small islands which support nesting colonies of Great, Snowy, Reddish, and Cattle Egrets, Tricolored Herons, Black-crowned Night-Herons, Roseate Spoonbills, Laughing Gulls, Royal, Sandwich, and Forster's Terns, and Black Skimmers. In migration or winter American Avocets and Marbled Godwits can be found here. To the left of the bridge is the open water and another chance to look through various gulls and terns. The first Long-tailed Jaeger in Texas was found here in 1971.

The next good stop is the Oryx Oil Field (3.5) on the right. The management usually allows entry at 8am and locks the gate by 2pm. It is best to check in at the building just inside the gate. As you drive in, look to the left to see if the gates are open, and be sure to note the current time that they will be locked. (While in here, stay away from well-heads, do not enter any fenced area containing a building, and turn around if you see hunters.) Two roads—one west and one east—go back about a mile to the Intracoastal Canal. On the way back you will pass ponds, sloughs, and marshes, good for ducks, spoonbills, and shorebirds. Check the brushy island and the row of Tamarisks near the first pond for night-herons. Most will be Black-crowned, but there are usually a few Yellow-crowned also. On the east side of the property is a three-acre woodlot of Hackberries. The road does not go all the way to the woods, and a quarter-mile walk across a moist field is needed. This woodlot is excellent during spring fall-outs and produced the first U.S. record of Yucatan Vireo in the spring of 1984. Give yourself plenty of time to be back at the gate by posted closing-time.

On the beach side of the peninsula are many access roads, some of which will allow you to drive on the beach, a good vantage point for observing shorebirds and other species riding the surf. In winter you may find all three scoter species, Red-breasted Merganser, Eared Grebe, and many Lesser Scaup.

Bob's Road (4.8) is at the north edge of the settlement of Crystal Beach. Turn right and follow this dirt road back to the bay. The marshes and ponds harbor most of the typical water birds; both American Swallow-tailed (rare) and Black-shouldered Kites have been seen hunting over the fields and woods during migration. A Curlew Sandpiper made a surprise visit here in the spring of 1984.

Bolivar Flats Shorebird Sanctuary (Houston Audubon Society), lying in the lee of the North Jetty at the entrance to Galveston Bay, is probably the best spot for shorebirds on the Upper Texas Coast. To reach it, turn left at Rettilion Road (opposite Loop 108) (8.0) to the beach (0.7). If the tide is low, drive to the right on the sand for about three-quarters of a mile until you reach the Houston Audubon Society fence. Do not drive beyond this point even if conditions permit. Park by the pilings and walk from there. Bring your scope. If the beach is not passable, you can walk, or go back to the highway and continue to 17th Street, which leads to the jetty. The view from the jetty is usually not as good as from the beach because of poor light conditions.

These tidal flats have an abundance of birds at all seasons. Most of the shorebirds to be found in the area occur here. It is one of the best places to find Snowy and other plovers, American Avocets, Black-necked Stilts, Red Knots, Marbled Godwits, American Oystercatchers, and both pelicans. Gulls and terns are well represented, as well as Reddish Egrets, Roseate Spoonbills, and other waders. After a rain the freshwater pools along the beach may have Hudsonian Godwit, Long-billed Dowitchers, Lesser Yellowlegs, and White-rumped, Baird's, and Semipalmated Sandpipers. Besides the rare shorebirds, also watch for rare gulls that have shown up, such as Great

Roseate Spoonbills
Shawneen Finnegan

Black-backed, Lesser Black-backed, California, and Glaucous Gulls. Between the highway and the beach you should see the resident Seaside Sparrows and Sharp-tailed Sparrows in the winter.

If you have plenty of time, there are other spots along this section of highway worth checking. Loop 108 makes a loop to the right through Port Bolivar and then returns to the highway. A fine place to find Yellow-crowned Night-Herons in winter can be reached by going to the other end of the loop and turning right. Just before reaching the bridge, stop by the 45-mph sign and look over the marsh to your right. You may have to stand on the bumper of the car to see them. Migrants and wintering sparrows like the trees and bushes about the houses in the town. The area around Fort Travis Seashore Park (camping; telephone: 409/766-2411) may be worth checking. French Town Road, another local access road on the right just before the ferry landing, is often worth the detour.

On the ferry—from Point Bolivar to Galveston   Paul J. Baicich

Bolivar Ferry

For a change of pace, continue to the end of the peninsula and take the free ferry to Galveston. After boarding, climb up to the observation deck. Check the pilings on the right for Neotropic and Double-crested Cormorants in winter and, with luck, Magnificent Frigatebirds in summer. As soon as the ship gets under way, there will be numerous gulls and terns following in its wake. During the three-mile, 13-minute ride, you will have ample time to study or photograph their graceful flight if you move to the rear of the ferry. This is an easy way to study gulls and terns, because they hover right overhead and you can compare their bills, feet, wings, and sizes. If you feed the gulls from the ferry, you will soon find that most of the other passengers have retreated to the safety of their vehicles. Be sure to wear a hat while doing this. Nearly all of the gulls seen in summer will be Laughing, but in winter there are also Herring, Ring-billed, and Bonaparte's. The year-round terns are Gull-billed, Forster's, Royal, and Caspian. They are joined in summer by Least and Sandwich and in migration by Common and Black; however, many of the seasonal terns occur as stragglers at other times.

In addition to the gulls and terns, you may see Black Skimmers and flights of herons and egrets. In winter there may be loons, grebes, and ducks. If you are lucky, a Bottle-nosed Dolphin may race along by the boat. These mammals were formerly abundant in the bay, but are decreasing rapidly.

The ferry crosses the main shipping channel for the ports of Houston and Galveston. You may pass huge ocean liners from all parts of the world. Farther along on the right is the sunken hull of a World War I ship made of concrete. Next to come into view on the right will be veterans of World War II, the submarine *Cavalla* and the destroyer escort *USS Stewart*. Then, on the left, you will see the Coast Guard Station and sometimes a ship owned by the Army Corps of Engineers.

You may ride back and forth on the ferry as long as you wish. Just leave your car in the parking lot to the left of the ferry landing and walk back on board.

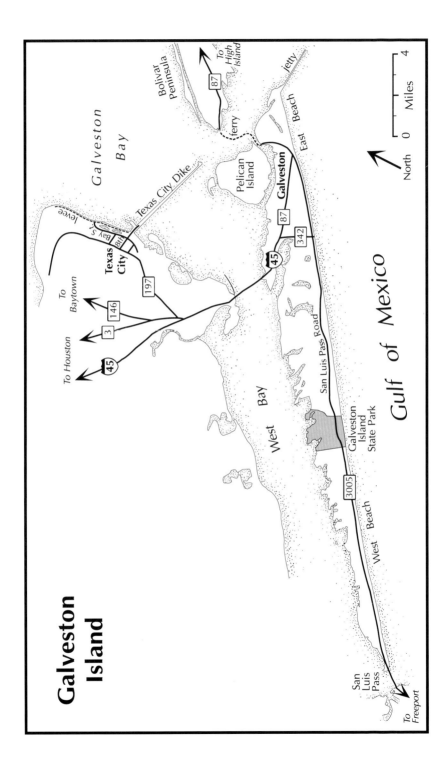

CHAPTER 6:
GALVESTON

Galveston Island has long been a mecca for birders, and despite private construction and government decisions to the detriment of wildlife, the island still offers some excellent birding. Over 300 species of birds have been found here, and most of the birding spots are easily reached by car.

Shorebirds are common; many of them winter in the numerous marshes and mudflats about the island. Gulls, terns, and Black Skimmers are abundant along the 32 miles of Gulf beaches, and thousands of colonial-nesting waterbirds such as herons, egrets, ibises, spoonbills, cormorants, gulls, and terns nest in the large rookeries on small islands in adjacent Galveston Bay. It is not easy to visit the rookeries because a boat is required, but most of the nesters can be seen feeding about the island.

A cold front moving through during migration—either spring or fall—may bring down an array of exhausted landbirds. When a front is combined with a heavy rain, the results are even more impressive.

Drive straight ahead on Ferry Road as you leave the ferry until you reach Highway 168 (0.9). Turn left here and angle back toward the Coast Guard base. A line of vegetation can be observed from the road. White-winged and other doves should be easy to locate, and Groove-billed Ani may show up here on occasion. Sparrows seem to like the area, too. Do not enter any fenced area even if the gates are open. Then retrace your route back to Ferry Road and continue southwest.

Soon you will reach Seawall Boulevard (0.7). This wide street follows the seawall, which was built after the 1900 hurricane flooded the island and killed over 6,000 people. Today, the boulevard is the principal avenue used by tourists. It is lined on one side by an assortment of hotels, motels, and restaurants, and on the other side by the beautiful Gulf of Mexico. In spring and summer the area can be very crowded with tourists and sun-worshipers. Galveston is the most popular beach resort on the Texas Gulf Coast.

To continue birding, turn left and follow Seawall Boulevard until it ends at the bay (2.0). You might want to drive up on the levee on the left for better views of the marshes, water, and fields on each side.

Just before the Boulevard ends you can turn right onto Boddeker Road (1.9) and go out toward R. A. Apffel Park (1.3) and the South Jetty (0.6). Along

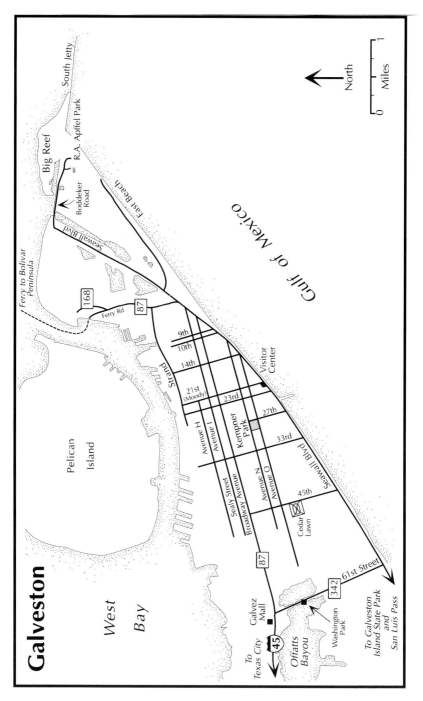

Galveston

the way there are small lagoons with shorebirds, waders, and ducks. Watch the area on the right for rails and check the ship channel for comparative looks at Double-crested and Neotropic Cormorants.

During the tourist season (April-October) a fee is charged to enter the beach at Apffel, but the booth may not be manned before 7am or 8am. The East Beach area is excellent for shorebirds, waders, gulls, and terns; low tide will expose extensive mudflats. This is an excellent area to observe most of the same species as are found on Bolivar Flats. It is a major wintering area for Piping and Snowy Plovers, Marbled Godwit, American Oystercatcher, Long-billed Curlew, Short-billed Dowitcher, and other species. White-rumped Sandpipers are regular migrants here.

In winter the South Jetty may have Spotted Sandpipers, Ruddy Turnstones, and, in some years, an occasional Purple Sandpiper. If you are a hardy rock-hopper, the end of the jetty is an excellent spot from which to watch for jaegers, Black-legged Kittiwakes, Northern Gannets, and other pelagic species, but you will be very lucky to see one.

You can return to town from the jetty by following the beach around its rim until you come to a paved road (1.1) that passes some high-rise condos (1.0). There will be ponds, marshes, and fields to check along this route back to Seawall Boulevard (0.9). Look for sparrows—Savannah, Le Conte's, Sharp-tailed, and Seaside.

At Seawall Boulevard turn left. (Galveston city streets are designated by letters—A to T, with the alphabet running NW to SE, Bay to Gulf, and by numbers running up as you go west. You will also discover that some of the streets have been given a second name, but the general grid prevails.)

While Seawall Boulevard is the primary tourist section, there is also an older downtown district. The Strand National Historic District, on the Strand and Mechanic Street between 20th and 25th Streets, has one of America's largest collections of 19th-century cast-iron architecture.

The Galveston Island Rail Trolley connects the Seawall with the Strand. It is a fine way to learn about the city's history. The trolley's south terminal is at the Visitors Center at Moody Avenue (21st Street) and Seawall Boulevard (2.3). The north terminal is at the Strand Visitors Center.

Galveston may have been officially founded by American entrepreneurs in 1856, but the first Europeans to land here were part of the shipwrecked Cabeza de Vaca party in 1528, and the pirate Jean Lafitte used the island for raids on Gulf shipping from 1817 to 1821. Throughout the 19th century, Galveston was probably the most important city in Texas, serving as the chief port and the leading financial center. The city boasts many firsts for the state: the first telegraph, first Catholic convent, first electric lights, first brewery, first free library, first medical school, and the first dial telephones. It also claims the oldest bank and one of the oldest newspapers.

You might want to check around the Court House at the corner of Moody (21st) and H Streets (0.9) for White-winged Doves, which can sometimes be found in the oak trees out front. This is where Galveston's White-winged Dove population was first established.

Another birding spot is Kempner Park. To reach it go back down 21st Street to Avenue O (0.6). Turn right and continue until you reach 27th Street (0.5). The park's attraction for birds has diminished considerably in the past few years, but it can still be good for migrant passerines. Like every other spot along the coast, it is at its best during a norther, particularly a wet one. Under ideal conditions, you may find many warblers, vireos, thrushes, and other migrants. Most of the time you can count on finding the dainty little Inca Dove, which can be located by listening for its characteristic two-note call, *no hope.*

Adjacent to the west end of the park is the Old Hutchins-Sealy Home, which is surrounded by huge trees and dense shrubbery. By walking along the fence, you may find some of the area's shyer birds, such as Chuck-will's-widow, Brown Thrasher, Veery, Yellow-billed Cuckoo, and some of the migrating warblers. A blind alley across 29th Street is often very productive.

Another residential area that can be interesting during migration is Cedar Lawn. This enclave of circles and half circles departs from the usual rigid Galveston street pattern, so wander or drive around. Entrance is from 45th Street between L and N Streets. From Kempner Park continue on O Street to 45th. Turn right and make the third left at Cedar Lawn (1.5). The residents here are used to seeing birders. *You should, however, resist any temptation to follow anything into anyone's yard.* When you fumble your way out of this area, consult the nearest street sign, get your bearings, and head north to Broadway and turn left (west).

Behind the Galvez Mall is another little-known spot. Turn north off Broadway at 61st Street (1.6) and go to the rear of the mall parking area. Drive along the edge of the scrub to the far corner and park near some old railroad tracks. Walk down these tracks for excellent views of several freshwater ponds. Look for grebes, herons, and ducks here.

At this point you have an option to visit the Texas City Dike. If that choice appeals to you, take the feeder road to Interstate 45 (1.5) and head over the causeway. (*Interstate 45 is also a quick route to Houston, and an alternate way to get into the next chapter.*)

TEXAS CITY DIKE

Most birders visiting the Galveston area in winter make the short trip to view waterfowl from the Texas City Dike, which can be reached by going northwest from Galveston on Interstate 45. The assemblage found there

Levee at Texas City   Paul J. Baicich

could include both Common and Pacific Loons, Red-breasted Merganser, and other ducks as well as stray gulls.

Leaving Galveston on Interstate 45 take Exit 5 onto a feeder road (5.0). This road, which parallels the highway, will give you a chance to bird the ponds on the right as you continue on to Texas City. This road bends to the right at Exit 7 (1.7), and merges with Highway 146, which branches immediately. Take Loop 197, the road to the right (0.5). Often there is good birding along the first mile or so of this route to the dike. Continue on Loop 197 to 6th Avenue N. (4.3), turn right, and proceed to where it ends at Bay Street (0.5). A left turn will take you to 8th Avenue N. and from there take a right turn at the traffic light to the dike (0.5).

The huge anchor by the motel at the base of the dike is a reminder of a disaster that occurred here in 1947. A French ship full of nitrates caught fire in the harbor, and the local citizens crowded the shore to watch it burn. It suddenly exploded, killing 576 people, wounding 5,000, and leveling a large part of the town. This 5-ton anchor was blown a half-mile from the ship.

The five-mile Texas City Dike extends straight out into Galveston Bay. It is a popular birding, fishing, and camping area, although facilities for the latter are limited. It is a fine place to study gulls, terns, and shorebirds. In winter Common Loons, Eared Grebes, and American White Pelicans are common; occasionally there is a Red-throated Loon, Horned Grebe, or Oldsquaw. For several years a Lesser Black-backed Gull wintered on the beach behind the first restroom and afforded many birders a lifer. Black-legged Kittiwake has been recorded, also. On leaving the dike, turn right and drive along the top of the levee on Skyline Drive. Many interesting ducks are usually in the long pond on the left. Watch the trees beyond this pond for Black-shouldered Kites and Northern Harriers. In winter both American and Sprague's Pipits can be

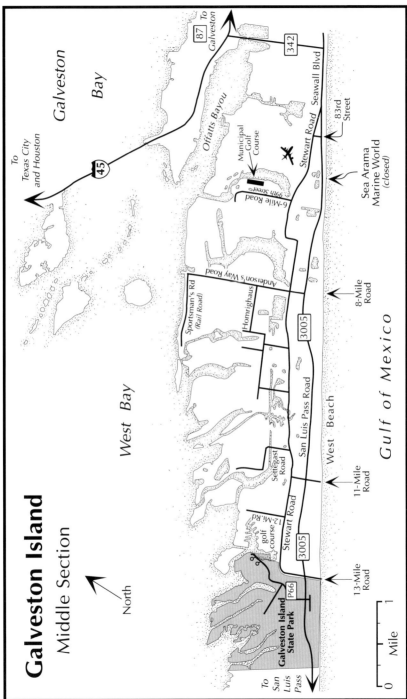

Galveston Island
Middle Section

North

found on the wide, sloping banks of the levee. You may have to hike around a bit to find them.

The levee-road goes 4.5 miles to a dead-end. To get off the levee, turn left at the fence (2.1), and cross the bridge. The road turns left onto Bay Street and leads back to Texas City. At 9th Avenue N. (1.9) turn right, then left onto Loop 197 and return to Galveston the way you came. (*Alternately, you can take Interstate 45 to Houston.*)

WEST GALVESTON ISLAND

If you have opted to stay in Galveston, return to 61st Street from the mall parking lot and go under Interstate 45. If you are returning to Galveston from Texas City, take exit 1A and turn right onto 61st Street. This will take you down a busy street and over Offatts Bayou. On the right is the Galveston County Boat Ramp, and a bit farther, a small city park, Washington Park (0.4 from Interstate 45), where you can escape the traffic and scan the water. A Pacific Loon is frequently here in winter, easily compared with the more numerous Common Loons. (Don't neglect to check the water on the east.) Continue down 61st and turn right onto Seawall Boulevard (1.2)

Some of the most productive birding areas on Galveston Island are at its west end. To reach them, continue down Seawall Boulevard. At 83rd Street (1.5) turn right, go one block, and turn left onto Stewart Road. The next seven-mile stretch of road can be very good for ducks, waders, shorebirds, and other migrants. (Some road signs are hard to read, have become victims of target practice, or are missing altogether. Pay attention to mileages here.) Go slow and pull over to stop wherever you see something interesting. Side roads can be productive, time permitting. The better ones are described below. You will soon pass Sea-Arama Marine World (the operation is closed, but the ponds are active) on the left (0.9).

Six-Mile Road (99th Street) is the first street that you will come to on the right (0.4). This will take you to the Galveston Island Municipal Golf Course on the right. Look there for Long-billed Curlew, Lesser Golden-Plover, Black-bellied Plover, Buff-breasted, Upland, and Baird's Sandpipers, and Killdeer. If it has rained recently, you may find landbirds in the small trees. Go back to Stewart.

Eight-Mile Road (or Anderson's Way) to the right (1.7) off Stewart Road is normally very productive. The pastures along the first part are good for plovers and shorebirds in migration, and for sparrows and pipits in winter. Near the end, another road goes off to the left (1.7). Its sign reads Sportsman's Road, but local birders call it the Rail Road because it is a good place to find Clapper Rails and, in season, Sora. Some of the other shorebirds which you can expect here in winter and migration are Common Snipe, Ruddy Turnstone, Long-billed Curlew, Greater and Lesser Yellowlegs, Willet,

Marbled Godwit, American Avocet, Solitary, Pectoral, White-rumped, Least, Stilt, Semipalmated, and Western Sandpipers, and Dunlin. Also common in the reeds, marshes, and backwaters are ducks, Great Blue, Little Blue, and Tricolored Herons, Cattle, Reddish, Great, and Snowy Egrets, White and White-faced Ibises, Roseate Spoonbill, and occasionally Wood Storks. In winter watch for Sharp-tailed Sparrow and in spring for Least Bittern. Near the turnaround (1.3) at the end of Sportman's Road you will see oyster bars in West Bay; at low tide these often attract American Oystercatchers. Also, check the bay for Magnificent Frigatebird, Red-breasted Merganser, Common Goldeneye, and just anything else that could show up.

On your way back down Eight-Mile Road turn off on Homrighaus Road (2.6) on the right. Here again you will be exposed to ponds, fields, and vegetation worthy of investigation. You can drive around wherever your interests take you and depend on the tall utility poles visible on Stewart Road to put you back on track.

Settegast Road is the next good road to check (2.7) along Stewart. It is on the right a mile past Ten-Mile Road, and you might reasonably expect it to be called Eleven-Mile Road, but that road is one-half mile farther along. Apparently, the highway department got confused. Just to confuse you further, local birders call it Nottingham Ranch Road. Anyway, check the pond on the right in summer for Least Bitterns and for Fulvous Whistling-Ducks during migration. Check the fields as you drive along toward the necessary left turn, then follow this along a well-grazed pasture. This area is excellent in spring for Black-bellied Plover, Lesser Golden-Plover, Long-billed Curlew, and Whimbrel. An Eskimo Curlew would probably love it. Be sure to check the small trees along the fence for migrants. For a number of years this area has produced a number of local vagrants—Curve-billed Thrasher, Western Meadowlark, Yellow-headed Blackbird, Pyrrhuloxia, Black-whiskered Vireo, Black-headed Grosbeak, and Lark Sparrow, among others. After satisfying yourself that none of these species is currently present, return once again to Stewart Road.

Continuing west on Stewart Road, you will soon pass Eleven-Mile Road. Farther along, there is another golf course (1.1) to be checked for "grasspipers." Stewart Road soon turns left and meets Termini Road (Farm Road 3005) (1.3). Turn right and drive a short distance to Park Road 66 (0.4). Turn into **Galveston Island State Park** (1,921 acres, camping, showers, fee; Route 1, Box 156A, Galveston, Texas 77554; telephone: 409/737-1222), with its coastal wetlands, salt meadows, coastal prairie, and 1.5 miles of beach, where birding can be very good. Stop at the park headquarters (on the beach side of Farm Road 3005) for a map and an informative elaborated checklist. The map has indicated the bird blinds, and, along with the checklist, Ted Eubanks has explained the uniqueness of the various habitats and the likely birds to be found in each. The Texas Park and Wildlife Department is currently attempting to restore habitat here, and to remove non-native trees and plants. The best areas are around the small ponds on the bay-side of the highway. The "Clapper Rail Trail", down a road to the west off the road leading to the north campground, is very good in winter for Hooded Merganser (found with some regularity), Marsh and Sedge Wrens, Palm Warblers, and Le Conte's and Sharp-tailed Sparrows. From the observation deck at the northeast extension of the trail, look for Common Goldeneye and Horned Grebe. (Parts of the trail are storm-damaged and await repair.) The nesting species found along the trail include Pied-billed Grebe, Gull-billed Tern, Black Skimmer, Black-shouldered Kite, Mottled Duck, Seaside Sparrow, Least Bittern, Clapper Rail, Purple Gallinule, Common Moorhen, Marsh Wren, and Common Yellowthroat. In midsummer, Magnificent Frigatebirds may roost on the posts over Carancahua Reef, visible from the north side of the campground located on the north side of the park.

Farm Road 3005 is the main road down the west end of the island. To follow the tour, you should continue toward San Luis Pass. At various points you can gain access to the beach. Red Knots, Piping and Snowy Plovers, and other winter shorebirds are easily found. At Indian Beach Road (3.0), you may want to check the ponds and inlets for as much as a mile. The area is good for ducks and shorebirds, but development threatens. Farther along on Farm Road 3005 you will cross ranchlands, which can be good for Lesser Golden-Plover, Long-billed Curlew, Whimbrel, and Upland, Buff-breasted, and Baird's Sandpipers in migration, and Sandhill Cranes in winter. In March of 1959 Ben Feltner found an Eskimo Curlew here. This co-operative bird stayed around for some weeks for all to see. It, or others, reappeared every April until 1965 and perhaps later. There are still occasional reports of this species from the area, but most of the sightings should be viewed with caution. When observed in the short-grass fields on Galveston Island, the Eskimo Curlew would feed with other shorebirds, with Lesser Golden-Plovers being its most likely companions. Recently, the Eskimo Curlew has been suspected

Ranchlands on West Galveston Island   Paul J. Baicich

Whimbrel
Eskimo Curlew
Shawneen E. Finnegan

Ben Feltner's Comments on Texas Eskimo Curlews:

In the early 1960s observations of Eskimo Curlew on the Texas Coast occurred most often on the western end of Galveston Island. Here its favorite habitat seems to be grassy fields that have been closely grazed by cattle. The consortium of birds that share this habitat with the curlew is made up primarily of Long-billed Curlews, Whimbrels, Upland Sandpipers, and [Lesser] Golden-Plovers.

All of the acceptable observations of this species have taken place between March 22 and April 29 with peak migration time seemingly being the last week of March and the first 10 days of April. On those happy occasions when the bird has been found here, it has usually stayed in the area for several days and, if not too frequently disturbed, has stayed more or less in the same location, making subsequent observations possible.

Because of its similarity to the Whimbrel, much has been made in the literature of the great difficulty in identifying it in the field. At a cursory glance it might be mistaken for a Whimbrel; however, it is easily separated by carefully noting its field marks. It is noticeably shorter, smaller, and finer-featured, and its bill is obviously thinner. On the whole it presents a rather delicate aspect. The Whimbrel's base color is grayish and cool-looking, while the Eskimo Curlew's is tan or light brownish, making it appear warm-colored. On the Whimbrel the head stripes are longer and more pronounced than on the Eskimo Curlew, which appears to have more of a separated crown than head stripes. The underwing and crissum of the Whimbrel are grayish. The underwing of the Eskimo Curlew is a very warm cinnamon-buff. The crissum may or may not be brownish-buff. The leg color of the Whimbrel is always light gray as is that of the Long-billed Curlew. The leg color of the Eskimo Curlews seen on the Texas Coast in spring is dark gray or brownish gray, not greenish as so often quoted in the guides.

The Eskimo Curlew behaves much the same as the Whimbrel in the field although when flushed it usually flies alone or with [Lesser] Golden-Plovers. On one occasion it exhibited a rather peculiar trait. As the observer approached a solitary bird feeding in an open field, instead of flushing, it squatted, froze like a snipe, and allowed approach to within approximately six feet. The observer was afforded the unique experience of watching a wild Eskimo Curlew literally at his feet.

to be nesting in its historic breeding range, in remote parts of the Northwest Territories, Canada.

To this day birders search the area every spring for Eskimo Curlews. Of course, if you are lucky enough to spot a bird which you identify as an Eskimo Curlew, be sure to make copious note, to take documentary photographs, and to inform other birders. Some appropriate habitat on the western end of Galveston Island continues to be maintained by the Texas Parks and Wildlife Department. A field thus maintained is called a "Curlew Meadow." It might as well be called a "Field of Dreams."

SAN LUIS PASS

Before crossing the toll bridge over San Luis Pass (8.7), turn off and go under it. Check out the boulders at the end of the bridge; Burrowing Owl wintered here recently. The sandbars in this area are used by migrating shorebirds, such as American Avocet, Red Knot, Baird's and White-rumped Sandpipers, and Marbled Godwit. At any season you should be able to find terns, gulls, Reddish Egrets, and usually Snowy Plovers. In summer there are also Wilson's Plovers. Magnificent Frigatebirds are sometimes seen from the bridge or on the pilings in West Galveston Bay.

Beyond the bridge, the road (now County Road 257) continues to parallel the beach along the peninsula to Surfside Beach (12.6). If the tide is low, you can drive carefully along the **wet** sand. There may not be many birds, but you never know.

Surf and White-winged Scoters, Magnificent Frigatebird, Northern Gannet, and Masked Booby are all rare along the coast, but all have been found in this section. At Surfside you can continue down the road beyond the bridge at Highway 332 (2.7) and over to the beach to the north jetty at the entrance to Freeport Harbor (1.7). During the Freeport Christmas Bird Counts, someone is stationed at the end of the jetty to watch for jaegers, kittiwakes, and Purple Sandpipers—often with success.

Return to the bridge access at Farm Road 332 (1.7) and cross a high bridge over the Intracoastal Waterway. On the far side there is a levee (1.8) along which you can drive in either direction. From this elevated viewpoint, ducks, waders, rails, and shorebirds can be seen in the marsh below. In winter Sprague's Pipits are often found on the level, grassy slopes to the right. At Farm Road 523 (1.8) turn left toward Freeport.

Here you have three good options: First, you can follow the next chapter's text for Houston and Vicinity by turning right onto Highway 36 from Farm Road 523. Second, you might wish to stick closer to the coast and skip to Chapter 8, for Freeport to Tivoli. And third, you could sample part of Chapter 8—for Freeport and up to the turn-off for Farm Road 2611—and then pick up the Houston chapter. All three options provide good birding opportunities.

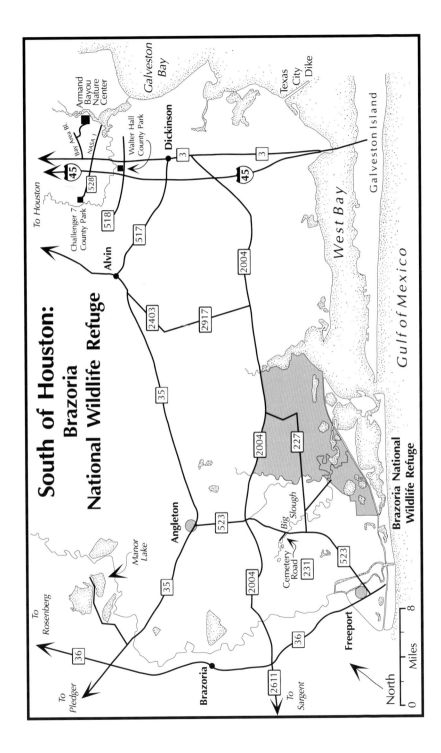

South of Houston:
Brazoria
National Wildlife Refuge

CHAPTER 7:
HOUSTON AND VICINITY

To reach birding areas close to Houston from the Freeport section of the regular coastal tour, turn right off Highway 36 onto Farm Road 2004 (which is the eastern counterpart of Farm Road 2611 of the regular tour). Much of this part of Brazoria County is devoted to ranching, and the numerous pastures here are good, in winter, for buteos, Black-shouldered Kites, Sprague's Pipits, and sparrows. You will pass wooded bottoms where you should look for Red-bellied and Pileated Woodpeckers, Blue Jay, Tufted Titmouse, Carolina Wren, and other eastern-woodlands species. After crossing Highway 288 twice (some 10 miles), watch for Farm Road 523 (3.6). Turn right here to explore an area along Big Slough. Watch for a small lane on the right known as **Cemetery Road** (3.9); it is also County Road 231. This road follows the near side of the slough to a peaceful little cemetery nestled in a grove of huge old oak trees along the banks of the bayou. To quote Jim Lane, "It is just the type of place where a birder might want to spend eternity." It is a lovely place—quiet except for the singing of many birds. The trees abound with Tufted Titmice, Carolina Chickadees, Northern Cardinals, and Blue Jays. Occasionally, Wood Ducks and Anhingas can be seen along the stream. The area is also good for migrants and for wintering birds such as Eastern Phoebe and Vermilion Flycatcher. You may even find an American Crow's nest high in one of the trees, decorated with colorful ribbons and plastic flowers borrowed from the grave-sites below.

Return to Farm Road 523. If you happen to be here on the first Saturday or Sunday of the month, you may want to visit **Brazoria National Wildlife Refuge**, located a short way southwest of here. This 40,854-acre refuge is currently open to the public **only** on the first full weekend of each month. Then, some of the refuge's seven miles of roads are designated as a tour route which visitors may drive in their own vehicles. There is also a good hiking-trail by the entrance. The gates are open on both days from 8am to 5pm. (There are plans to expand the hours of open operation, between November and April. To verify any new hours call the Fish and Wildlife office in Angleton at 409/849-6062.) To reach the refuge, turn right to County Road 227 (1.8). Turn left (east) and drive to the gate on the right (1.7). In 1991, the refuge tripled its size, adding an additional 29,000 acres of varied habitats;

public use facilities and hiking-trails are planned in these new areas. The refuge provides habitat for wintering migratory waterfowl and other wildlife. Snow Geese are the most numerous geese, with Greater White-fronted, Canada, and Ross's present in lesser numbers. Some 15,000 to 20,000 ducks of 24 species are also found here. The refuge's bird checklist includes 30 migrant warbler species and 13 species of wintering sparrows. Birds which commonly nest on the refuge include Black-crowned Night-Heron, ten species of herons and egrets, White Ibis, Roseate Spoonbill, Mottled Duck, Black-shouldered Kite, Clapper Rail, Common Moorhen, Wilson's Plover, Black-necked Stilt, and Forster's and Least Terns. Black Skimmer, Horned Lark, Seaside Sparrow, and Boat-tailed Grackle also nest. Less common are Least Bittern, Black and King Rails, and Purple Gallinule. After a fire here in 1969, a number of tiny nests were found in the ashes. The eggs from these nests were identified as those of Black Rails. Other nests have since been found. (But be alert for venomous snakes if you are walking through grass off the road!)

To resume the side trip, return to Farm Road 2004 and continue east to Farm Road 2917 (19.0). Along the way you will pass through many pastures where, in winter, you can find American and Sprague's Pipits and Vesper, Savannah, Le Conte's, Henslow's (rare), and Grasshopper Sparrows. You will probably have to walk the fence-lines to flush them out. Look to the south opposite the Amoco Refinery for a pair of resident White-tailed Hawks. At FM 2917 turn left to FM 2403 (7.4), then right to Highway 35 (4.6) and right again to Alvin (3.3). Here, take Farm Road 517 to Dickinson on Highway 3 (9.0). Turn left (northwest).

After passing Farm Road 518 (4.4), start watching on the left for Walter Hall County Park (0.5). In storm-free weather, when there are no impressive concentrations of migrants along the coast, this area may be good for them. The resident birds are typical of the southeastern woodlands. In early April Swainson's and Worm-eating Warblers often stay in the dense underbrush at the east end of the park—an area which can also hold Rusty Blackbirds during wet winters.

On leaving the park, continue on Highway 3 to NASA Road 1 (2.0). To the right are the Johnson Space Center and Space Center Houston, the new multi-media visitors' center. (A visit to the center is worthwhile—you will learn a great deal about the NASA space program.) To the left is Farm Road 528, which you can take to check out Challenger 7 County Park. To do this, drive past Interstate 45 (1.0); soon after you pass under the power line, the entrance to the park will be on your left. A resident White-tailed Hawk has often been found perched on one of the power-line supports. It has most often been found on the power line that borders the east side of the park. This is the northernmost record for this species. In winter look for Groove-billed Anis in the park's brushy areas. Migrant warblers abound here during migration. Return to Interstate 45, turn right at the interchange, and continue northwest toward Houston.

Nearby **Armand Bayou Nature Center** (fee; PO Box 58828, Houston, Texas 77258; telephone: 713/474-2551), with exhibits and bookstore, can also offer productive birding. The preserve contains 1,900 acres and is the most beautiful wild area remaining in heavily-developed Harris County. The Center's hours are: Wednesday 9am to dusk, Thursday and Friday 9am to 5pm, Saturday dawn to 5pm, Sunday noon to dusk, and closed Monday and Tuesday. To reach Armand Bayou Nature Center, continue on Interstate 45 to Bay Area Boulevard (1.0). Turn right and continue past the county park (2.5) to the entrance gate on the right (1.5).

The Center's naturalists are helpful and knowledgeable. There are six trails, which vary in length from 0.1 to 3.0 miles, which you may follow through the woods and along the bayou. One is a prairie trail leading to a recreated turn-of-the-century farm site. The Center's bird checklist contains 220 species.

Migrants can be plentiful, and such residents as Barred Owl, Eastern Screech-Owl, and Pileated Woodpecker can usually be seen at any season. Shorebirds, waders, and waterfowl utilize the bayou and the surrounding mudflats, which were created by subsidence. Black Vultures often roost in the trees; both Ospreys and Black-shouldered Kites have nested. Organized bird-walks are conducted every weekend (late morning and early afternoon on Saturday, early afternoon on Sunday). For information about these and other education and nature programs, call 713/474-2551.

To continue, or to return to Houston, turn left onto Bay Area Boulevard upon leaving the Center and continue straight through to Interstate 45 (4.0).

HOUSTON

If you should be in downtown Houston during migration, check the trees in front of City Hall at the corner of Smith and Walker Streets. Normally, 10 to 15 species can be found if one gets there before 8am. When a rare one is discovered, it cannot get away before you see it well. Over the years some 30 species of warblers have been recorded here, including a rare Connecticut Warbler. This area is particularly good for migrating Chuck-will's-widows, which can be flushed from tree to tree.

Houston has 225 parks—most are highly developed, but some have extensive natural areas. **Memorial Park** (1,468 acres) on the west side of the city along Memorial Drive is the biggest and best municipal park for birding. It has extensive tracts of pine/oak forest where typical eastern-woodland birds can be found. The best birding is in the area south of Memorial Drive to Buffalo Bayou, the southern boundary. Some of the resident birds are Yellow-crowned Night-Heron, Barred Owl, Pileated and Red-bellied

Woodpeckers, Blue Jay, Carolina Chickadee, Tufted Titmouse, Carolina Wren, Great-tailed and Common Grackles, and Northern Cardinal. In summer there will be Great Crested and Acadian Flycatchers, Eastern Wood-Pewee, Wood Thrush, White-eyed Vireo, Pine and Hooded Warblers, Northern Parula, Summer Tanager, and Orchard Oriole. In winter, look for Northern (Yellow-shafted) Flicker, Yellow-bellied Sapsucker, Hermit Thrush, Gray Catbird, Brown Thrasher, House and Winter Wrens, Yellow-rumped Warbler, and White-throated Sparrow. During the spring and fall there are

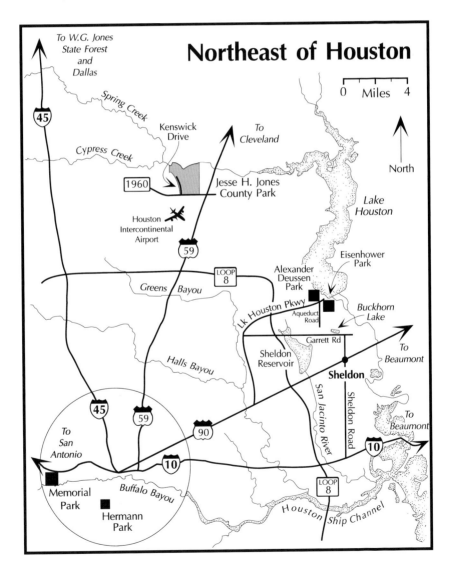

many migrants—you can often find warblers here in calm weather when there are few along the coast.

Hermann Park (398 acres) off South Fannin Street can also be productive, but it is more developed. The major attraction is the free zoo. If you cannot find any wild birds, go over and watch the large collection in the flight-cages and tropical aviary. The Houston Museum of Natural Science is also located in Hermann Park.

AREAS NORTH OF HOUSTON

After being dry for several years, the Sheldon Reservoir Wildlife Management Area has been reflooded and can be an excellent place for wintering ducks and geese. To reach it leave the city on Interstate 10 East. After some 14 miles turn left onto Sheldon Road (exit 783). Follow that road north for 7.0 miles until it ends at Garrett Road; then turn left. Off to the right you will soon see a cypress-studded swamp known as Buckhorn Lake. This is a good place for finding Wood Duck, Anhinga, Little Blue Heron, Red-headed Woodpecker, and, in summer, Prothonotary Warbler, although you will probably need a scope to see most of them. After 1.9 miles, you will come to Aqueduct Road, where you can turn right, then left (1.9) onto Lake Houston Parkway to reach **Alexander Deussen Park**, or right to **Eisenhower Park** on Lake Houston. Only Deussen Park is open to camping, but you should be able to find the typical eastern-woodland birds in either. In the uncleared areas of Eisenhower Park, where the brush is thick and moist, you may see Hooded and Kentucky Warblers in summer. Also nesting are Red-shouldered Hawk, Barred Owl, Red-headed and Pileated Woodpeckers, Belted Kingfisher, Eastern Bluebird, and Orchard Oriole among others.

The headquarters for Sheldon Reservoir is to the left of Garrett Road just 0.2 mile past Aqueduct Road. Marshy fields and willow-studded levees provide a number of different habitats. To reach the reservoir itself, continue up Garrett Road for another 1.5 miles. When you reach the west jetty of the lake on the left, stop and scan the water for ducks and geese. The geese usually stay in the fields along the east side of the refuge and are hard to see, but occasionally a large flock will billow into the air.

Be sure to check the tree snags and the marshy areas. Anhingas, and often a Neotropic Cormorant, can usually be found perched in the dead trees. In winter there may be Double-crested Cormorants, Osprey, and even Bald Eagles. The marshes are normally bedecked with herons, egrets, coots, Common Moorhens, and in summer with Purple Gallinules. This is an excellent area for Little Blue Herons. They probably nest nearby, because in late summer there are many in the white or white-blotched plumage of young birds. At the western edge of the reservoir, there is a path on the right side of the road. It follows the levee around the northern end of the lake and leads

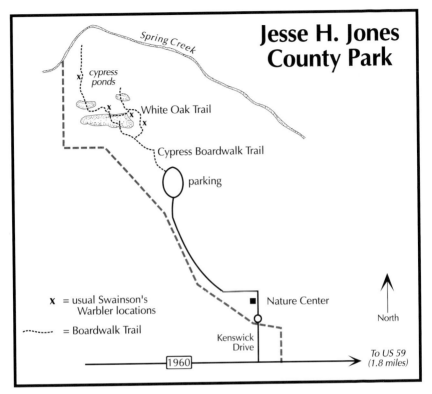

Jesse H. Jones County Park

Spring Creek

cypress ponds

White Oak Trail

Cypress Boardwalk Trail

parking

x = usual Swainson's Warbler locations

•••••••• = Boardwalk Trail

Nature Center

North

Kenswick Drive

1960

To US 59 (1.8 miles)

into a good area for landbirds. The wet tangle of willows and cypress on the left just as you start on the trail is usually good for Prothonotary Warblers in summer and for Swamp, Lincoln's, and White-throated Sparrows in winter. To the left, Fauna Road follows the levee for several miles to a parking lot and access area at the southwestern corner of the lake. You can also park anywhere along the road and walk up onto the levee.

To continue to other areas, drive west on Garrett Road or Lake Houston Parkway to Beltway 8 and turn right for some 9 miles to US Highway 59. Turn right (north), then left onto Farm Road 1960 (5.0), which is just beyond Houston Intercontinental Airport. (This intersection may also be reached by driving north from the city on US Highway 59.) In 1.8 miles turn right onto Kenswick Drive and watch for the small green sign indicating the 225-acre **Jesse H. Jones County Park** entrance (20634 Kenswick Dr., Humble, Texas 77338; telephone: 713/446-8588). There are long trails and boardwalks through thickly-forested cypress swamps in this 225-acre park. Several good spots for finding Swainson's Warblers are found along the park's Cypress Boardwalk Trail.

The 1,725-acre **W.G. Jones State Forest** north of Houston is the most famous place in the state for finding Red-cockaded Woodpeckers and Brown-headed Nuthatches. To reach it go north from Houston on Interstate 45 for some 35 miles, then turn left onto Farm Road 1488 toward Hempstead. After 1.4 miles you will see the headquarters on the right (telephone: 409/273-2261). This is an experimental forest managed by Texas A & M University, sectioned into numerous plots where various growing methods are tried. Most of the trees are Shortleaf and Loblolly Pines, but there are also

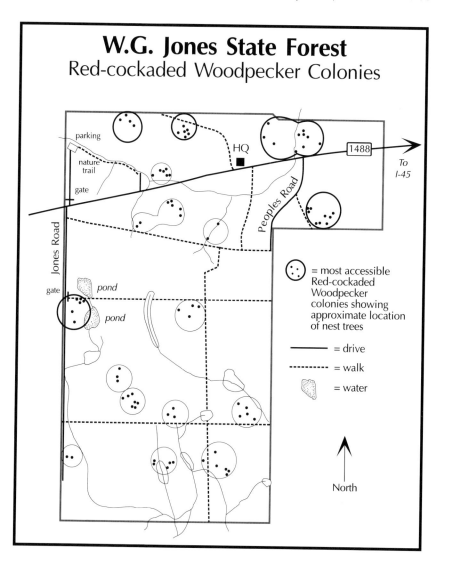

W.G. Jones State Forest
Red-cockaded Woodpecker Colonies

plantings of Slash Pine, Arizona and Bald Cypresses, and Eastern Cottonwood. Some plots are used for experimental wildlife food plantings. One large section has been left in a natural state, and here you can find numerous species of hardwoods. The foresters have laid out a nature trail and printed a pamphlet to help you to identify the 50 or so plant species. Brown-headed Nuthatch is common throughout the forest, but Red-cockaded Woodpecker is restricted to areas with old pines that are infected with red-heart disease. Recently, the Piney Woods Wildlife Society encircled nest trees with orange bands when they censused the birds. The people at the office can recommend some of the better areas. Two of the most consistent spots are along the Sweetleaf Nature Trail, and east of Jones Road beyond the gate and near the two ponds. Two good colonies are just south of the park's northern boundary just north of the nature trail. Listen for the calls or pecking sounds. The birds are most active in the early morning. There is a parking area for those who want to walk the nature trail. Monday through Friday, you must pick up the key at the office between 8am and 5pm—this is located at the gate just before and to the right on the west boundary. The gate is left open from Friday evening until Monday morning. You may walk into the forest anytime, but

Red-cockaded Woodpecker
Charles H. Gambill

parking is limited except at headquarters. You can drive Jones Road along the western boundary and Peoples Road to the south (just east of headquarters). After a short distance, take a left at the Y to an accessible colony of Red-cockaded Woodpeckers.

Numerous other eastern-woodland birds are common here. At the right time of year, you may find as many as eight species of woodpeckers, as well as Blue Jay, Carolina Chickadee, Tufted Titmouse, Carolina Wren, Eastern Bluebird, Pine Warbler, and in summer Chuck-will's-widow, Great Crested and Acadian Flycatchers, White-eyed and Yellow-throated Vireos, Indigo and Painted Buntings, and others. You may also find Swainson's, Parula, Black-and-white, Yellow-throated, Kentucky, and Hooded Warblers, and perhaps a Louisiana Waterthrush.

KATY FARMLANDS

The **Katy Farmlands** west of Houston offer a different set of birds. This area is rapidly being engulfed by the city's urban sprawl, but good birding can still be found in spring, fall, and winter. To reach the farmlands, leave the city on Interstate 10 West and drive some 17 miles to the Highway 6/Addicks turnoff (exit 751). Turn right (north) to Patterson Road (2.0); then turn east to the south entrance of **Bear Creek Park** (1.0). Although much of the dense undergrowth attractive to birds has been removed in recent years, some fine habitat still remains along the creek's banks. Follow Bear Creek Drive to Golbow (0.8) and turn right. The big trees around the picnic area and the wooded bottoms are attractive to eastern deciduous-woodland species in summer. At this season you might find Wood Duck, Barred Owl, White-eyed, Solitary, Yellow-throated, and Red-eyed Vireos, Northern Parula, and Kentucky and Hooded Warblers. Red-shouldered Hawk is a common resident. In winter you should find Brown Creeper and Golden-crowned Kinglet. You just may see a Winter Wren, Rusty Blackbird, or a Purple Finch if you search hard. Wintering sparrows are fairly common. In migration you could find almost anything.

Exit from the park's north side and turn left (west) onto Clay Road. After you cross South Mayde Creek (7.4), you begin to leave the urban sprawl and enter a world of sorghum, soybeans, and rice. In spring, when the rice fields are flooded, look for migrant shorebirds including Lesser Golden-Plover, Upland, Stilt, Baird's, Buff-breasted, and White-rumped Sandpipers, Hudsonian Godwit, and Wilson's Phalarope. In stock ponds or on top of rice-field levees, look for Fulvous and Black-bellied Whistling-Ducks. You may also see good flights of Swainson's and Broad-winged Hawks. In summer Scissor-tailed Flycatchers and Dickcissels abound. In autumn check the large flocks of Brown-headed Cowbirds for Yellow-headed Blackbirds. Look, too, for rice-harvesting combines in October. Their blades flush

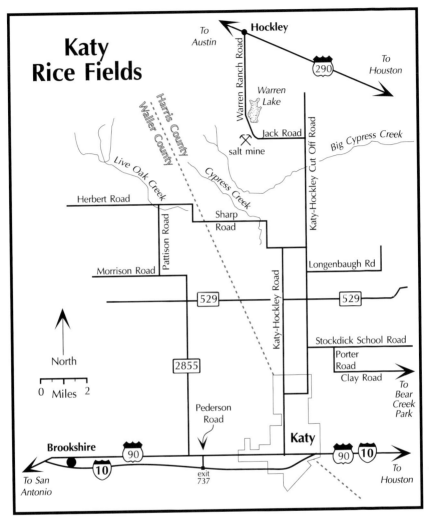

Katy Rice Fields

rails—mostly King and Sora, but also, occasionally, Virginia and Yellow. In winter look for raptors such as Northern Harrier, Red-tailed Hawk, and American Kestrel, and, in the hedgerows, accipiters. Eastern Bluebird, American and Sprague's Pipits, and Savannah (predominant), Grasshopper, Le Conte's, Vesper, Lark (rare), and Lincoln's Sparrows occur, as well as huge concentrations of geese, including Greater White-fronted, Canada, and Snow. Among the latter search for the uncommon but increasing Ross's. Pick them out in flight by their diminutive size—fully one-third smaller than a Snow—or, on the ground, by their rounded head and shorter bill with a vertical dark strip next to the head—not the Snow's "grin patch". (At close range, or through a scope, this shows as a warty base to the bill.) Always look for rarities while on this 70-mile loop trip.

At Porter Road (2.3) turn right. Check the weedy fields here for more sparrows and certain catfish ponds on the left for whistling-ducks. (By standing on top of your vehicle, you can get a look at these private ponds.) At Stockdick School Road (1.0) park at the corner and walk the dirt track straight ahead (north) if it is not posted. It, too, can be very good for sparrows, including Le Conte's.

Turn left (west) to Katy-Hockley Cut-Off Road (1.0), where you will turn right (north). The fields in this area are plowed flat and are especially good for flocks of Buff-breasted Sandpipers in spring. When the rice fields along this road are flooded, they should be checked for geese and shorebirds. Turn right onto Longenbaugh Road (3.0) and check the flooded rice fields for more of the same, plus a possible Bald Eagle which may be feeding on injured, flightless ducks and geese. Drive to the road's end; then retrace your route to the Katy-Hockley Cut-Off Road. Turn right and continue north to Big Cypress Creek (4.1). This crossing is famous for owls—Eastern Screech-Owl in particular. At Jack Road (1.2) turn left (west) to Warren Ranch Road (1.8), which begins where the road starts to curve north (and where a salt mine is on your left). Continue to an overlook on your right for Warren Lake (1.0). At night, Jack Road hosts numerous hunting Barn Owls (which may nest in the mine or in its buildings) and, on the fenceposts in spring, Whip-poor-wills. Watch the power towers which parallel Warren Ranch Road for perching raptors, including Red-tailed ("Harlan's") Hawk and Ferruginous Hawk. The lake has diving ducks, Bald Eagles, and, in late fall, migrating Franklin's Gulls. Check the hedgerows across the road from the overlook for flocks of White-crowned and Harris's Sparrows.

Return to Katy-Hockley Cut-Off Road, then backtrack south to Katy-Hockley Road (4.3), and turn west. At the stop sign (1.0) continue straight onto Sharp Road. After the bend to the right, watch the roadsides for more sparrows, including Song and an occasional Harris's (November and December seem best—before waterfowl hunters invade en masse.) In the numerous red-berried Yaupon bushes, look for Cedar Waxwings, Pine Siskins, American Goldfinches, and Field, Fox, Song, White-throated, White-crowned, and Harris's Sparrows. Rarities found along Sharp Road have included Burrowing Owl, Sage Thrasher, and Green-tailed Towhee. Upon leaving Harris County and entering Waller County, Sharp Road changes to a dirt road (4.1) and continues to twist and turn among the rice fields. (Sharp Road also changes its name at the county line and becomes Herbert Road.) At Pattison Road (2.8) the dirt road ends. Scan north of this intersection for White-tailed Hawk and Crested Caracara. Turn left (south) onto Pattison Road, and, at the bridge over Live-Oak Creek (0.2), check the brushy area for Fox Sparrow and, at dawn or dusk, Barred Owl. Continue slowly driving south along Pattison Road. In mid-winter the birds in the plowed fields here include Horned Lark, American and Sprague's Pipits, and, occasionally, Lapland Longspur. Rarities along this stretch have included Mountain Plover and McCown's Longspur. Pattison Road ends at Morrison Road (2.7). Jog east for a mile and then south for another mile to where Morrison Road becomes Farm Road 2855. Continue south on this road to Highway 90 (6.0) while watching for whistling-ducks, White-tailed Hawk, and, in the wet ditches, King Rail. Jog east to Pederson Road (0.5), then south to Interstate 10 (0.7) (exit 737). To complete the loop, return east to Houston.

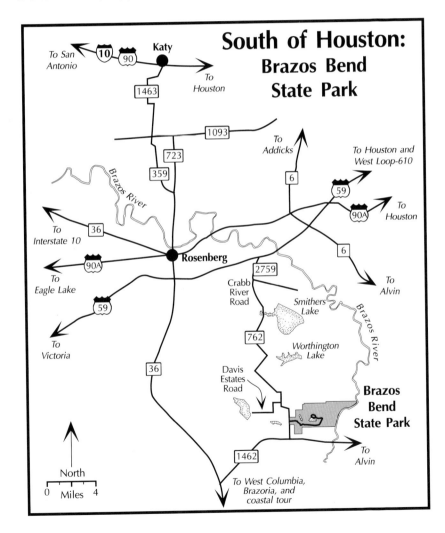

South of Houston: Brazos Bend State Park

Though it is just outside the range of this book, you may wish to consider a side-trip to the Attwater Prairie Chicken National Wildlife Refuge. This is the best place for Greater Prairie-Chicken in the area, though reservations are needed to observe the birds on their leks (February through April). Take Interstate 10 westward to Sealy. Details are provided in the "Specialties" section of this book.

BRAZOS BEND

Brazos Bend State Park (4,897 acres; fee; camping, picnicking, restrooms with hot showers; 21901 FM 762, Needville, Texas 77461; telephone: 409/553-3243) lies just 35 miles southwest of downtown Houston in Fort Bend County. The park is reached from Houston via US Highway 59 South. From West Loop I-610, take US Highway 59 South (Victoria exit) to Crabb River Road (Farm Road 2759) (18.0). *Or, if you are coming into Houston on Interstate 10 from the west, go south on Highway 6 (exit 751) to US Highway 59 (12.0), and turn right to Crabb River Road, a distance of some 7 miles.* Turn left onto Farm Road 2759 for 1.9 miles to Farm Road 762. Turn right (south) to the park entrance on your left (15.9). While driving this road in winter, watch the utility poles for hawks—mostly Red-tails. The park is very productive—with 290 species of birds on its checklist—because it is located at the convergence of four major habitats of the Upper Texas Coast: freshwater ponds, marshes, and the Brazos River; Spanish-Moss-draped live-oak woodland; bottomland hardwoods; and coastal prairie. Brazos Bend State Park is noted as the best inland area for incredible views of most of Texas's waterbirds, including breeding Anhingas, Black-bellied Whistling-Ducks, Least Bitterns, White Ibises, Roseate Spoonbills, and Purple Gallinules. There is a very large heron rookery north of the observation tower on the east side of Pilant Lake. The herons and waterbirds are relatively tame and frequent even the paths of the park. Some of Texas's specialty landbirds can be easy to find here as well, such as breeding Northern Parulas in the Spanish Moss-covered oaks and abundant Prothonotary Warblers in the willows along the dike trail to the observation tower and beyond. Barred Owls call all day long, and Pileated Woodpeckers frequent the oaks in the Elm Lake picnic area. Mississippi Kites breed here, and Red-shouldered Hawks are resident. There are large, permanent vulture roosts; Broad-winged Hawks rise with the thermals in spring.

Other nesting birds include Common Moorhen, Mottled and Wood Ducks, Eastern Screech-Owl, Eastern Kingbird, Acadian Flycatcher, White-eyed, Yellow-throated, and Red-eyed Vireos, and Hooded and Swainson's (rare) Warblers. American Redstarts and Painted and Indigo Buntings also have been found here in summer and may nest.

Wood Stork
Gail Diane Luckner

Other wintering birds include 24 species of waterfowl, American Woodcock, Vermilion Flycatcher, Rufous-sided Towhee, and Chipping, Field, Vesper, Le Conte's, Fox, Song, Swamp, and White-throated Sparrows.

Other birds of interest that have been recorded at the park are American Swallow-tailed Kite, Golden and Bald Eagles, Black-billed Cuckoo, Black and Say's Phoebes, Pyrrhuloxia, Rusty Blackbird, and Sharp-tailed Sparrow (rare). Rarities included a Ringed Kingfisher that was found one spring at Elm Lake. A Northern Jacana was reported once. Masked Duck has appeared on a couple of occasions. Old Horseshoe Lake should be checked, since it is less explored, and is the best spot for nesting Black-bellied Whistling-Ducks. In winter these ducks roost at 40 Acre Lake.

In late summer Wood Storks can be found in the old sulphur-mine ponds in the Davis Estates oil field. This area can be reached by driving north for 2 miles on Farm Road 762 from the park entrance. Turn left (west) onto Davis Estates Road and proceed 3.8 miles on the dirt road. Cross the large cattle-guard to where the dikes are on both sides of the road. *Please do not go over these dikes because the property off the road is private and misuse of the area will jeopardize continued access to these birds.* In winter the surrounding fields harbor thousands of Snow Geese with numerous Ross's

Geese, ducks, and hundreds of Sandhill Cranes. Tundra Swans are occasionally seen in the north pond. The westernmost pond across from the old buildings is the best for viewing ducks. Look along the road for wintering sparrows and American and Sprague's Pipits. Resident White-tailed Hawks, Crested Caracaras, and Black-shouldered Kites, as well as an occasional wintering Ferruginous Hawk, frequent the Davis Estates and the surrounding area. Bald Eagles sometimes perch on the abandoned oil derricks.

Another spectacular sight in winter is to witness the huge morning blackbird fly-out. The multitude leaves the roosts at sunrise—Christmas Bird Count estimates of their numbers range up to 5 million grackles, American Crows, Red-winged and Brewer's Blackbirds, and Brown-headed Cowbirds. The best place to observe this spectacle seems to be just south of Brazos Bend State Park on Farm Road 1462.

Any spring or fall trip here can produce a large passerine (especially warbler) list. And, without any trouble at all, you will be able to look eye-to-eye with an American Alligator. For information, call the park office at 409/553-3243.

For birders who interrupted their coastal tour to take this Houston and Vicinity side-trip, the following directions will take you back toward Freeport, where you can continue the tour down the coast: From the Brazos Bend State Park entrance, drive left (south) on Farm Road 762 to Farm Road 1462 (1.5). Turn right and follow it to Highway 36 (7.0). Turn left (south) and continue through West Columbia and Brazoria, down to the intersection of Highway 36 and 1495 (35.8). Alternately, you may have already birded Freeport and want to pick up the next chapter's text at San Bernard National Wildlife Refuge. In that case, as you drive down Highway 36, watch for Farm Road 2611 (some 5 miles after Brazoria) on your right.

From Freeport
South to Palacios

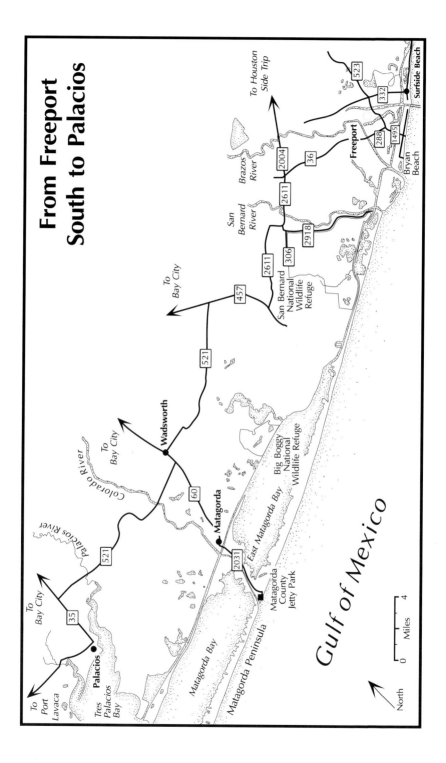

CHAPTER 8:
FREEPORT TO TIVOLI

If you are following this route after covering the Galveston Chapter (Chapter 6) you will have left Surfside Beach behind you, and will have turned westward on Farm Road 523, crossed the canal and cleared the traffic light. Then bear left onto Farm Road 1495 (1.2) toward Freeport. The main business district of Freeport is visible on the right as you cross the bridge (1.1), but continue straight ahead on Pine Street to Highways 288 and 36 (1.2). If you

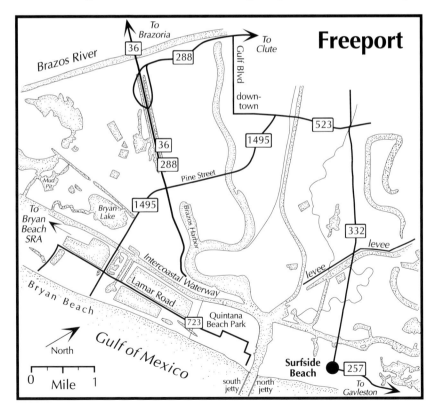

have arrived at this chapter from Houston (Chapter 7) you will have driven down Highway 36 to this same intersection.

Drive down Farm Road 1495, crossing the Intracoastal Waterway via a swing bridge to Bryan Beach, where you can usually find a few shorebirds. It seems to be a good spot for Snowy Plovers. At low tide, you can drive to the right (south) down the beach, or to the left (north) toward the harbor's south jetty at the north end of the Quintana Beach County Park (day-use fee). The park may also be reached by driving north three miles on County Road 723 (Lamar Road) or driving to the end of Lamar Road and turning right to the south jetty. Return on FM 1495 across the Intracoastal Waterway and turn left onto Highway 288, which is bordered by ponds. Mottled Ducks and Least Grebes nest here. White and White-faced Ibises occur in winter. At the Brazos River stay on Highway across the bridge (1.3). (The Brazosport Center for the Arts and Science in nearby Clute is worth checking if time permits.)

For the next dozen miles of so you will have the opportunity to check for Red-shouldered Hawk, Pileated Woodpecker, and Black Vulture. At Farm Road 2611 (9.7) turn left. Then turn left onto Farm Road 2918 (4.2), following signs toward the **San Bernard National Wildlife Refuge**. At County Road 306 (1.1) turn right to the field office entrance (1.3) where you can pick up a map and checklist. The entrance to good habitats is another mile down County Road 306 on the left. San Bernard National Wildlife Refuge is the only one of the three area refuges administered from one office which is open to the public on a regular basis (National Wildlife Refuge Complex, PO Drawer 1088, 1216 North Velasco, Angleton, Texas 77516; telephone: 409/849-6062). The other two refuges of the Complex are Brazoria National Wildlife Refuge (northeast of Freeport, and open only on the first full weekend of every month, and there are plans for increased openings) and Big Boggy National Wildlife Refuge (southwest of San Bernard National Wildlife Refuge and currently not open to the public at all). San Bernard's 24,455 acres have been open to the public (dawn to dusk seven days a week) for a few years now. By driving the roads you can see waders, rails, shorebirds, and Seaside Sparrows in the *Spartina* marshes. Try the three-mile Moccasin Pond Loop for starters. And there are a few good hiking-trails. White and White-faced Ibises occur on the refuge in fall. Yellow Rails are found during the winter months. (There are plans for an approved rail observation site and rope-dragging area on the refuge.) Black Rails probably nest at San Bernard. Snow Geese are the most numerous of the thousands of geese wintering here, while Greater White-fronted, Canada, and Ross's occur in lesser numbers. With luck you will find Crested Caracara in winter. Also, 24 species of ducks are listed on the refuge checklist. Thirteen species of sparrows winter on the refuge, and some 30 species of warblers are found during migrations. Nesting birds include many herons, egrets, rails, gulls, terns, and six species of the blackbird family. Four spoil islands in the Cedar Lakes area are noteworthy, providing nesting habitat for many Tricolored Herons, Cattle Egrets, Laughing Gulls, Royal Terns, and Black Skimmers.

Return to Farm Road 2611 and continue south. Turn right onto Farm Road 457 (9.1) and then left onto Farm Road 521 (6.2). At Wadsworth (15.6) Farm Road 521 turns left, running jointly with Highway 60 for 1.5 miles, then angles off to the right. Continue straight on Highway 60 to Matagorda, and then turn left on Farm Road 2031 (10.5) past the Intracoastal Waterway to **Matagorda County Jetty Park** on Matagorda Peninsula, and to the Gulf (6.6). Here you can swim and camp on the beautiful beach or explore the island. The birds here are about the same as elsewhere on the Gulf with Least Terns being rather common. Magnificent Frigatebirds are often seen hovering over the shrimp boats offshore; you can watch for them from the newly refurbished jetty. Groove-billed Anis frequent the Tamarisks along the road. In winter Short-eared Owls can sometimes be flushed from the marsh, and in summer Western Diamond-back Rattlesnakes are found on the dunes. The sparse grass on the dunes would hardly seem like good habitat for snakes, but with a little luck you may find one.

To continue the tour, return to Farm Road 521 and follow it southward until you can turn left onto Highway 35 (18.6). As you continue south, there are many roads leading to towns and settlements on the bays. Each is fun to explore, and you may find some good camping and birding spots, but the birds will probably be about the same as those you have already seen.

At a flashing light at the edge of Palacios, Highway 35 turns right (west) (5.2). Continue to Farm Road 172 (15.5), and turn left (south) toward Olivia. Look for Sandhill Cranes in winter on the pastures in this area. Turn left onto County Road 159 (4.4), which ends in two-and-a-half miles at Carancahua Bay (the site of "old" Port Alto and good at low tide for shorebirds). At the first crossroad you can turn right and watch for Curve-billed Thrashers in this area of brushland. At the end of this road turn right and watch for Cassin's Sparrows making their display flights from April to July. Back at Farm Road 172 you can turn left and check the county park and picnic area, scanning Keller Bay in winter and spring for migrants and loons, grebes, and mergansers. Return north on Farm Road 172 to Farm Road 2143 (3.4) and turn left onto Highway 35 (4.5).

North of Lavaca Bay is a wooded area great for spring migrants from mid-April to mid-May. **Bennett Park**, a 40-acre county park (primitive camping) is set in an oxbow bend of Garcitas Creek, and offers picnicking, fishing, and primitive camping. It is a magnet for northbound migrants, with its lush canopy and thick understory. Mark Elwonger says "passerines are more numerous and perhaps easier to find here than in more open sites to the south and west. They apparently like to follow the riparian corridor offered by Garcitas Creek and the Navidad River." To reach the park, turn right (north) onto Farm Road 1593 (1.7). At Lolita (11.4) turn left (west) onto

Farm Road 616, drive through Vanderbilt (4.8), and at LaSalle (3.8) turn right onto County Road 325. Cross the tracks, and at the T-intersection (0.7) follow County Road 325 left. Turn left on County Road 326 (1.3) to the entrance to the park (1.0).

Back at Highway 35 continue southwest through Point Comfort and turn off to the old causeway on the left (1.5) to check for Common Loon, Horned Grebe, Common Goldeneye, Osprey, and American Oystercatcher in proper season. Continue across Lavaca Bay on Highway 35 to Port Lavaca and turn left at the lighthouse (3.3). This squat lighthouse was built in 1858 on Half Moon Reef in Matagorda Bay, moved later to Point Comfort and then to its present location where it is currently used for meetings. Pull into the parking lot of the **Port Lavaca Lighthouse Beach and Bird Sanctuary** (camping; fee). The park has a long fishing pier and the Formosa Wetlands Walkway and

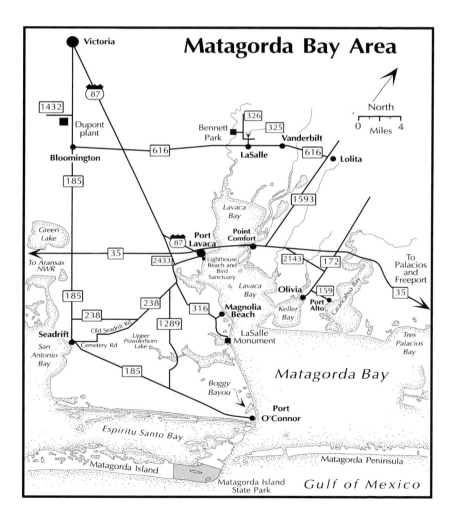

Formosa Wetlands Walkway and Birding Pavilion   Paul J. Baicich

Alcoa Birding Pavilion. From here you may scan the bay for loons, grebes, cormorants, waterfowl, and pelicans. The 2000-foot-long boardwalk is fabricated entirely of recycled materials—two million plastic milk jugs (80 percent) and fiberglass (20 percent). It is currently the largest structure in the world built entirely of recycled plastic products. Common Moorhen, Clapper Rail, and Seaside Sparrow are resident here.

To continue the tour, drive west on Highway 35 and turn left (south) onto Farm Road 2433 (4.8). A rather different area can be found along the road to Port O'Connor. Much of the land here is still in the prairie state, although there are some rice fields and ponds. In winter, Snow and Greater White-fronted Geese, Sandhill Cranes, and hawks are common. In spring migration the pastures and fields abound with Lesser Golden-Plovers, and you may find Upland, White-rumped, and Buff-breasted Sandpipers, and Hudsonian Godwits. There is plenty of habitat for Eskimo Curlews, but, since none has been reported here, maybe the birds do not know about it.

At Highway 238 (1.4) turn right, and when this road turns right (1.7), continue straight ahead onto Highway 316 toward Magnolia Beach and Indianola on Lavaca and Matagorda Bays. If you are here in April or May, check the flooded rice fields for shorebirds. Near the end of the road is a marshy area where Black Rails have been heard, especially in spring. At the end of the road (9.0) is a monument to Rene Robert LaSalle, who gave the United States its first claim to Texas as part of the Louisiana Purchase. (Notice that the monument is about three-quarters of an inch off the center of its foundation, the result of the storm wave-surge during Hurricane Carla in 1961.) The ruins of the once-thriving port of Indianola, destroyed by storms and fire by 1886, are actually underwater 400 yards off the beach at this point.

Return to Highway 238 and turn left. At Farm Road 1289 (0.9) turn left again to check more rice fields and Upper Powderhorn Lake (7.5). A stop at the Powderhorn Lake bridge to scope the adjacent wetlands and "lake" is usually worthwhile. Roseate Spoonbills are present there much of the year.

At Highway 185 (3.7) turn left to Port O'Connor (7.0), then right to the boat dock and ferry to **Matagorda Island State Park** (PO Box 117, Port O'Connor, Texas 77982). Matagorda Island lies about six miles offshore and is separated from the mainland by Espiritu Santo and San Antonio Bays; it can be reached only by chartered or private boats or passenger ferry. The ferry currently runs about three times a day on Saturdays and Sundays. (Call the Texas Parks and Wildlife Department office at Port O'Connor to check the current schedule: 512/983-2215.) There are no stores, so take water and all other necessary items. Primitive camping is allowed, and although motor vehicles are not permitted, you can take bicycles to the island. The aforementioned inconveniences are by design to maintain the island's most cherished features—its isolation and its windswept, near-pristine environment. The State Park encompasses 7,325 acres, though the Department actually manages a vast 53,000 acres. (The U.S. Fish and Wildlife Service now owns most of the island, and manages the Matagorda Unit of the Aransas National Wildlife Refuge on the island's far end [see the next chapter]. The Nature Conservancy originally secured some of this land that was later picked up by Fish and Wildlife.) There are over 80 miles of

Wilson's Plover
Shawneen E. Finnegan

beach, roadways, old military airport runways, and mowed pathways. Every weekend, weather permitting, a shuttle vehicle makes round-trips from the ferry dock on the island to the Gulf beach (fee).

Wildlife here consists of many fish, numerous crustaceans, three species of amphibians, and over 30 species of reptiles (including 19 species of snakes). The island supports a very small number of mammals, the most numerous being White-tailed Deer and Raccoons. There have also been over 320 species of birds recorded, including wintering Whooping Cranes, Peregrine Falcons, and Short-eared Owls. During spring (March-May) and fall (mid-July-October) migrations, songbirds by the thousands find the clumps of Tamarisks and Silver-leaf Sunflowers a temporary haven for resting on their long journey to their nesting areas to the north or wintering areas to the south. Many winter over, and some 37 species nest on the island, including White-tailed Hawk and Black-shouldered Kite. Horned Larks, Wilson's Plovers, and Least Terns nest on the old runways.

Wood Storks show up from their nesting colonies in Mexico along with buoyant Magnificent Frigatebirds. At any season, when the weather turns bad, look gulfward for species such as Masked Booby, Northern Gannet, Surf Scoter, and any other temporarily displaced pelagics. With increased public access and birder interest, Matagorda Island is guaranteed to become one of the best birding spots in Texas.

Port O'Connor is a small town, but it has nice cafes and several motels. At the north end of Washington Street you will find a mudflat which is good for shorebirds on Boggy Bayou. It is permitted to walk along the shoreline at low tide, but above the high-tide mark is private property. To get to more birding, stay on Highway 185 and skirt the south side of the peninsula. White-tailed Hawks can be found along this highway all year, and Magnificent Frigatebirds can occasionally be seen in summer. Keep an eye out for Whooping Cranes; if you are very lucky some may stray over from Aransas National Wildlife Refuge 20 miles across the bay.

At Seadrift (17.7) turn right onto Cemetery Road. After two miles, this jogs left, then right, and becomes Old Seadrift Road. Start checking the canals and flooded rice fields (April-May) along this section of road for White-faced Ibis, Marbled Godwit, Black-bellied and Fulvous Whistling-Ducks, King Rail, and many shorebirds, including Lesser Golden-Plover and Upland Sandpiper. At Farm Road 238 (7.8) turn left to return to Highway 185 (6.5). Turn right onto Highway 185 and proceed northwest.

The Union Carbide Seadrift Plant is located on the right near the junction of Highways 185 and 35. The side-road to look for is on the left of Highway 185 (5.6); it leads a short distance to the Company clubhouse and skeet range. This is where a Masked Duck and an immature Northern Jacana were discovered in mid-December 1992. Although Union Carbide welcomed birders at the time,

Dupont Eagle-watching Tower   Paul J. Baicich

future birders will require permission to enter the property from the company Human Resources Administrator (telephone: 512/553-2213).

Continue across Highway 35 on 185 toward Victoria to the far side of the E.I. Dupont Victoria Plant, where a Bald Eagle nest can be viewed at a distance. To visit the Bald Eagle Observation Tower, turn left onto Farm Road 1432 (Pickering Basin Road) (16.7). A wetland-restoration project is planned for the low area to the left (1.6); turn left at the Dupont back gate (0.3). The tower, built by Dupont in 1990, is just ahead up the hill (0.3). There are five known Bald Eagle nests within approximately 50 miles, but this one at Dupont provides the best viewing opportunity. Nesting occurs from December into March, though the birds are in the area from September through April. The Dupont Victoria Plant has won both conservation awards and the appreciation of birders for its habitat improvement and environmental protection projects. A good number of other species are also observed from this tower.

Return to Highway 35, via Highway 185, and turn right (south) onto Highway 35. You will soon come to an entirely different habitat, a fresh-water marsh. The Guadalupe Delta Wildlife Management Area, run by Texas Parks and Wildlife (2601 N. Azalea, Suite 31, Victoria, Texas 77901, telephone: 512/576-0020), is located here (1.5) along the Guadalupe River. A Hog Bayou Nature Trail is planned for the future. Current access is available only on special request. The Guadalupe/San Antonio drainage here is the dividing line between closely related eastern and western species such as Eastern and Western Kingbirds, Tufted and "Black-crested" Titmice, Red-bellied and Golden-fronted Woodpeckers, and Brown and Long-billed Thrashers. The drainage is also the southern limit for American Crow, Downy and Pileated Woodpeckers, Prothonotary Warbler, and Northern Parula. Wood Storks frequent this area in summer.

Beyond Tivoli (5.9) (Tie-VOLE-ee) you will want to turn left onto Farm Road 239 (2.0) toward Aransas National Wildlife Refuge, but, first, you may want to continue south for a mile and check the farm fields on the right. For many years—from January through April—these fields served as a booming-ground for Greater Prairie-Chickens. Recent clearings for agriculture are reducing the number of sightings considerably. However, some birds have been recently seen for an hour or so at dawn between the "Y" and the grain elevators. *Under no circumstances should you walk into the fields.*

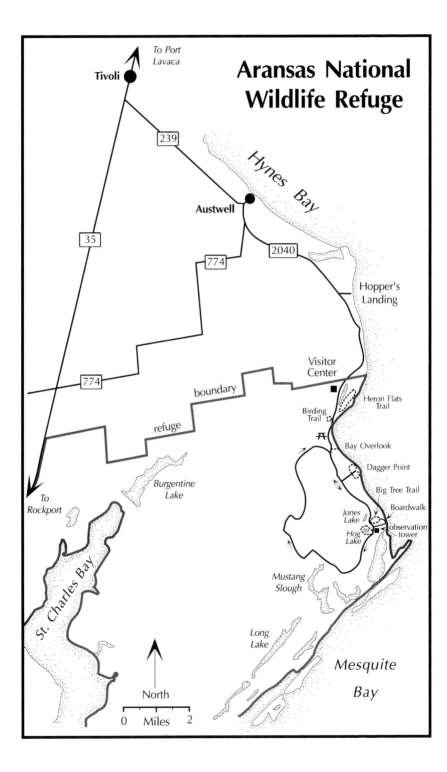

CHAPTER 9:
ARANSAS NATIONAL WILDLIFE REFUGE

From southbound Highway 35, turn left onto Farm Road 239 and follow the signs to **Aransas National Wildlife Refuge** (PO Box 100, Austwell, Texas 77950; telephone: 512/286-3559), 12 miles to the east. Watch for White-tailed Hawk and Crested Caracara along the way. Check the plowed fields around Austwell (4.3) in season for Upland and Buff-breasted Sandpipers. Just after Austwell, turn left on Farm Road 2040 (1.2)

The refuge is open from sunrise to sunset, and the birding is best at these extremes of the day. Stop at the Interpretive Center (8:30am-4:30pm daily) (6.6) for a map and a bird checklist. You will probably want to pick up a very informative new book by Barry Jones called *Birder's Guide to Aransas*, and other books and pamphlets, and will certainly want to see the display on the Whooping Crane. In summer you might ask if any Buff-bellied Hummingbirds have been visiting the hummingbird feeder. There may also be some Inca Doves near the Center. A few foot-trails begin near the Visitor Center. The Rail Trail is located across the road from the Center. It is a short, grassy trail good for King Rails. (This trail hooks up with the Heron Flats Trail described below.) Take plenty of insect repellent along with you; the refuge abounds with mosquitoes and chiggers.

This 54,829-acre sanctuary on the Blackjack Peninsula is best known as the winter home of the endangered Whooping Crane. The numbers of this bird have been alarmingly low in recent history. In 1941 there were only about 15 wild birds wintering in Texas. The numbers began to creep up, but they crashed again in 1954 to 21 individuals. (The nesting-grounds at Wood Buffalo National Park in Canada's Northwest Territories were not found until the same year, 1954.) Numbers have gone up since then—with some exceptions, such as the unexplained loss of 25% of the flock in 1972. Today the numbers are more hopeful; some 136 Whooping Cranes wintered in the area during the 1992-1993 season. There have always been natural losses of Whooping Cranes, but today their lives are challenged by man-made obstacles, oil and chemical spills, irresponsible hunters, or even being "loved

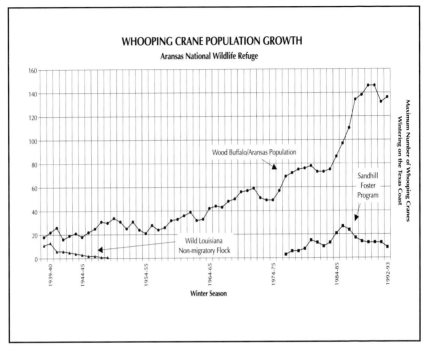

WHOOPING CRANE POPULATION GROWTH
Aransas National Wildlife Refuge

to death" by observers. Their survival is always brought into question during their twice-yearly, 2,500-mile migration between Aransas and Wood Buffalo. (This is one reason why there has been continued work on the possibility of "creating an alternate wild flock" somewhere—first a failed attempt for an Idaho/New Mexico foster program, and now a new effort in central Florida.)

From late October to early April most of the wild population of this rare bird stays on the grassy saltflats in isolated areas on the bayside fringe of Aransas. For most of this time they inhabit 400- to 600-acre territories where pairs or families feed, preen, and rest. In March and early April you may see the birds engage in courtship—bowing, wing-flapping, and leaping. In late March and early April the territorial behavior breaks down and the cranes begin to leave in families or small groups.

In order to protect the cranes, the interior of the refuge is closed to the public. However, there is a tall and impressive observation tower along the Tour Loop Drive. Generally, in season, a few cranes can be seen as specks in the distance from the tower, but by using one of the tower's telescopes or, better yet, your own, you may see a number of cranes and other birds sufficiently well. The Whooping Cranes can also occasionally be seen feeding elsewhere on the refuge. In fact, when the refuge conducts prescribed burns in certain areas, the Whoopers may be observed feeding on exposed acorns. Still, the best way to see the Whooping Cranes fairly close is by boat from the Rockport area. (*For details on boats, see the next chapter.*)

While Whooping Cranes are the most sought-after birds on the refuge, there are many others which you will want to look for. Nearly all of the species of waders found in Texas can usually be seen feeding in the marshy slough along the main road or on the adjacent shallow margins of San Antonio Bay. You may also see Roseate Spoonbill, Wood Stork, Sandhill Crane (winter), White and White-faced Ibises, and Clapper Rail, as well as numerous grebes, ducks, and shorebirds. In fact, the Aransas checklist boasts 389 species, with some very exciting sightings. In 1988, a female Crimson-collared Grosbeak and a Clay-colored Robin, both from Mexico, appeared. There are at least three records for Tropical Parula and at least five records for Masked Duck, too.

The Heron Flats Trail (0.5) beyond the Interpretive Center provides an excellent opportunity to view the largest number of waterbirds, including occasional Whooping Cranes. In summer check the Turk's-Cap Lilies here, and elsewhere in the refuge, for possible Buff-bellied Hummingbirds. (You may want to pick up an excellent interpretive booklet for use on this trail.)

Just past the Heron Flats parking area is a short Birding Trail (0.2) that passes through lush stands of Virginia Live Oak. It is especially good for landbirds during migration. The refuge picnic area (0.5) can also be good for landbirds. Some of the likely resident landbirds include Red-tailed Hawk, Tufted ("Black-crested") Titmouse, Carolina Wren, White-eyed Vireo, and Eastern Meadowlark. In summer you may also find Common Nighthawk, Scissor-tailed Flycatcher, and Painted Bunting; in winter, Eastern Phoebe, Vermilion Flycatcher, Yellow-rumped Warbler, Rufous-sided Towhee, and Savannah, Vesper, and other sparrows. *During migration, expect anything.*

At Jones Lake (2.9) on the right you can make a short stop to scan the area from a wooden observation platform. From here you can see all sorts of waders, ducks, and even rails sometimes. Look for Common Moorhen and Purple Gallinule.

From the tower at the end of the two-way road (0.5), you can scan the tree-tops for hawks and the marshes for cranes. You will certainly want to linger at the tower; there is also a nearby boardwalk passing through saltmarsh. From the left of the boardwalk's end there is a trail which connects with the Big Tree Trail. This winds through a Virginia Live-Oak patch attractive to migrant landbirds. The Hog Lake trail which is on the other side of the Tour Loop Road will bring you along the edge of a lake bed. Look for bitterns, Yellow-crowned Night-Heron, ducks, King Rail, and Purple Gallinule. Even when the area is dry, there will be some water by the wooden observation deck.

What you do not find from the tower and surrounding trails, you may find along the next twelve miles of the Tour Loop Road, which continues past the tower as a one-way road and winds through the brush and grasslands. Watch for White-tailed Hawk (rare) and Crested Caracara. You may also find Nine-banded Armadillos poking around in the fields and along the edge of the road. By approaching from the downwind side, you can usually get very close to them. Collared Peccaries (Javelina) are here, too; the best spot for them is around the picnic area. Bobcats are common throughout the refuge, but are seldom seen. This tan-with-pepper colored cat may be seen in late afternoon as it bounds across the road. White-tailed Deer are plentiful. The non-native hogs seen on the refuge are wild domestic pigs that have crossed with introduced Wild Boars, producing large and powerful creatures.

As you finish driving the Tour Loop Road (10.8), it may be dusk. You might see or hear Great Horned Owl or Pauraque by the Interpretive Center and refuge exit. Your headlights may pick up the Pauraque's orange eyeshine along the roadside.

Observation Tower on Tour Loop   Harold R. Holt

If there is still light on leaving the refuge, go back on Farm Road 2040. Shortly, you will find a small road to the right (3.0). At the end (0.4) is a boat launch called Hopper's Landing where you can find a small RV park (hook-ups). Back on FM 2040, continue north and watch on the right for a large pond (1.0), sometimes good for herons, egrets, cormorants, and waterfowl including Black-bellied Whistling-Duck. In fall, winter, and spring watch all along this road and the next, especially in plowed fields, for Upland and Buff-breasted Sandpipers, Crested Caracara, Sandhill Crane, and Lesser Golden-Plover (spring only). Turn left onto Farm Road 774 (2.6) and left again onto State Highway 35 (9.0) toward Rockport. In the past an occasional Greater Prairie-Chicken has been seen near this intersection during winter months, at dusk or dawn, especially near the rest stop on Highway 35 (2.6). (If you still have not seen a White-tailed Hawk or a Crested Caracara, though, continue west on Farm Road 774 for 7 or 8 miles. This is an excellent area for raptors and a good one for Wild Turkey.) Continuing south on Highway 35, you will come to Cavasso Creek (5.2). Sora, rails, Purple Gallinule, Common Moorhen, and other marsh birds can be found here. Watch also for American Alligators.

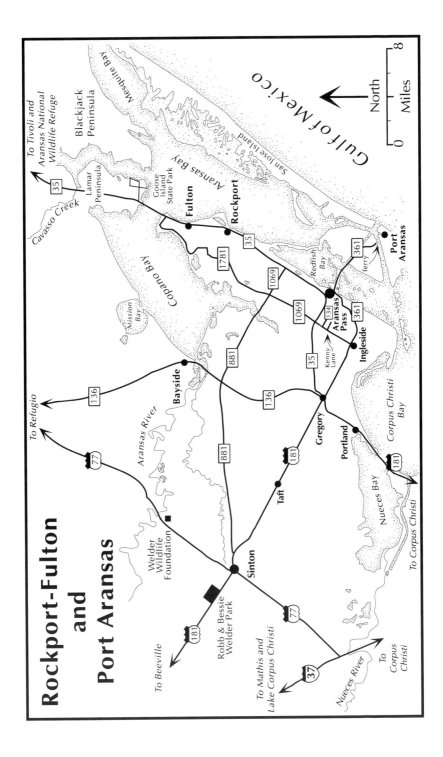

Rockport-Fulton
and
Port Aransas

CHAPTER 10:
ROCKPORT-FULTON AREA

As you go southward on Highway 35 toward Rockport you are traveling the length of the Lamar Peninsula. You are also approaching an area that has long been a mecca for birders—the Lamar Peninsula and, to the south, the Rockport-Fulton area. Along with the migrant wonders of the area and the wintering species, there are resident, year-round birds that should interest virtually any birder. Among these residents are Least Grebe (uncommon), Brown Pelican, Neotropic Cormorant, Reddish Egret, Roseate Spoonbill, Black-bellied Whistling-Duck, Mottled Duck, Black-shouldered Kite, White-tailed Hawk (uncommon), Crested Caracara (uncommon), Snowy Plover (uncommon), American Oystercatcher, Gull-billed and Sandwich (rare in winter) Terns, Inca Doves, Common Ground-Dove (rare), Greater Roadrunner (uncommon), Groove-billed Ani (rare), Pauraque, Buff-bellied (rare in winter), Ruby-throated (rare in winter), and Black-chinned (rare) Hummingbirds, Golden-fronted (uncommon) and Ladder-backed Woodpeckers, Long-billed (uncommon) and Curve-billed (rare) Thrashers, Pyrrhuloxia (rare), Olive (rare), Cassin's, Field, Lark, Grasshopper, and Seaside Sparrows, and Bronzed Cowbird (uncommon).

Approaching Copano Bay on southbound Highway 35, watch on the left for Park Road 13 (5.5 miles from Cavasso Creek in the previous chapter) just before the Sea-Gun Resort. Park Road 13 leads to Goose Island State Park (1.4). Rather than turning right to the state park, continue straight ahead on Main Street until it ends at the water's edge (0.4). Turn left (north) along St. Charles Bay. You will soon (0.3) reach 4th Street, where there is a pond along the northwest side of the intersection. This is the **Fourth Street Pond**; look for an opening just a few yards from the 4th Street intersection for a clear view. On the opposite side of the pond Black-crowned Night-Herons roost, sometimes with a Yellow-crowned Night-Heron. Early in the morning one can listen for Soras in migration; also watch for ducks and Purple Gallinules. The Tamarisks lining the pond and other trees in the area can attract many migrating warblers.

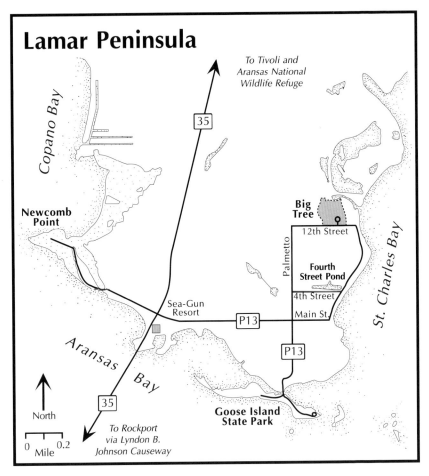

Lamar Peninsula

To Tivoli and
Aransas National
Wildlife Refuge

Copano Bay

35

Newcomb
Point

Big
Tree

12th Street

Palmetto

Fourth
Street Pond

4th Street

St. Charles Bay

Sea-Gun
Resort

P13

Main St.

P13

Aransas Bay

North

35

To Rockport
via Lyndon B.
Johnson Causeway

Goose Island
State Park

0   0.2
Mile

Continuing north, waders and shorebirds can be seen in numbers along the beach to your right. The road will soon turn left on 12th Street and approach the Big Tree, the national champion Virginia Live Oak, on the north side of the road (0.8). Continue west and turn left at the first road, Palmetto, (0.4) which will now take you straight into **Goose Island State Park** (camping, hot showers, fee; Star Route 1, Box 105, Rockport, Texas 78382; telephone: 512/729-2858)(1.2). The park is located at the southern tip of Lamar Peninsula at the conjunction of Aransas, Copano, and St. Charles Bays. It is a small park (314 acres), but very productive, as the park checklist which you can get at the entrance will indicate. The roads will lead you to a variety of habitats, and there is a hiking-trail through the woods. This area, along with the Fulton-Rockport area, has some of the best birding along the entire Texas coast. The habitat variety here makes it an excellent place to observe waterbirds, waterfowl, shorebirds, and passerines—both in migration and in residence. During low tide, shorebirds find St. Charles Bay, the shallowest of the area's bays, great for feeding. During migrations, especially in spring, the live-oak thickets attract many passerines, with warblers being especially abundant. The area also has marshes that are good for rails and gallinules, and open meadows.

The winter bird population is excellent and varied. Aransas Bay has diving birds—Eared Grebe, Lesser Scaup, Common Goldeneye, Bufflehead, and various other ducks—as well as Common Loon and Double-crested Cormorant. Because this bay is shallow, it also attracts the dabbling-ducks. Look for American White Pelicans across the bay on sandspits or feeding in the shallows near the Aransas National Wildlife Refuge on Blackjack Peninsula. Occasionally, a family of Whooping Cranes can also be seen feeding there. Canada Geese feed and rest on the bays. Herring, Ring-billed, Bonaparte's, Laughing, and Franklin's (rare) Gulls are found in winter over the water, as are Forster's, Royal, and Caspian Terns.

Upon leaving Goose Island State Park, turn left on Park Road 13 to return to Highway 35. Directly across the highway is a paved road leading to Newcomb Point. (This is also known as "No Man's Land.") The caliche road to the left (0.5) is not very good and *should not be traveled in wet conditions*, but the birding is excellent. The mudflats and saltmarsh (0.8) are favorite areas for Least Bitterns, rails, plovers, sandpipers, and Seaside Sparrows.

ROCKPORT-FULTON

Continue south on Highway 35 and cross Copano Bay on the Lyndon B. Johnson Causeway to the Liveoak Peninsula, on which **Rockport** is located. Not only is it a birder's paradise, but it is also a resort town and a base for part of the Gulf coast shrimp fleet. Rockport has a wide variety of habitats that attract many bird species in every season, but particularly during spring migration. Connie Hagar, who moved to Rockport in 1935, made daily birding rounds to document the bird life. Her routine—continued for 35 years—opened the eyes of the growing numbers of birdwatchers to the fact that Rockport is one of the most productive areas on the entire Texas coast. The diminutive Connie Hagar put Rockport on the birding map, and by the time she died, in 1973, the place had become a magnet for birders as well as for birds. The list of species recorded for the area has now reached almost 450!

Any road in the vicinity offers birding possibilities, but one of the better roads is Farm Road 1781 (2.6), the first one leading to the right (west) as you leave the L.B.J. Causeway. Follow Farm Road 1781 along the west side of the peninsula as it passes good stands of Virginia Live-Oaks and thickets which harbor small landbirds. Check out the small ponds along the way—there is a possibility of a Least Grebe. A good saltwater marsh and pond are on your right (0.9); Neotropic Cormorants often perch on the posts in this pond. Warblers and other migrant passerines can be found in the oak groves, and the grazed pastures attract Black-bellied Plover, Lesser Golden-Plover, Upland, Baird's, and Buff-breasted Sandpipers, and Long-billed Curlew.

At the intersection of Farm Road 2165 (5.5), keep right on Farm Road 1781. Turn right at the next fork (0.6) onto Rattlesnake Point Road toward Copano Cove. At the entrance to the cove (2.0) turn left to Pouzee's Pier (0.3) located at the end of the road—a great place to study ducks, shorebirds, and waders. There is usually an American Oystercatcher somewhere in the area.

Return to Farm Road 2165 and turn right. An ideal spot to observe passerines in migration and summer is Memorial Park (1.4) on your right. At Highway 35 (1.0) turn left, and then right into Rockport Beach Park (0.5). To your right is the Texas Maritime Museum (fee), open l0am to 4pm Wednesday through Saturday, Sunday 1pm-4pm (closed Monday, Tuesday). The Rockport-Fulton Area Chamber of Commerce facility is just west of here on Business 35. Here you can obtain a copy of *Birder's Guide to Rockport/Fulton* which contains maps and a bird checklist.

Since 1989 there has been a "Hummer/Bird Celebration" in town during the first part of September. It is run as a special project of the Tourism Development Council of the Rockport-Fulton Area Chamber of Commerce with the help of area birders and birding organizations. Extending over a long weekend, it includes speakers, workshops, vendors, and field trips. (For more information, contact the Chamber at PO Box 1055, Rockport, Texas 78381; telephone: 512/729-6445 or 800/242-0071.)

Turn left down the beach into the recreation area (fee), where you can usually find gulls, terns, shorebirds, Reddish Egrets, and maybe Snowy, Piping, and Semipalmated Plovers. A small area set aside for a bird sanctuary has an observation tower. Black Skimmers and other waterbirds nest on the islands in Little Bay.

Return to Highway 35 and turn right. At the north edge of town at the split in the road, ease right and follow the road that goes along the water toward Fulton Beach (0.6). This road closely borders the bay and passes the **Connie Hagar Wildlife Sanctuary**, where there is a pull-off on the right (0.4). The sanctuary is at its best in winter, when there are numerous loons, grebes, and waterfowl in the bay.

Keep left at the Y-intersection (0.7) (the right fork goes out to residential Key Allegro). Farther along, the road winds through patches of freshwater marsh, which harbor rails and bitterns, to the Sandollar Pavilion (1.7) where Captain Ted Appell docks his boat, the *Skimmer*. This is a fairly new (1986) 46-passenger craft (its popular predecessor, the *Whooping Crane*, has been retired) especially designed to operate in two feet of water, with ample inside seating, an observation deck, restrooms, and a cruising speed of 25 knots or

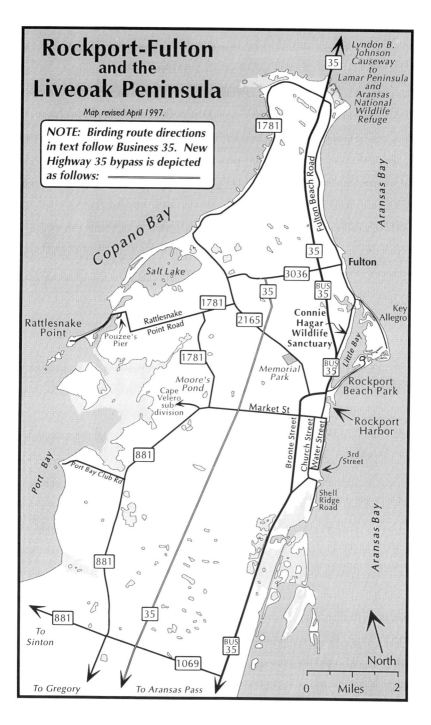

Rockport-Fulton
and the
Liveoak Peninsula

Map revised April 1997.

NOTE: Birding route directions in text follow Business 35. New Highway 35 bypass is depicted as follows: ═══

Lyndon B. Johnson Causeway to Lamar Peninsula and Aransas National Wildlife Refuge

35

1781

Fulton Beach Road

Aransas Bay

Copano Bay

Salt Lake

35

Fulton

3036

BUS 35

1781

Rattlesnake Point Road

35

2165

Connie Hagar Wildlife Sanctuary

Key Allegro

Rattlesnake Point

Pouzee's Pier

Little Bay

1781

Moore's Pond

Memorial Park

BUS 35

Cape Velero subdivision

Market St

Rockport Beach Park

Bronte Street

Church Street

Water Street

Rockport Harbor

881

3rd Street

Port Bay

Port Bay Club Rd

Shell Ridge Road

881

Aransas Bay

35

881

To Sinton

BUS 35

North

To Gregory

1069

To Aransas Pass

0   Miles   2

more (Capt. Ted's Whooping Crane Tours, Star Route 1, Box 225J, Rockport, Texas 78382; telephone: 512/729-9589 or 800/338-4551). The boat's speed means less running-time and more time for birding and photography. A boat trip to Aransas National Wildlife Refuge is a great way to see Whooping Cranes, Roseate Spoonbills, numerous herons, egrets, ibises, shorebirds, and usually an American Oystercatcher. From November 1 to April 1 the 30-mile round trip is made daily on the *Skimmer*, except on Tuesday, 7:30am to noon. Afternoon trips are also available with a minimum of ten persons, 1pm-4pm. The cost of the trip is refunded if no Whooping Crane is seen.

At least three other boats run regular trips (with slightly different schedules and routes) for the Whooping Cranes and other birds out of Rockport Harbor, not out of the Sandollar Pavilion. Ray Little leads the tour on the large motorized catamaran *Wharf Cat*, with a high top deck good for viewing. The boat will hold up to 90 people and has many amenities. Since it is a catamaran, the *Wharf Cat* has twin hulls which provide extra stability. At least one daily trip is scheduled—on Tuesdays, though, it runs out of Port Aransas. (Fisherman's Wharf, PO Box 387, Port Aransas, Texas 78373; telephone: 512/749-5760 or 800/782-BIRD). Captain John Howell's *Pisces* (49 passengers; 1019 North Allen, Rockport, Texas 78382; telephone: 512/729-7525 or 800/245-9324) and the *New Pelican* (47 passengers; 34 Turning Basin, Rockport, Texas 78382; telephone: 512/729-8448) are also based in Rockport Harbor. It is a good idea to call for reservations and to

Reddish Egret
Gail Diane Luckner

check on current schedules, minimum loads, and prices. You should find something to suit you. And you can always arrange for a personalized trip—for up to six passengers—with other services (e.g., Capt. Jim Friebele: 512/729-5676).

From April through June 1 most of these boats will also make visits to rookeries (some administered by the National Audubon Society) on the shell-islands in the bay. You will see thousands of birds nesting, as well a very large Reddish Egret rookery. Other birds seen on these trips should include nesting Cattle and Snowy Egrets, Tricolored and Little Blue Herons, Roseate Spoonbill, White Ibis, Brown Pelican, Gull-billed, Forster's, Least, Sandwich, Royal, and Caspian Terns, and Black Skimmer.

To continue the tour, follow Fulton Beach Road north, birding as you go. The road ends at Highway 35 (2.0), just south of Farm Road 1781. Turn left and proceed to the junction of Business 35 (5.6). Take this to Market Street (0.6) and turn left one block to Water Street. Bird the bayside for ducks, gulls, terns, and, at low tide, for herons, egrets, and shorebirds on the bars. Continue to the street-end at Third Street (1.0), turn right one block and then left onto Church Street. Soon the road swings right, but bear left and immediately turn left. At the bay, the road turns right and ends at Shell Ridge Road. Birding here is usually good for all waders, including Reddish Egret.

Return to Church Street and continue straight ahead on it to Market Street (1.0). Turn left to the traffic light (0.3). At this point Market Street becomes Farm Road 881. Continue straight ahead and at the intersection with Farm Road 1781 (2.0), turn right on 1781 for a short distance and watch on your left for Moore's Pond (0.3). This can be good at times for Black-bellied and, occasionally, even Fulvous Whistling-Ducks, Least Grebe, and Neotropic Cormorant. Return to Farm Road 881 and turn right. Follow 881 (as the road makes a curve to the left) to a sign on the right marking the Cape Velero Subdivision (0.4). This is a private road. *Birders are tolerated, but do not block the road (keep your right tires off the pavement when parked) and give all residents the right of way.* Cassin's Sparrows are sometimes heard in summer in the dry, grassy areas as they do their skylarking song. Migrating shorebirds stop in the wet meadows, so check in May for White-rumped Sandpiper and Hudsonian Godwit. There are excellent wetlands along this road. Look for White-faced Ibis, Greater White-fronted, Snow, Ross's (rare), and Canada Geese, Black-necked Stilt, herons, egrets, and Roseate Spoonbill. Return to Farm Road 881 and turn right.

Other migrating shorebirds such as Lesser Golden-Plover, Upland, Baird's, and Buff-breasted Sandpipers, Whimbrels, and Long-billed Curlews prefer the drier pastures such as those found along Port Bay Club Road (2.2) which dead-ends on the right. In spring you are sure to see a great display of wildflowers and Cassin's Sparrows skylarking, and, in winter, Vermilion Flycatcher. At Farm Road 1069 (3.0) you have a choice of following 881 westward toward Sinton and the center of San Patricio County, or keeping straight ahead for Aransas Pass.

Louisiana Waterthrush
Gail Diane Luckner

WEST OF ROCKPORT

Taking Farm Road 881 west toward Sinton should provide you with good Sandhill Crane views in winter. At the intersection of 881 and Farm Road 136 (7.0) you might also drive northward toward Bayside to check some extensive salt marshes (4.0). Here you may find Wood Storks in summer and fall, and a whole array of birds, including herons, egrets, plovers, and sandpipers. It is especially good at low tide. Return to 881 and proceed westward to Sinton (15.2).

The Sinton Settlement Ponds are found by traveling into Sinton on U.S. Highway 181 to Scofield Avenue, immediately past the railroad tracks (1.3). Turn right and after three blocks, turn right again onto East Main Street. Drive two blocks and turn left (0.4). Follow the dirt road alongside the railroad tracks until you come to a fence (0.2). Park here and walk through the gate in the barbed-wire fence to the left. The Settlement Ponds are on the left. The Main Group Bird Club maintains an observation blind at the ponds. Waterfowl and wading birds, especially in winter, can be found here.

Return to US Highway 181 and turn right. Continue on US Highway 181 through town, following 181 right on San Patricio Avenue (0.6). Robb and Bessie Welder Park is up US Highway 181 just northwest of town (2.4). The entrance is on the right. Robb and Bessie Welder Park houses the golf course. The park can be particularly good for migrants, and there is a developing native plant area on the southeast corner of the park adjacent to the pond. To get to the pond area, take a series of rights until you get to a dirt road; walk down to the pond.

Return to US Highway 181 and turn left to the overpass for US Highway 77 northbound (1.5). The Welder Wildlife Foundation (PO Box 1400, Sinton, Texas 78387; telephone: 512/364-2643) northeast of Sinton on Highway 77 (7.4). This private research station has excellent facilities for biological studies, and it also can be a good birding spot, though access is restricted. On Thursday afternoons there are tours of the facilities for the general public; group tours may be arranged for other times.

After visiting here you can drive back to Sinton, and from there eastward to Aransas Pass via U.S. Highway 181 to Ingleside, and FM 361 to Aransas Pass.

Alternately, from the junction of Farm Roads 1069 and 881, continue on Farm Road 1069 toward Ingleside. After crossing Highway 35 (4.3), watch on the left for County Road 134 (1.9). This dead-end street has lily-grown swales and ponds, where Least Bitterns, Common Moorhens, and Purple Gallinules nest, and many ducks winter. After one-half mile, return to the main road, continue to Kenny Lane (0.7), and turn left. Check the marshes for Least Grebe, White-faced Ibis, Mottled Duck, and Cinnamon Teal. During migration watch for Fulvous and Black-bellied Whistling-Ducks, Wilson's Phalarope, American Avocet, Black-necked Stilt, and Upland, Stilt, White-rumped, Pectoral, Solitary, Least, Western, and Semipalmated Sandpipers; also, check the live oaks for warblers.

At the stop-sign, turn left onto Highway 361 (2.0) and proceed to Aransas Pass (2.7). Follow Highway 361 when it makes a right turn toward Port Aransas. You will soon be on the Dale Miller Causeway, which crosses a shallow bay that is filled with sandbars. Here you can find American Oystercatcher, Reddish Egret, Snowy Plover, and other shorebirds. In winter it is good for ducks, American Avocets, and Marbled Godwits. With a great deal of luck in summer, Sooty Terns might be seen feeding over the bay, particularly on the left side of the road. A few pairs nest yearly in the region.

Beyond the Dale Miller Causeway is the free ferry to Port Aransas.

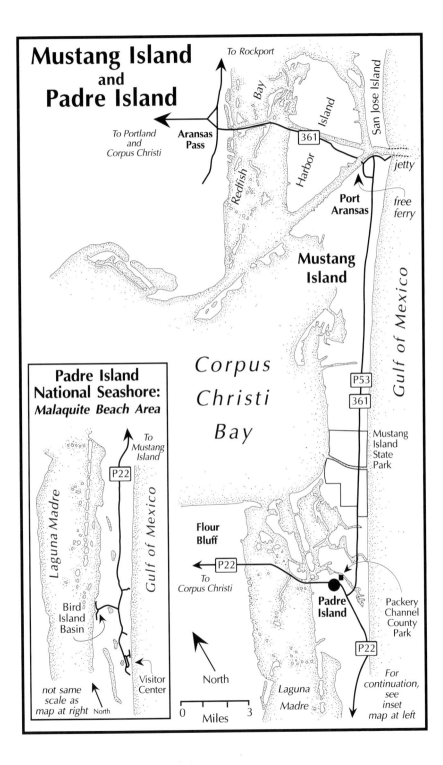

CHAPTER 11:
MUSTANG AND PADRE ISLANDS

As you ride the free ferry (6.5) into Port Aransas, watch for Bottle-nosed Dolphins. After docking, continue on Cotter Avenue until you reach the jetty (1.5). Gulls, terns, and shorebirds can be seen sitting on the beach or flying along the channel. This is a good spot to study Sandwich Terns; Sooty Tern has also been found here. The jetty bears an interesting assortment of starfish, crabs, sea anemones, and snails. There is a campground down the beach to your right (fee). Since the jetty extends several hundred yards out into the gulf, it provides the birder with a good opportunity to scan for pelagic species such as Northern Gannet (winter), Masked and Brown Boobies, Magnificent Frigatebird, all three jaegers, and Sooty Tern. In winter Bonaparte's Gull and Eared Grebe can be seen swimming near the jetty.

The waters of the Gulf of Mexico represent a largely unexplored facet of Texas coastal birding. The edge of the continental shelf diverges from the Upper Coast, making travel times to good pelagic birding habitat prohibitive. The Coastal Bend is considerably closer to the shelf edge, with the lower coast closest of all. Unfortunately, there are no regularly scheduled trips to Texas waters from Port Isabel on the Lower Coast. Most of the pelagic work has been done from the snapper fishing vessel *Scat Cat*, which operates from Port Aransas. Masked Booby, Pomarine Jaeger, and Cory's and Audubon's Shearwaters are becoming known as regular visitors offshore in late summer and fall. Those birders interested in exploring the Gulf can accompany the fishermen on their Red Snapper excursions for $40 (a reduced rate for birders who do not fish). The phone numbers for Fisherman's Wharf at Port Aransas are 512/749-5760 and 512/749-5448.

It is possible to reach St. Joseph Island and North Jetty. The boat (fee) leaves from and returns to Woody's Boat Basin (telephone: 512/749-5252) hourly from 6:30am to 6pm. Retrace your route to the first stoplight on Alister Street (1.0), turn left, and continue south on Alister Street (which becomes State Highway 361 and also Park Road 53) down **Mustang Island**.

101

This island is a part of the great barrier beach system that stretches almost the full length of Texas. It is composed mostly of sand dunes with a scant cover of grass. With so little vegetation, landbirds are not common, but there are plenty of shorebirds on the many mudflats, tidal marshes, and bays. You can go over to the Gulf by the Port Aransas Airport exit (2.5) to scan the shoreline for Red Knots, Sanderlings, Whimbrels, and plovers. There are several other access roads to the Gulf also, where you can drive on the **wet** sand. Primitive camping is also allowed here. Shell collectors find many species on the gulf beach, and other kinds are found on the muddier banks of the bay.

Farther south on the island is **Mustang Island State Park** (10.6) (fee, camping;PO Box 326, Port Aransas, Texas 78373; telephone: 512/749-5246). Pick up a bird checklist. Birding is good, not only on the gulf beach and jetty, but also in the dunes, grasslands, bayside waters, marshes, and tidal flats. In winter look for loons, grebes, pelicans, cormorants, and ducks, along with the resident herons, egrets, ibises, gulls, and terns. Oystercatchers, plovers, curlews, sandpipers, and godwits are found on the bayside flats. In winter also watch for Short-eared Owls feeding over the grasslands. The telephone poles along the highway make good perches for Ospreys and for White-tailed and Ferruginous Hawks. Spring migrants can be especially numerous near here during inclement weather that can force birds to land. Such fall-outs bring in many warblers, tanagers, orioles, grosbeaks, and buntings as well as a possible Bobolink or two.

Upon leaving the park, turn left to continue south on 361. Turn left at Park Road 22 (4.8) for **Padre Island National Seashore** (9.6) (fee; telephone: 512/937-2621). The birds here are usually the same as those on Mustang Island, but the sand dunes are higher, more majestic, and undeveloped. In addition, there are nature trails, a campground with cold showers, and miles and miles and miles of beautiful beach. The best birding is along this beach, which can be reached by driving to the end of the paved road and then carefully on the beach along the **wet** sand. Stop at the Visitor Center (2.7) for a bird checklist, information, maps, and books. Shortly the pavement will end (0.8). It is ordinarily possible to drive down the beach about five miles past the end of the road. Mile Post Five is the end of the two-wheel zone. Beyond this point, conditions are suitable for four-wheel drive vehicles only, and malleable patches of broken shells and soft sand can swallow up even these vehicles. (Before taking a four-wheel drive journey farther down the beach, you would be advised to consult with a park ranger about what to expect.) The remaining 55 miles of beach south to the Mansfield Channel may yield migrating Peregrine Falcons, peaking in late September and early October. There are also some nesting Snowy Plovers and wintering Piping Plovers among other birds. While scanning the beach beyond mile 16 you might get an eyeful; nude bathing, though prohibited by the Park Service, does seem to go on nonetheless.

The Padre Island National Seashore is the site of an ongoing effort to bring back the endangered Kemp's Ridley Sea Turtle from the brink of extinction. Young hatchlings have been "imprinted" on the Padre Island beaches in hopes that they would return as adults to nest. (Report sea turtle sightings to the National Seashore office.)

Before leaving the park, check the Laguna Madre side of the island via the road to Bird Island Basin, 2.6 miles north of the Visitor Center. The spoil banks here, along both sides of the Gulf Intracoastal Waterway, provide nesting areas for a great number of birds, such as herons, egrets, ibises, Black Skimmer, Laughing Gull, Caspian, Royal, and Gull-billed Terns, and American White Pelicans.

After passing the entrance station (0.9) and leaving the National Seashore (1.3), stay on Park Road 22 past Park Road 53/State Highway 361 (9.6), then watch on the right for small **Packery Channel County Park** (0.5). Here you can drive up close to the mudflats and study waders and shorebirds.

As you return toward Park Road 22, turn left onto Sand Dollar Avenue to a scattered housing development with numerous vacant lots which contain native and ornamental plantings along with several oak mottes. This six-square-block area is one of the primary migrant traps in this region. When local birders speak of "Packery," they are not speaking of Packery Channel County Park, but of this small **Packery Area Housing Development**. Any spring weekend will find several birders wandering the streets here, all wearing binoculars and hopeful looks. Beginning in late March, and continuing through at least mid-May, any inclement weather can produce hordes of flycatchers, swallows, thrushes, vireos, warblers, and tanagers here as they actively replenish their fuel supply on insects and larvae.

Though other times of year can be productive, spring passage is very special here. *Walk the streets, confining your activities to the roadsides, and respecting the private property of the residents.* Some of the neighborhood residents are birders. This neighborhood has been the site of several rarity sightings in recent years, so be on the alert. Seen in the past few years have been American Swallow-tailed Kite, Sulphur-bellied Flycatcher, Gray Kingbird, Black-whiskered Vireo, Black-throated Blue Warbler, Townsend's Warbler, Western Tanager, Bobolink, and Hooded Oriole.

After finishing birding here, return to Park Road 22, turn right and continue across the Kennedy Causeway. Once you have crossed the high bridge you can find places where you can stop to view the numerous shorebirds. At the west end of the bridge you will see a section of beach on the south section of the highway closed to vehicle traffic. This is to protect the nesting area of Black Skimmers. Look for these birds with their young in June and July. Least Terns can usually be found nesting here, too.

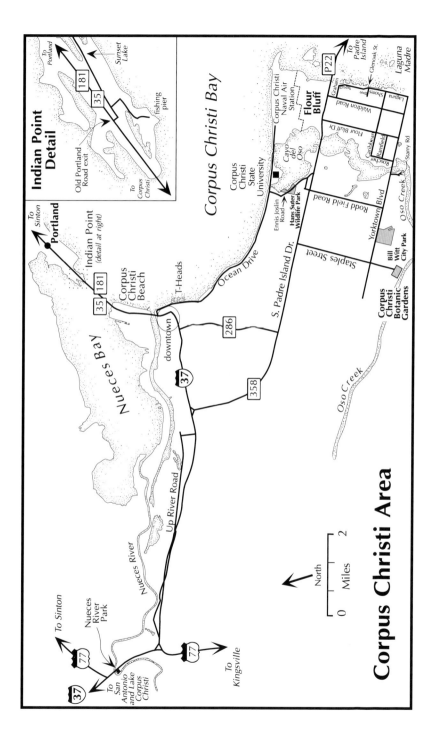

Indian Point Detail

Sunset Lake

To Portland

181

35

Old Portland Road exit

fishing pier

To Corpus Christi

Corpus Christi Bay

Nueces Bay

To Sinton

Portland

Indian Point *(detail at right)*

181

35

Corpus Christi Beach

T-Heads

downtown

37

Ocean Drive

286

358

S. Padre Island Dr.

Staples Street

Corpus Christi State University

Ennis Joslin Road

Hans Suter Wildlife Park

Cayo del Oso

Corpus Christi Naval Air Station

Flour Bluff

Flour Bluff Dr.

Waldron Road

Rodd Field Road

Yorktown Blvd

Bill Witt City Park

P22

To Padre Island

Glenoak St.

Shores

Laguna Madre

Laguna

Gotham

Rocher

Caribbean

Ramfield

Starry Rd

Oso Creek

Corpus Christi Botanic Gardens

Oso Creek

Up River Road

Nueces River

Nueces River Park

To Sinton

77

37

To San Antonio and Lake Corpus Christi

77

To Kingsville

North

Miles

0   2

Corpus Christi Area

CHAPTER 12:
CORPUS CHRISTI

As you cross the Laguna Madre on the Kennedy Causeway, Park Road 22 becomes South Padre Island Drive at the west edge of the Encinal Peninsula, and you enter the **Flour Bluff** section of Corpus Christi (4.5). Take the first exit, Waldron Road (0.6), turn left, proceed to Graham Road (0.5), and turn left again to Laguna Shores Road (0.5). Here, at the west edge of the Laguna Madre, check both sides of the road for waders and shorebirds. There is a large fresh-water pond at the southwest corner of this intersection that can have numerous wintering ducks. Proceed south (right) on Laguna Shores Road, continuing to check the mudflats and tidal pools on both sides of the road. The small islands at the edge of the bay are nesting areas for several species, including Wilson's Plover and Gull-billed and Least Terns. Other species which can be found on Laguna Shores might include American Oystercatcher, Snowy, Piping, and Semipalmated Plovers (migration and winter), Black-necked Stilt (year-round), Greater and Lesser Yellowlegs (except summer), Long-billed Curlew, Marbled Godwit, Ruddy Turnstone, Sanderling, Semipalmated (migration), Western, and Least Sandpipers, and both dowitchers. Shorebird populations here sharply increase during migration and winter months. Watch also for Reddish Egret in both color morphs.

Turn right on Glenoak Street (1.6) for half a block to check a large freshwater pond which hosts resident Black-crowned Night-Herons, Mottled Ducks, and numerous wintering ducks, including Green-winged Teal, Northern Pintail, Northern Shoveler, Gadwall, American Wigeon, large flocks of Redhead, Lesser Scaup, Bufflehead, and Common Goldeneye, as well as a few Hooded Mergansers.

Continue south on Laguna Shores to Yorktown Boulevard (1.4) and turn right. Continue past Flour Bluff Drive (2.0), and look for a large pond on the left, which is on private property. You may scope from the roadside for nesting Fulvous and Black-bellied Whistling-Ducks, resident White-faced Ibis, and Mottled Duck. Return to Flour Bluff Drive and proceed north (left) to Caribbean Drive (1.0). The patches of scrub-oak along the following three streets—Caribbean, Ramfield, and Yorktown Boulevard—can be excellent for migrants and wintering landbirds. The small grass-lined ponds in the area may produce Neotropic Cormorant, Black-crowned Night-Heron, or, if you are very lucky, a Masked Duck. The best way to cover the area is to make a series of figure-eights up and down the roads.

Return to Yorktown Boulevard and turn right; drive beyond Oso Creek to Starry Road (1.0). Turn left and proceed slowly down this dead-end dirt road which passes by a corral area. This spot will usually have large mixed blackbird flocks. Look for Brewer's Blackbird (winter) and Yellow-headed Blackbird (migration). There will be three small ponds where the road bears left (0.5). The small pond on the left may have nesting Purple Gallinule in summer. Watch the roadside scrub here and along Yorktown Boulevard for Groove-billed Ani at most times of year.

Retrace your path to Yorktown Boulevard and turn left. Continue northwest until you reach Bill Witt City Park (2.7). The short grass athletic fields can have numbers of Lesser Golden-Plovers, and Baird's and Buff-breasted Sandpipers in spring. Continue to Staples Street (0.8), and turn left and follow the road to the 264-acre **Corpus Christi Botanical Gardens** (1.2) (fee). The ornamental and flowering plants attract Ruby-throated and Black-chinned Hummingbirds. Mesquite and a variety of other native woody plants are along the walking trail. Look for Groove-billed Ani, Long-billed and Curve-billed Thrashers, White-eyed Vireo, and Pyrrhuloxia. There is a 12-acre pond with cattails and sedges which attracts many birds, including Least Grebe and a variety of ducks. A new thatch-covered observation

Trail along Cayo del Oso   Harold R. Holt

Black Skimmer
Gail Diane Luckner

platform is at the pond. Look for King and Virginia Rails in winter and spring. Check the nearby trees for Couch's Kingbird; this is about as far north as it regularly gets on the Texas Coast. Also check out the shoreline of the adjoining Oso Creek for grebes, Tricolored Heron, Roseate Spoonbill, and shorebirds.

Return to Yorktown Boulevard and turn right and then left onto Rodd Field Road (2.0). Cross under Padre Island Drive (1.8), turn right onto McArdle Road (0.2), and at Ennis Joslin Road (0.5) turn left to **Hans Suter Wildlife Park** (1.1), situated on the edge of Cayo del Oso. This shallow lagoon is the best place in the area to find shorebirds, waders, and waterfowl. Take the excellent boardwalk; from it you can scan the bay for Roseate Spoonbill, Reddish Egret, Stilt Sandpiper, American Avocet, Black-necked Stilt, and other shorebirds. A Jabiru thrilled birders here for two weeks in September 1981. For several years in a row, a Ruff wintered here.

Follow Ennis Joslin Road until it merges with Alameda Street and ends at Ocean Drive (0.9). Turn right toward Corpus Christi State University to get a different view of Cayo del Oso and to reach other shorebird spots. Turn left to reach downtown Corpus Christi.

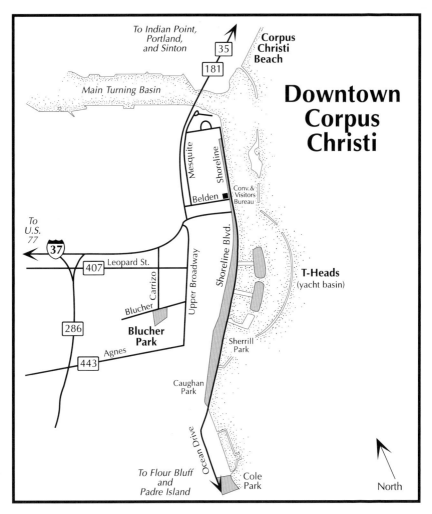

To Indian Point,
Portland,
and Sinton

35

181

Corpus
Christi
Beach

Main Turning Basin

Downtown
Corpus
Christi

Mesquite

Shoreline

Belden

Conv.&
Visitors
Bureau

To
U.S.
77

37

407 Leopard St.

Shoreline Blvd.

Upper Broadway

Carrizo

Blucher

286

**Blucher
Park**

Agnes

443

T-Heads
(yacht basin)

Sherrill
Park

Caughan
Park

Ocean Drive

To Flour Bluff
and
Padre Island

Cole
Park

North

CORPUS CHRISTI

Corpus Christi, an attractive city of 265,000, is perched high on a bluff overlooking the bay. Since it is close to many birding areas, it makes a fine place to spend a vacation—its friendly residents will surely make you welcome. Even if you do not have a car, there are good birding areas within walking or bussing distance. As you reach downtown, Ocean Drive becomes Shoreline Boulevard. On the right is Cole Park, and just beyond on the downtown bayfront off Shoreline Boulevard you will find three man-made wharves called T-Heads; try this bayfront area in winter for pelicans, cormorants, ducks, and sandpipers. Immediately behind the downtown section, next to Central Library off Carrizo Street, is Blucher Park, a major stopover for migrating passerines and hummingbirds. The local Audubon Outdoor Club of Corpus Christi conducts bird-walks every Saturday and Sunday during April at Blucher Park; join the group from 7:30 to 9:30am.

After passing the yacht basin on North Shoreline Boulevard (7.2), turn left onto Belden Street toward Interstate 37. The Convention and Visitor Bureau is located here on the corner (1201 North Shoreline Boulevard, Corpus Christi Texas 78403; telephone: 512/882-5603 and 800/678-6232). Pick up a free pamphlet, *Birding the Corpus Christi Area*, which includes a bird checklist.

If you wish to explore the north side of the bay, take Highway 35/181 toward Sinton, and cross over the high bridge. Directly on your right is Corpus Christi Beach, with an RV park located at its north end. Beyond this park 2.0 miles is the exit (Old Portland Road) off the Nueces Bay Causeway leading through the marsh to Indian Point (0.4). The area has two boardwalks which lead into the marsh, and a new fishing pier at the end of the road. This is a great place for finding and observing waders, rails, Black Skimmers, gulls, and terns. In migration many passerines are found, also. The Old Portland Road continues east along Sunset Lake from the turn-off for an additional 2.2 miles, but the road is very rough and is sometimes closed. To return to Corpus Christi, go back to the causeway, turn left on the frontage road, and use the underpass (0.9) (check the islets and marsh on the east side) to reach the southbound lane of the causeway.

To continue the tour, take Interstate 37. (Keep in the right-hand lanes for the first mile or you will find yourself southbound on Highway 286.) Leave the freeway at exit 5 and go right onto Corn Products Road (10.1); then turn left onto Up River Road (0.6). You will soon come to an isolated arm of the Nueces Bay known as **Tule Lake** (1.2). Park, with care, along the shoulder of the road. The lake's brackish water alternates between fresh and salt, depending on the rain and the tides, so you will often find different birds here from one visit to the next. The mudflats are usually good in winter and migration for ducks, Wilson's Phalarope, Semipalmated, Piping, Snowy, Wilson's, and Black-bellied Plovers, Greater and Lesser Yellowlegs, Marbled Godwit, American Avocet, Black-necked Stilt, and Least, Stilt, White-rumped, Baird's, Western, and Semipalmated Sandpipers, and Dunlin. There are also waders here, and in the evening they come in great numbers to roost. Wood Storks are almost always present in July, August, and September. These birds may be joined by mixed flocks of what may seem to be a million or more cowbirds, grackles, and blackbirds.

Continue on Up River Road until it goes under the freeway (2.9). Jog left and then right on the lateral road, which soon becomes Up River Road again. You will cross a sparsely-developed area of brush, where you may find Pyrrhuloxia and Groove-billed Ani. At Violet Road (2.4), turn left to Leopard Street (0.4), and then turn right; watch on the left for the **Hilltop Community**

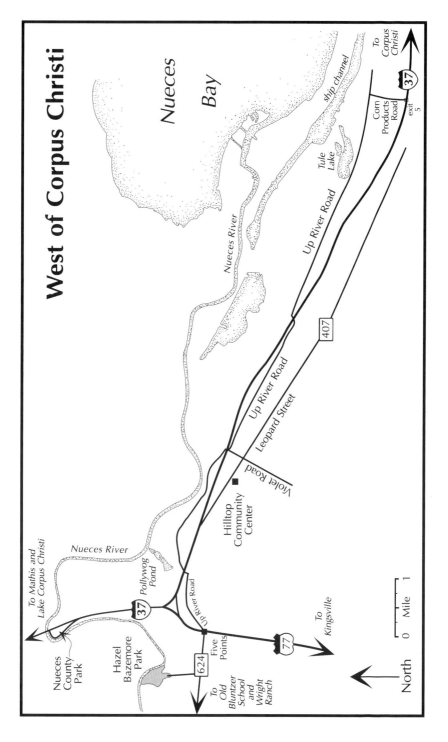

West of Corpus Christi

Center (0.3) (open daylight hours). A half-mile nature trail leads through native-brush habitat, which is excellent for migrating and resident species. Return to Violet Road, turn left, and continue over the freeway. Turn left onto Up River Road; park by the small wildlife sanctuary sign (2.1) on the right. The area between the road and the Nueces River is used as a settling-basin by the City Water Department, and has been designated a wildlife sanctuary. Local birders refer to it as **Pollywog Pond**. There is actually a series of ponds here, which are alternately flooded and dry. The flooded ponds usually have a good assortment of ducks, grebes, and shorebirds. Least Bitterns nest here, and in winter you should find King, Virginia, and Sora Rails. Be sure to check the willows on the right side of the channel for vireos, warblers, sparrows, Groove-billed Anis, and White-winged Doves. At dusk large numbers of herons and egrets come in to roost, and, occasionally, you may see Neotropic Cormorants and Anhingas. You can walk for about a mile along the levees to the river.

Continue straight on Up River Road, past Sharpsburg Road, and past the junction with Interstate 37 (1.9). Stay on the frontage road and you will reach the public boat ramp (0.9). Follow this road as it makes a loop under the freeway by the river and through **Nueces County Park** on the Nueces River (camping, fee). The birding can be good here in winter. Stay on this road and rejoin the freeway southbound toward Corpus Christi, then turn right onto Highway 77 South (exit 14) (2.0).

After you have turned right onto Highway 77 South, you will come to Five Points (0.5). Turn right onto Farm Road 624, and right again to visit the excellent **Hazel Bazemore County Park** (0.6) (ask for map and bird checklist). Especially check the sanctuary under the bluff for Groove-billed Ani, Carolina Wren, Curve-billed and Long-billed Thrashers, and Olive and Lark Sparrows. Small landbirds can be common here during migration, particularly hummingbirds. Fairly often you will find Black-shouldered Kites.

If you do not plan to go farther south at the moment, you can visit an interesting area around Lake Corpus Christi, where a few of the western and Mexican species can be found. To continue the tour to Kingsville (30.0 miles on Highway 77 South) and the Lower Coast, skip the following chapter.

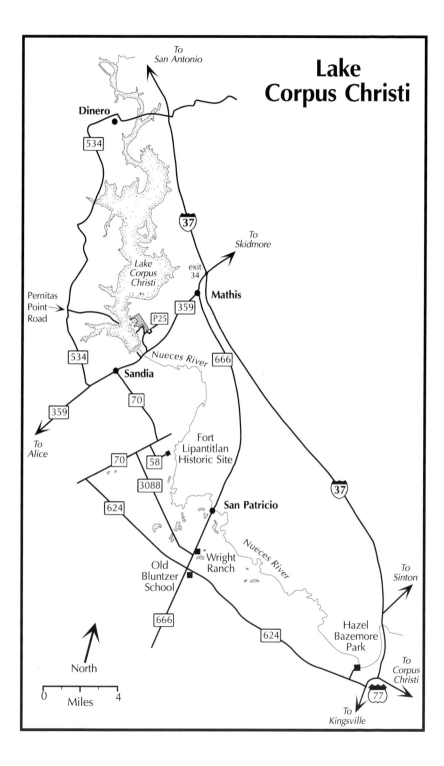

Lake
Corpus Christi

To
San Antonio

Dinero

534

37

To
Skidmore

Lake
Corpus
Christi

exit
34

Mathis

Pernitas
Point
Road

P25

359

534

Nueces River

666

359

Sandia

70

359

70

58

Fort
Lipantitlan
Historic Site

To
Alice

3088

624

San Patricio

Nueces River

37

Wright
Ranch

Old
Bluntzer
School

To
Sinton

666

Hazel
Bazemore
Park

624

To
Corpus
Christi

North

77

0   Miles   4

To
Kingsville

CHAPTER 13:
LAKE CORPUS CHRISTI

Lake Corpus Christi is located on the Nueces River (new-A-ces) at the edge of the chaparral belt that covers much of southcentral Texas. The birdlife is somewhat different from that along the coast. The resident birds are more typical of those found farther south and west of Corpus Christi. If you do not plan to visit the Rio Grande Valley, it is worth your time to drive out to the lake.

To reach the lake go west on Interstate 37 from the intersection of U.S. Highway 77. Leave the Interstate at the Skidmore exit (21.0) (exit 34) near Mathis. Turn left onto Business Route 359 westbound, and then right onto Park Road 25 (4.5), which leads to **Lake Corpus Christi State Park** (camping, hot showers, fee; PO Box 1167, Mathis, Texas 78368; telephone: 512/547-2635). As soon as you start on this road, look to the left for the entrance to the wildlife sanctuary below the dam. You can walk along the service road to explore most of the area. The sanctuary is wetter than the surrounding area and has a few willows. Swamp, Lincoln's, and White-throated Sparrows can be found here in winter; Northern and Orchard Orioles, Brown-crested Flycatcher, Blue Grosbeak, Painted Bunting, and Yellow-billed Cuckoo are likely in summer. On a rainy day in spring, the bushes may be hopping with warblers.

The park is in a drier area of mesquite, where you can find White-winged and Inca Doves, Common Ground-Doves, Golden-fronted and Ladder-backed Woodpeckers, Curve-billed and Long-billed Thrashers, Greater Roadrunner, Pyrrhuloxia, and Olive Sparrow. Along the lake there are always a few coots and, usually, Black-bellied Whistling-Ducks. In winter there should be numerous other ducks and grebes, except on weekends, when the place is overrun with picnickers and fishermen.

Return to State Highway 359 and turn right. At once you are on the Nueces River Bridge, crossing the river that was once the boundary between Texas and Mexico. Look for a turn on the right (0.5) for the **Wesley Seale Dam**, and proceed about one-half mile to the south end of the dam. Here you can park and walk some 300 yards below the dam to a cattail marsh, which often has Least and American Bitterns, Common Yellowthroat, and Marsh Wren. After some 200 yards, you will find the river, where there may

Wesley Seale Dam   Harold R. Holt

be coots, Common Moorhens, Purple Gallinules, gulls, terns, and sandpipers. You may find Texas Horned Lizards ("Horned Toads") eating ants on the hard, dry ground; at the water's edge there might be a large Diamond-backed Water Snake or a Checkered Garter Snake. Green Treefrogs often call from the trees. Walk down the right bank of the river for another 100 yards to the east, and you will find yourself in a thick grove of Virginia Live-Oak, Prickly Ash, Hackberry, and American Elm. You will also find some large Pecan trees here, the *nueces* or nuts that give the river its name.

These thick woods are excellent for Barred, Great Horned, and Barn Owls, Eastern Screech-Owls, Carolina, Bewick's, and House Wrens, Eastern Bluebird, Ladder-backed and Golden-fronted Woodpeckers, Curve-billed and Long-billed Thrashers, Red-winged and Brewer's Blackbirds, and Olive Sparrow. In winter look for Northern Flicker, Yellow-bellied Sapsucker, Brown Thrasher, and Lincoln's, White-crowned, and White-throated Sparrows. In summer, you might find Northern (Bullock's) and Orchard Orioles, Painted Bunting, and Brown-crested Flycatcher.

Return to State Highway 359 and turn right. Drive through Sandia (1.3) and continue to the intersection of Highway 359 and Farm Road 534 (1.9).

Turn right (north) and follow FM 534 to a paved road on the right marked **"Pernitas Point"** (4.7). Turn right and drive through some excellent dry chaparral habitat, mainly on the left side. Stop occasionally to look for Harris's Hawk and Crested Caracara, which may be perched on any tree or

Nueces River below dam   Harold R. Holt

post. The vegetation of Catclaw, yucca, and several associated plants and cacti can hold an interesting array of birdlife. Look and listen for White-winged Dove, Ladder-backed Woodpecker, Ash-throated Flycatcher (spring and summer), Verdin, Bewick's Wren, Curve-billed Thrasher, Pyrrhuloxia, Olive Sparrow, Green-tailed Towhee (winter), Cassin's Sparrow, and Black-throated Sparrow.

Continue to the entrance of Pernitas Point (2.5), a lakeside community which is currently not as developed as its network of streets. The road you are traveling becomes Trail Ridge, and several short side streets can be walked or driven for more birds and wildlife of the chaparral. This is all private property, so keep to the roads. Species should be about the same as in the Pernitas Point Road area.

As you explore around the housing development, you may find Golden-fronted Woodpecker and Great Kiskadee in the areas of larger trees and ornamental plantings, especially near the lakeshore. A population of Green Jays is also present here, and this has been an easy area in which to find Greater Roadrunner. In migration, the numbers of residential birds can be supplemented by numerous landbirds—vireos, warblers, tanagers, and sparrows.

Return to Farm Road 534 (2.5). If you wish to search for more birds of the dry chaparral, turn right and continue to Dinero (19.2) on the west side of the reservoir. In Dinero you stand a good chance of finding Groove-billed Ani,

Harris's Hawk, Cactus and Bewick's Wrens, Couch's Kingbird, and Cassin's and Black-throated Sparrows. With luck, you may find Scaled Quail. Look for Black-bellied Whistling-Ducks in the ponds. During spring migration, there are usually large flights of Swainson's and Broad-winged Hawks, and Mississippi Kites.

Back in Sandia (6.8 if you did not go up to Dinero), turn right onto Farm Road 70. You will drive through mostly farmland. Knolle Dairy, along the way, is reported to have one of the largest herds of Jersey cows in the world. If that fact does not udderly delight you, maybe the numerous Bronzed Cowbirds and Lark Sparrows will. In spring the gently rolling hills are covered with truly spectacular splashes of Texas Bluebonnet and Indian Paintbrush. In winter look for Lark Buntings, American Goldfinches, and Savannah, Grasshopper, Vesper, Field, and White-crowned Sparrows. In April Clay-colored Sparrows can be abundant, and in summer Scissor-tailed Flycatchers and Dickcissels are common. Shortly after this road makes a sharp turn to the right (4.6), watch on the left for the entrance to **Lipantitlan State Park** (Lee-PAHN-tit-lahn) (primitive camping), which is on CR 58. Turn left here and proceed to where you will take another left (1.2) to the park entrance (1.2). The park was named for the Indians who once occupied the

Green Jay
F.P. Bennett

area. This small area can be good for Eastern Bluebirds and Vermilion Flycatchers in winter and for other residents of the mesquite brushlands at any time. Return to Farm Road 70 and soon turn left onto Farm Road 3088 (1.4), and then left onto Farm Road 666 (5.9). Watch on the right for a fenced lake at the Wright Ranch (0.1). If there are any whistling-ducks in the area, this is where you will find them. Black-bellied is resident, although more common in summer; Fulvous occurs in migration. Several large American Alligators live in the lake and can be seen sunning themselves, usually on the south bank. Across the road you will see a thicket and a swale, which are good for both night-herons, Anhinga, Verdin, and Tufted ("Black-crested") Titmouse. A mile to the north, or sometimes directly to the south, you can wonder at a herd of the almost extinct Long-horned Cattle.

Turn around and go back past Farm Road 3088, then turn left onto Farm Road 624 (0.7) at the old Bluntzer School. Watch on the left for a canal and an inconspicuous sign marking the road into Hazel Bazemore County Park (8.9) described in the last chapter.

When you reach U.S. Highway 77 (0.9), turn onto it—Interstate 37 is to the left and Kingsville is to the right.

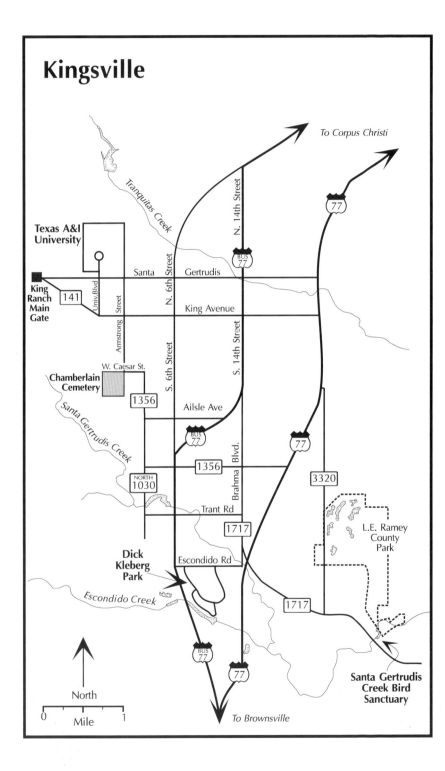

Kingsville

Texas A&I University

King Ranch Main Gate

141

Univ.Blvd

Armstrong Street

Santa

Gertrudis

King Avenue

N. 6th Street

N. 14th Street

S. 6th Street

S. 14th Street

Brahma Blvd.

Tranquitas Creek

Santa Gertrudis Creek

Chamberlain Cemetery

W. Caesar St.

1356

Ailsle Ave

BUS 77

1356

NORTH 1030

Trant Rd

1717

Escondido Rd

Dick Kleberg Park

Escondido Creek

BUS 77

77

To Brownsville

To Corpus Christi

77

BUS 77

77

3320

L.E. Ramey County Park

1717

Santa Gertrudis Creek Bird Sanctuary

North

0   Mile   1

CHAPTER 14:
KINGSVILLE AND VICINITY

The city of Kingsville was named for Richard King, founder of the 825,000-acre King Ranch (said to be the country's largest privately-owned ranch). Richard King started the ranch in 1852 with an original purchase of 75,000 acres. Kingsville itself got its start in 1904 as King Ranch Station, when the St. Louis, Brownsville, and Mexico Railroad laid tracks across the vast ranch. Now, with a population of 25,000, Kingsville is best known as the headquarters for the King Ranch, but it is becoming increasingly known as a fine birding locale, with abundant numbers of many species.

Many of the specialties of Kleberg County, in which Kingsville is located, and Kenedy County to the south, are species which are near the northern limit of their nesting ranges in this area. These species include Black-bellied Whistling-Duck, Harris's Hawk, White-tailed Hawk, Ferruginous Pygmy-Owl, Buff-bellied Hummingbird, Great Kiskadee, Brown-crested Flycatcher, Cave Swallow, Green Jay, Tropical Parula, Pyrrhuloxia, Olive Sparrow, and Audubon's Oriole.

The entrance to Santa Gertrudis, the headquarters division of the King Ranch is located some 3.5 miles west of Highway 77 on Highway 141 (King Avenue). Watch on the left for the white gatehouse. Some birders will be disappointed to learn that the self-guided tours on the property were discontinued in the late 1980s, but visitors can still ride the Guided Tour buses (fee) which run daily 10-3 and Sundays 1-4. (These are general tours, devoted to the history and work of the ranch, especially the breeds developed here—the Santa Gertrudis cattle and Old Sorrel Quarter-Horses. The busses will not stop for you to take a leisurely look at a bird.) There are also 4-to-5 hour "VIP Wildlife Tours" where you can get some better looks at some area specialties, such as White-tailed Hawk, Crested Caracara, Great Kiskadee, Green Jay, and Pyrrhuloxia. Reservations must be made at least a week in advance, and the cost is currently $40. To reserve a spot on this kind of tour call 512/592-8055. (Another way to see the birds on the ranch is to sign up for a bird tour with Victor Emanuel Nature Tours [VENT]. These tours start and end in Corpus Christi, include a trip for the Whooping Cranes, and spend a couple of days on the King Ranch, including one on the ranch's productive Norias Division. They run at various times from late February to mid-April and will seek out much-desired birds such as Ferruginous Pygmy-Owl, Northern Beardless-Tyrannulet, Tropical Parula, and Audubon's Oriole. Other VENT trips are run on some weekends on the Santa Gertrudis and Laureles Divisions of the ranch and are shorter, but are not as bird-oriented. Arrangements may be made by calling the Austin, Texas-based bird-tour company at 800/328-VENT.)

When you leave the King Ranch gate, drive straight ahead (east) on Santa Gertrudis Boulevard to University Boulevard (0.8) and the **Texas A & I University** campus. Look around here for White-winged and Inca Doves and Great Kiskadee at all seasons; Western Kingbird, Purple Martin, and, in the tall palms lining the campus, Hooded Oriole during breeding season.

Buff-bellied Hummingbird, a South Texas specialty, can be encountered almost anywhere described in this chapter (from Kingsville itself to the rest stops down Highway 77). The problem is, that given the variability of undergrowth and flowering plants in the area, from year to year it is difficult to know exactly where to look. Often you will hear the bird's high-pitched and squeaky metallic voice before seeing it.

Continue east on Santa Gertrudis Boulevard to Armstrong Street (0.2). Turn right to **Chamberlain Cemetery** (1.1), located at the end of the street. The large trees in the cemetery provide habitat for many species, including nesters such as Golden-fronted and Ladder-backed Woodpeckers, Great Kiskadee, Brown-crested Flycatcher, Green Jay, Tufted ("Black-crested") Titmouse, and Curve-billed Thrasher. You may also find Lesser Nighthawk here. Spring migration is good here for passerines, with a good variety of flycatchers, vireos, warblers, orioles, and sparrows.

When leaving the cemetery, turn right (east) onto West Caesar Street, then right onto Farm Road 1356 (0.2). When FM 1356 turns left (1.0), continue straight ahead on County Road 1030N. At Santa Gertrudis Creek (0.4) pull over and check for possible wading birds, shorebirds, or waterfowl. Continue down 1030N and turn left onto Trant Road (0.1). (Be particularly careful at the unprotected railroad crossing.) At Business 77 (0.4) turn right. Continue to Escondido Road (0.5) and turn left . After about 100 yards, turn right into **Dick Kleberg Park**.

This county facility has open water, native brush, oaks, and grassland. Resident birds include Golden-fronted and Ladder-backed Woodpeckers, Great Kiskadee, Green Jay, Tufted ("Black-crested") Titmouse, Curve-billed and Long-billed Thrashers, Pyrrhuloxia, and, possibly, Olive Sparrow. Bronzed and Brown-headed Cowbirds are often very numerous. Migration brings vireos and warblers of many species. In winter you should be able to find Black-shouldered Kite, many Vermilion Flycatchers, and usually good flocks of American Pipits. If you are lucky, a Sprague's Pipit may be found foraging in the short grass. On the small lake you may find the infrequent Least Grebe or Anhinga. Double-crested and Neotropic Cormorants frequent the lake and may sometimes be seen side by side. Mottled Duck is present year-round, and is joined in winter by a good variety of other waterfowl. A nesting colony of Barn and Cave Swallows is located under the bridge at the north end of the lake from March into September.

Upon leaving the park from the exposition exit, turn right (east) onto Escondido Road. Escondido Road will make a sharp left, cross a creek, and intersect with Farm Road 1717 at a stop sign (0.4). Turn right, stop again, and cross Highway 77. Continue east on Farm Road 1717 to the **Santa Gertrudis Creek Bird Sanctuary** (1.8) on your left. Some 130 species of birds have used the wet area, small pond, and extensive cattail marsh for part or all of the year. The area can be birded by walking along the levee to the observation stand. Some nesting species are Least Grebe, Black-bellied Whistling-Duck, Mottled Duck, Purple Gallinule, Common Moorhen, American Coot, and Red-winged Blackbird. You may want to check the wooded area to the left (west) and across the road for Green Jay, Brown-crested Flycatcher, Great Kiskadee, and Curve-billed Thrasher. At the pond area in winter look and listen for Eared Grebe, American Bittern, herons, egrets, a variety of ducks, hawks, Sora, King and Virginia Rails, gulls, terns, Marsh and Sedge Wrens,

Harris's Hawk
Gail Diane Luckner

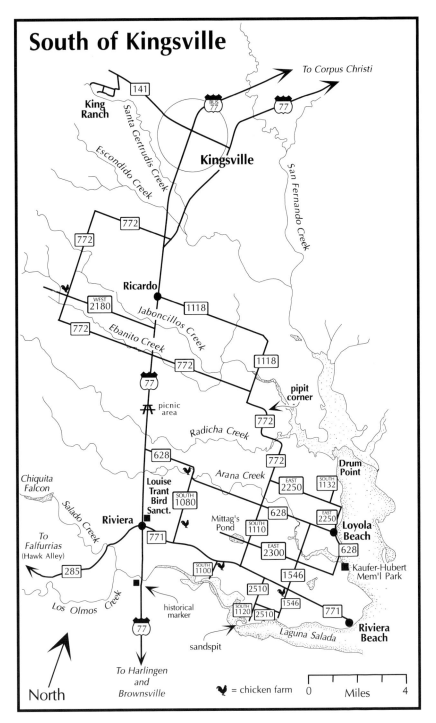

South of Kingsville

To Corpus Christi

141

King
Ranch

BUS
77

77

Kingsville

Santa Gertrudis Creek

Escondido Creek

San Fernando Creek

772

772

Ricardo

WEST
2180

1118

Jaboncillos Creek

772

Ebanito Creek

772

77

1118

pipit
corner

picnic
area

772

Radicha Creek

628

772

Drum
Point

Louise
Trant
Bird
Sanct.

Arana Creek

EAST
2250

SOUTH
1132

Chiquita
Falcon

SOUTH
1080

628

EAST
2250

Salado Creek

Riviera

Mittag's
Pond

SOUTH
1110

Loyola
Beach

To
Falfurrias
(Hawk Alley)

771

EAST
2300

628

285

SOUTH
1100

1546

Kaufer-Hubert
Mem'l Park

2510

Los Olmos Creek

historical
marker

SOUTH
1120

1546

2510

771

77

sandspit

Laguna Salada

Riviera
Beach

To Harlingen
and
Brownsville

= chicken farm   0   Miles   4

North

and Swamp and Lincoln's Sparrows. At the culvert under Farm Road 1717 look for nesting Cave, Barn, and Cliff Swallows in summer.

Return to Highway 77 and turn left (south). At the sign directing you to the Presbyterian Pan American School, turn right (1.7). This is Farm Road 772. Continue west, crossing Business 77 (0.1), and passing in front of the school (0.4). Check for Common Ground-Doves as you drive through all the roads in this area. Brushy areas may provide looks at Green Jay, Great Kiskadee, Long-billed Thrasher, Curve-billed Thrasher, Cactus Wren, Olive Sparrow, Pyrrhuloxia, and, in summer, Groove-billed Ani, Painted Bunting, Hooded Oriole, and possibly even Audubon's Oriole. A Black-vented Oriole from Mexico visited nectar-feeders nearby between June and October 1989.

Continue on FM 772 as it turns left (south) (3.1). After 3.0 miles, you should see the long sheds of a chicken farm. This is one of several "chicken factories" which you will see on this tour. (All may not be operating at the same time.) Daily, from about 9am to noon, the dead chickens are removed from their brooder houses and dumped in a field where local scavengers will feast on them. Look right (west) beyond the first field to the chicken dumping-ground. Vultures and hawks will be scattered about the area if the pickings are good. There should be plenty of Crested Caracaras here. Locally known as the "Mexican Eagle," this handsome scavenger takes advantage of the handouts of half-a-dozen chicken farms. You may catch a Crested Caracara in the act of stealing a meal from one of the other raptors—a not-uncommon trait of this striking bird. Some of the largest concentrations of this species ever recorded in the United States have been found in the vicinity of the commercial chicken farms in Kleberg County. Along with the Crested Caracaras, you may also find numbers of White-tailed and Harris's Hawks, as well as Turkey and Black Vultures. In winter a few Red-tailed Hawks and Ferruginous Hawks can be observed feeding here, also. Another way to view this dumping-ground is to continue south to County Road 2180W (0.2), turn right (west), and go to the orange-colored fenceposts (0.3). Set up your spotting scope and look from the road, directly to the north, about one-third to one-half mile. Local birders know that the chance of studying Harris's and White-tailed Hawks in juvenal and sub-adult plumages is excellent here. It is said that the easy-pickings at the "chicken factories" are particularly appealing to the less-experienced younger hawks. (After you've finished here, you may have to drive another 0.2 mile to a place where you can turn around on the narrow road.)

Return to Farm Road 772 and turn right (south), following it as it turns left (east) (1.0) to Highway 77 (4.0). Cross the highway and continue east on Farm Road 772. As you drive these back roads, watch, especially on fences, for Common Ground-Dove, Long-billed and Curve-billed Thrashers, Pyrrhuloxia, and Lark Sparrow. In summer look for Groove-billed Ani, Scissor-tailed Flycatcher, and Painted Bunting (a common nester in brushy areas). Keep following Farm Road 772 (right) at the T-intersection (Farm Road 1118 goes left) (4.0). Shortly the road turns left (0.3), and at a long right curve (0.8) which cuts off a former right-angle turn, look within this grassy triangle for Sprague's Pipits (December through March). You may park on the old road, where there is little traffic, and scan for the pipits. *Do not harass these birds.* Just north of the old road is a small pond surrounded by trees and a farm field beyond that is often flooded. These areas may be good for a variety of birds in winter.

As you continue on Farm Road 772, the road soon makes another left turn to cross Radicha Creek, where another Cave Swallow colony (March–August) is located under the bridge (1.5). Just beyond, the road turns right (south) to County Road 2250E (1.6). Turn left (east) onto County Road 2250E; then make another left turn onto County Road 1132S (2.2), and drive north(1.0) to where the road turns right (east) (0.2). Here, the pavement will go down the bluff and will give way to caliche (be very careful driving on this surface after a rain). Turn left on the caliche road to continue on to **Drum Point** on Cayo del Grullo, a finger of Baffin Bay. The road ends after a mile. Many herons and egrets are found here during most of the year; waterfowl winter in large numbers, with Buffleheads in the hundreds and Lesser Scaup in the thousands. Reddish Egrets are present—the white-morph constitutes about ten percent of their total numbers. American White Pelicans can be numerous. Shorebirds may be found year-round. Wilson's Plovers, Willets, Black-necked Stilts, and Least Terns nest here, also. Roseate Spoonbills and Black Skimmers frequently add to the interest of the site. During spring (April) and fall (September) migrations you may see tens of thousands of swallows and Purple Martins within a few hours as they fly past, sometimes at eye-level.

Return to County Road 2250E and turn left (east) (0.7), then right as the road turns south to Farm Road 628 at Loyola Beach. Take the road that angles left (not the sharp left turn) to Arana Creek and **Kaufer-Hubert Memorial Park** (1.3). The mouth of Arana Creek just before you enter the park is usually full of herons, egrets, and shorebirds. Wilson's Plovers commonly nest. During migration, and in winter, you may even find Semipalmated, Snowy, and Piping Plovers on the mudflats. In fall Buff-breasted Sandpipers may be found on the flats, despite the fact that they normally prefer short-grass pastures. Yearly visitors—Greater and Lesser Yellowlegs, Short-billed and Long-billed Dowitchers, Black-necked Stilt, American Avocet, Solitary, Spotted, Semipalmated, Western, Least, White-rumped, Baird's, Pectoral, and Stilt Sandpipers, Sanderling, Dunlin, and Wilson's Phalarope—are easily found in migration. American White Pelicans are resident here.

In the brushy areas of the park look for nesting species—Inca Dove, Common Ground-Dove, Bewick's Wren, and Olive Sparrow. Also commonly found are Golden-fronted and Ladder-backed Woodpeckers, Great Kiskadee, Green Jay, Long-billed and Curve-billed Thrashers, and

Cactus Wren. Along the bayfront you will see many of the same species seen at Drum Point. In January 1989 such South Texas rarities as Greater Scaup and Black and Surf Scoters were found here. At the back of the park is a large RV park with hookups (fee). Inside the RV park are two ponds, where a variety of shorebirds and waterfowl can be found in winter. (Birders are allowed in here, but please be sure to check in at the office first.)

Upon leaving the park, turn left onto Farm Road 628, which turns right (0.4) to Farm Road 1546 (1.5). Turn left (south); beyond Farm Road 771 (1.2) you will find another chicken farm on the left (0.2). Here, especially in the mornings, you should watch for raptors and vultures feeding on the dead-chicken bodies. Take Farm Road 1546 south to Farm Road 2510 (0.7); turn right. In summer, watch among the sunflowers along these roads for Lesser Goldfinches. Where Farm Road 2510 turns right (0.9), turn left onto a dirt/caliche road (County Road 1120) for about a mile. Watch the trees here for Harris's Hawks. You will see a long sandspit, which extends far out into Laguna Salada, the estuary of Los Olmos Creek, and the westernmost branch of the Baffin Bay complex. (Locally, the area is known as "Site 55.") Although the road continues out onto the spit, it is best to walk. Wilson's Plovers nest here, as do some Laughing Gulls and Willets. Also resident are Reddish Egrets of both color morphs, and other herons. Many migrant shorebird species are found in good numbers, as well as Franklin's Gulls. In winter look for such species as Red-breasted Merganser, Osprey, and Bonaparte's Gull. Rarely, an Oldsquaw may be found, and in 1988 a very rare Eurasian Wigeon was seen here. In summer, especially if it is a stormy day, you might be lucky to find a Magnificent Frigatebird, or who knows what! Part of this area is a Texas A & I University Biological Station.

Return north on County Road 1120 and Farm Road 2510 and turn left (west) onto Farm Road 771 (1.8). Turn right (north) onto County Road 1110S (1.0), drive to County Road 2300E (1.0) where you turn left to check out Mittag's Pond (0.2). The pond is a large, but intermittent, pothole—sometimes holding water for years at a time, but sometimes completely dry. When it is wet, the pond extends both north and south of County Road 2300E. Once, about 600 Fulvous Whistling-Ducks were found here; another time it held 36 Cinnamon Teal. Return to Farm Road 771 and turn right (west). At County Road 1100S (1.0) you can check for raptors at yet another chicken farm.

Continue west on 771; at County Road 1080S (2.0) turn right (north). You will soon see another chicken farm (0.7) on the right. Continue north on 1080S to Farm Road 628 (1.9). Turn left (west) on 628. Just after you round the curve, check on your left for the fifth—and final—chicken farm (0.5). Continue west on 628 to Highway 77 (1.8). Turn left (south) on Highway 77 to Louise Trant Bird Sanctuary on the northeast side of the small town of Riviera (Re-VEER-ah).

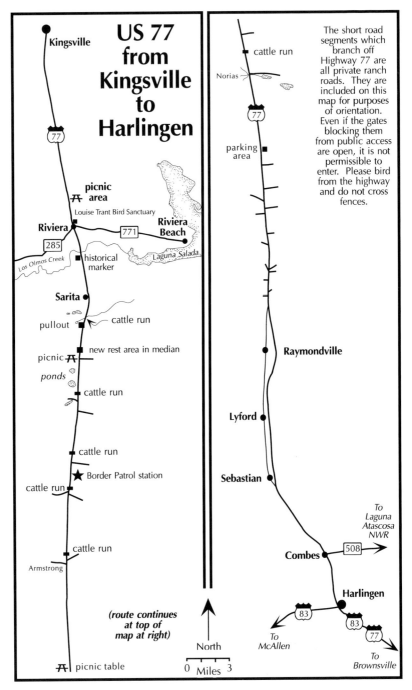

US 77
from
Kingsville
to
Harlingen

Kingsville

77

picnic
area

Louise Trant Bird Sanctuary

Riviera

285

771

Riviera
Beach

Los Olmos Creek

historical
marker

Laguna Salada

Sarita

pullout — cattle run

picnic — new rest area in median

ponds

cattle run

cattle run

★ Border Patrol station

cattle run

cattle run

Armstrong

**(route continues
at top of
map at right)**

North

0   Miles   3

picnic table

cattle run

Norias

77

parking
area

The short road
segments which
branch off
Highway 77 are
all private ranch
roads. They are
included on this
map for purposes
of orientation.
Even if the gates
blocking them
from public access
are open, it is not
permissible to
enter. Please bird
from the highway
and do not cross
fences.

Raymondville

Lyford

Sebastian

To
Laguna
Atascosa
NWR

Combes

508

Harlingen

83

83

77

To
McAllen

To
Brownsville

In the early 1900s a developer bought some land from the King Ranch and founded an agricultural community called Riviera and a resort called Riviera Beach. These communities never really recovered from a hurricane back in 1916.

The **Louise Trant Bird Sanctuary** is a small wetland maintained by the Audubon Outdoor Club of Corpus Christi which has produced some interesting sightings. In winter such regulars as Sora, American Coot, and Common Moorhen are found along with Neotropic Cormorant, large numbers of Cattle Egrets, and various herons and other egrets. Yellow-headed Blackbirds may stop off in large flocks during spring migration. The only Kleberg County record of Red-billed Pigeon was here in 1988. In the spring of 1985, a Masked Duck was found here.

A worthwhile detour, for those heading south, starts at Riviera. Highway 285, between Riviera and Falfurrias, is better known to local birders as "Hawk Alley". Check out the bridge over Salado Creek (1.5) for nesting Cave, Barn, and Cliff Swallows. Farther along Highway 285, the terrain becomes more arid; it is productive for numerous predator species, especially Crested Caracara, White-tailed Hawk, and Harris's Hawk. During migration (March-April and late August through mid-October) it may be excellent for migrating buteos, kites, and other raptors. If you don't plan to make it all the way to Falfurrias (20.5), at least drive 5 to 8 miles out Hawk Alley.

HIGHWAY 77

As you continue south on Highway 77, be sure to check your gas. You can get gas at Riviera, and there is currently one station at Sarita (on the northbound side of Highway 77), seven miles farther south, but it is then another 50 miles until the next service station. This stretch of Highway 77 offers some of the best roadside birding in south Texas. During most seasons you should try to bird here in the early morning, so that you will arrive before the temperature really climbs. In winter, however, early mornings may produce fog.

As a final note before you begin this stretch, be aware of intermittent ponds all along this route. Depending on recent rainfall and the time of year, flooded fields and ponds may appear or disappear cyclically. A few of these spots will be mentioned in the remainder of this chapter, but this does not guarantee that they will all be there or, perhaps more importantly, that others might not appear along your route. These sites can be good for a variety of species, including Least Grebe, Pied-billed Grebe, Sandhill Crane, Common Moorhen, Purple Gallinule, American Coot, White-faced Ibis, Wood Stork, egrets and herons of many species, ducks of all kinds, gulls and terns, and many shorebird species (e.g., both dowitchers and both yellowlegs, Common Snipe, White-rumped, Western, and Least Sandpipers, Killdeer, Black-necked Stilt, and American Avocet). If there are perches nearby, look for Vermilion

Flycatcher, Eastern and Say's Phoebes, and Great Kiskadee. Checking all likely-looking wet spots on this route can make for productive birding.

You will now cross Los Olmos Creek south of Riviera (2.0); just beyond (0.3) is a historical marker pull-off. In spring and summer Hooded Orioles nest in the palm trees here. At the flashing yellow light in Sarita (3.3), turn right to the courthouse (0.1), and turn right again to several ponds (0.5), which can be productive. Sarita is the largest town in Kenedy County, with a mere 185 people. (Virtually all of the county is occupied by ranches and oil fields.) Continuing south on Highway 77, stop to see a rather large colony of Cave Swallows—together with Cliff and Barn Swallows—nesting under a cattle-run (1.7).

For many years the biggest attractions along this stretch of highway were Ferruginous Pygmy-Owl and Tropical Parula. The owl has not been found from the highway since the 1980s, but the Tropical Parula has become an occasional nester. It is wise to check all of the rest areas with mottes, however, if time permits. In these oak mottes you should find a selection of the subtropical passerines—Couch's Kingbird, Brown-crested and Ash-throated Flycatchers, Green Jay, Tufted ("Black-crested") Titmouse, Long-billed and Curve-billed Thrashers, and Olive Sparrow.

Hawks are also a big attraction along Highway 77. The residents are Crested Caracara and White-tailed and Harris's Hawks. During migration seasons you may also see thousands of Broad-winged and Swainson's Hawks and some Mississippi Kites. The main push of the Broad-wings comes in late March and late September, Swainson's come through in early April and early October, and the kites trickle through in late April and August. In winter you may find Ferruginous Hawks, though they are not common. (The very light phase of the Red-tailed that is found here is often mistaken for a Ferruginous.)

Along the fence-lines look for Wild Turkey, Greater Roadrunner, Golden-fronted and Ladder-backed Woodpeckers, Western and Couch's Kingbirds, and Vermilion Flycatcher. You may also want to check culverts and cattle-runs for swallow colonies during breeding season. Cave Swallows are always a possibility.

The accompanying map shows a number of ranch roads branching off east and west of Highway 77. Many maps of this area will show "towns" of Norias and Armstrong, but Norias is just the headquarters of the Norias division of the King Ranch and Armstrong is the headquarters of the Armstrong Ranch. *All of the private roads along this long stretch of Highway 77 are gated, and you should not enter them even if you find an open gate.* Some of the old rest areas have stiles over the barbed-wire fence—compensating, no doubt, for the lack of sanitary facilities (the one new rest area on this route is the exception). While people cross fences for this purpose (watch your step!), Texas landowners take trespassing very seriously—you are well-advised not to wander around looking for birds on this or any private property.

Shortly after the large swallow colony there is a pull-off (1.0). At rare times in recent years Northern Beardless-Tyrannulets have been found feeding in the trees here. There is another pull-off in a short distance (0.4) where you can check for Couch's Kingbirds and other songbirds. There are also occasional Summer Tanagers in this and other oak mottes in Kenedy County.

Next, there will be a large modern rest stop in the median (3.0). (This is the only "rest" area with any rest rooms.) At this site Tropical Parulas have nested since 1990. Look for them in the oaks and Mustang Grape vines; they can sometimes be found with small feeding flocks of titmice. If you miss the Tropical Parula, you can at least enjoy the Hooded Orioles nesting in palms lining the walkway, and Green Jays and Wild Turkeys that may be seen eating acorns under the oaks. Watch also for Lesser Goldfinches here.

There is a pull-off with a picnic table on the right just beyond the rest stop (0.6), followed by a pond (1.0), and shortly by another pond (0.6). These two ponds and other intermittent ponds along Highway 77 may produce both Black-bellied and Fulvous Whistling-Ducks in the spring and fall; Mottled Ducks are to be expected at any time. Least Grebes may also surprise you.

And as far as surprises go, you may also see a dark gray mammal with devilish-looking horns, the size of a small horse, with high shoulders and low hindquarters. This is a Nilgai, an exotic antelope imported from India. The hornless female is smaller and browner. Other "normal" mammals along this route might include White-tailed Deer, two species of ground-squirrel, Javelina, Coyote, Bobcat, Black-tailed Jackrabbit, and Evening and Brazilian Free-tailed Bats.

At **Raymondville** (41.1) you have left Kenedy County behind you and will abruptly enter the irrigated fields of the Lower Rio Grande Valley. Most of the birds here will be Great-tailed Grackles, Brown-headed Cowbirds, and House Sparrows, but Black-shouldered Kites are often seen hovering over the pastures. If the fields are smoothly plowed without clods or vegetation, you may find Mountain Plovers in late winter and early spring, although they are rare.

Check the rows of Tamarisks—if you can find a row on some undisturbed side road; there may be a good assortment of warblers, vireos, and other migrants. Try walking down the row, flushing the birds before you. Eventually, they will fly back, and you will get a second look. If there is a rare one, walk quietly back and forth until you really get a good look.

Continue south to Combes and turn left (east) onto Farm Road 508 (16.5) toward Rio Hondo. At Farm Road 106 (9.0) turn left and go straight through the town. Follow Farm Road 106 for 10 miles to the first sign for Laguna Atascosa National Wildlife Refuge.

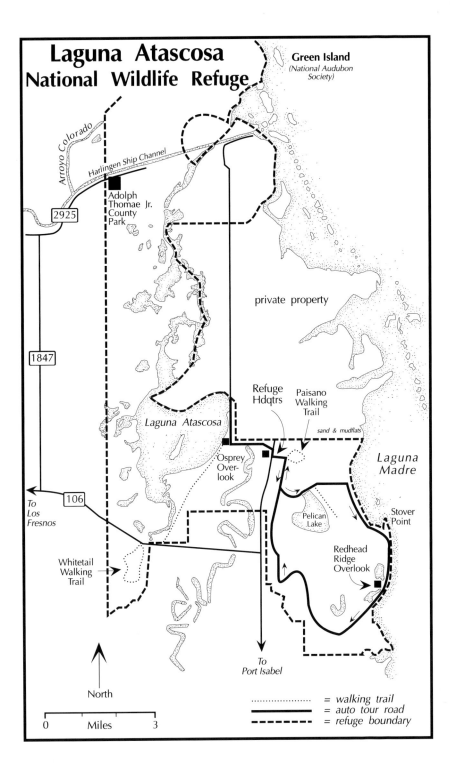

Laguna Atascosa
National Wildlife Refuge

Green Island
(National Audubon
Society)

Arroyo Colorado

Harlingen Ship Channel

2925

Adolph
Thomae Jr.
County
Park

1847

private property

Refuge
Hdqtrs

Paisano
Walking
Trail

sand & mudflats

Laguna Atascosa

Osprey
Over-
look

Laguna
Madre

106

To
Los
Fresnos

Pelican
Lake

Stover
Point

Whitetail
Walking
Trail

Redhead
Ridge
Overlook

North

To
Port Isabel

0   Miles   3

.... = walking trail
━━━━━━━ = auto tour road
╍╍╍╍╍ = refuge boundary

CHAPTER 15:
LAGUNA ATASCOSA
NATIONAL WILDLIFE
REFUGE

Laguna Atascosa National Wildlife Refuge (fee area; 45,190 acres) is covered in the 1992 edition of the ABA/Lane Guide entitled *A Birder's Guide to the Rio Grande Valley of Texas,* as are sites described in the next chapter. However, the area is so nearby, so productive, and so much an important birding section of the Texas Coast, that it merits repeated treatment here.

Laguna Atascosa National Wildlife Refuge (PO Box 450, Rio Hondo, Texas 78583; telephone: 210/748-3607) was originally set aside in 1946 as a wintering-ground for ducks and geese, but the refuge is now managed for a more varied wildlife spectrum. A total of 392 species of birds have been recorded here, including the endangered Aplomado Falcon (a release program was instituted here in 1985), Peregrine Falcon, Piping Plover, (Southern) Bald Eagle, and Brown Pelican. Many other species found only in the Lower Rio Grande Valley can be seen here. In the fall, a half-million ducks descend on the refuge along with thousands of Snow Geese, hundreds of Sandhill Cranes, and countless shorebirds and other winter visitors.

Spring migration begins in mid-April and can be a spectacular sight when a strong northern wind and rain farther up the coast keep the warblers grounded for a day. Migrant warblers filling the trees and Scissor-tailed Flycatchers lining the fencerows, combined with returning summer residents like Brown-crested Flycatcher calling from tree-tops and colorful Blue Grosbeak and Painted and Indigo Buntings, make a memorable sight.

The refuge lies along the inland side of placid Laguna Madre and is protected from the sometimes stormy Gulf by the sand dunes of Padre Island. Brushlands, prairies, saltflats, mudflats, bays, and freshwater ponds on the refuge all attract a variety of wildlife. Two self-guided road tours (open daily from sunrise to sunset) and four hiking-trails can bring you to all of these areas. (If you also wish to visit a remote part of the refuge not open to vehicles, you can join one of the monthly birding field trips in winter. The trips are contingent upon the availability of staff. Reservations are taken beginning the first of each month and fill up quickly.) *Use of tape recordings to attract wildlife is prohibited within the Refuge.*

Shortly after passing the first refuge sign (10 miles east of Rio Hondo on Farm Road 106) you will come to the first of four walking trails. **Whitetail Trail** (5-mile loop, parking area on right) is a primitive trail maintained on an irregular basis. It goes through an area of mesquite and grass that is most productive in early morning. Greater Roadrunners, Bewick's Wren, Blue Grosbeak, and Painted Bunting nest here. In winter you will find numerous sparrows. Keep in mind that the refuge's brushy areas are renowned for their high population of Western Diamond-backed Rattlesnakes.

The Visitor Center, located 7 miles from the first refuge entry sign, is open from 10am to 4pm daily October-April, weekends only in September and May, and is closed June through August. Maps, checklists, books, and wildlife information are available here. Some of the best birding can be found in the area around the Center itself. Green Jay, Tufted ("Black-crested") Titmouse, and Golden-fronted Woodpeckers fly from tree to tree in the parking lot and picnic area. White-tipped Dove and Buff-bellied Hummingbird visit the feeders at the front of the building. Behind the building at the far end of the parking lot is a tree-lined gully famous for its nesting Yellow-green Vireos. For at least three years a pair of these vireos nested here; they or their offspring just might return to the area. This is also a good spot to check out Great Kiskadee, Couch's Kingbird, Brown-crested Flycatcher, and spring warblers.

Mesquite Trail (1.5-mile loop) begins at the west end of the parking lot. It will yield a good selection of birds. White-tailed Deer and Nine-banded Armadillos stroll along this path in early morning or late evening, and signs of Coyote are present at any time of day.

Bayside Drive begins to your right just before you reach the Visitor Center parking lot. This 15-mile paved road has many turnouts so you can stop to view the birds as you travel through various habitats. The first half-mile passes through dense thickets of thornbrush where Plain Chachalacas call out each morning. Greater Roadrunner, Pauraque, Golden-fronted and Ladder-backed Woodpeckers, Verdin, Bewick's and Cactus Wrens, White-eyed Vireo, Long-billed Thrasher, and Olive Sparrow prefer this dense, thorny growth. You may want to leave your car in the Visitor Center parking lot and walk the first part to increase your chances of seeing these birds in winter, or Groove-billed Ani, Yellow-billed Cuckoo, White-winged Dove, Couch's Kingbird, and Painted Bunting in spring and summer. Varied Buntings have nested here, but they are difficult to find. Javelinas sometimes are seen as they nibble on the Prickly-Pear Cactus pads along the roadside.

The parking area for **Paisano Trail** is on your left shortly after the road curves to the south. The short (1.5-mile) paved trail passes through thorny trees and shrubs once typical of South Texas. Huisache, Tepeguaje, Allthorn,

Ladder-backed Woodpecker
Charles H. Gambill

Granjeño (Spiny Hackberry), and others provide food and shelter to wildlife in this part of the country where little native cover remains. Plain Chachalaca, doves, sparrows, Verdin, buntings, deer, and even Bobcat are frequently seen along this route. A side trail leads through the Granjeño Research Natural Area, a small wilderness area set aside for biological study.

To continue the tour, go south for a mile to the junction of the one-way loop. Turn left and watch the open prairie and surrounding trees for Aplomado Falcons. They began to be released at the Refuge in 1985, and may yet establish themselves in the area. Look for other raptors here, too. A mile past the junction you will come to Pelican Lake, a fresh-water impoundment in wet years. In winter, various ducks and pelicans can be found, and in spring and summer, you can see Black-bellied Whistling-Duck. Least Grebes are uncommon throughout the year, but may be more regular in summer. As you continue, check the brush along the road for Curve-billed Thrasher and Cactus Wren. Grassy areas should have Savannah, Vesper, White-crowned, possibly Le Conte's, Grasshopper, and Field Sparrows in winter, Clay-colored in April. Both Cassin's and Botteri's are permanent residents, but you will probably have to hear them singing to tell them apart.

When the road reaches the **Laguna Madre**, pull out to your left and check the area to the north with a scope carefully. All along the shore you are likely to find Great Blue, Little Blue, and Tricolored Herons, Great, Snowy, and Reddish Egrets, Roseate Spoonbill, Laughing Gull, Forster's, Royal, Sandwich, and Caspian Terns, and Black Skimmer. In winter or during migration there may be Common Loon, Eared Grebe, American White Pelicans in huge numbers, Wood Stork, Double-crested Cormorant, Piping, Semipalmated, and Black-bellied Plovers, Greater and Lesser Yellowlegs, Red Knot, Long-billed and Short-billed Dowitchers, Dunlin, Long-billed Curlew, Marbled Godwit, American Avocet, and Least, Stilt, Semipalmated, and Western Sandpipers. In summer look for Black-necked Stilt, Least Tern, Neotropic Cormorant (uncommon), American Oystercatcher, or Magnificent Frigatebird (rare).

Redhead Ridge Overlook is worth the short hike to top of the hill for a view of South Padre Island, the Laguna Madre, and the surrounding ponds. Local hunters may recall a time when Redheads literally filled the bay. The ducks were easy targets from this high ridge.

After following the shoreline for some three miles, the road veers away and crosses several other habitats. First there is the *Spartina* marsh, where Clapper Rails and Seaside Sparrows live. In winter there may be King and Virginia Rails, Sora, and Sedge Wren. The road then enters an arid grassland with scattered patches of mesquite and yucca that bloom in February. White-tailed Hawks and Crested Caracaras have nested here. In summer look for Common and Lesser Nighthawks, Blue Grosbeak, White-winged Dove, Couch's Kingbird, and Painted Bunting; in winter, Vermilion Flycatchers; and Cassin's and Botteri's Sparrows at any time of year.

The saltflats are next. Wilson's Plovers nest here, and in migration Lesser Golden-Plover and Upland and Buff-breasted Sandpipers use the area. The road swings north and crosses open areas where you can again look for hawks, sparrows, and Long-billed Curlews before returning to the beginning of the loop.

The two-mile **Lakeside Drive** starts just past the Visitor Center. Turn left and follow the road a short distance to where it crosses a resaca (an old river bend, now maintained artificially). You may find Bufflehead, Northern Shoveler, or other ducks in winter, Roseate Spoonbill, egrets, herons, American Avocets, Black-necked Stilt, Least Grebe, and Caspian Terns and Black Terns (in migration) at other times, depending on season and water levels.

Past the resaca, check every bird that looks like a grackle to be sure that it isn't a Groove-billed Ani. Eastern Meadowlarks sing from the surrounding fields in winter and Dickcissels in spring. An area on your left was planted with seedlings by volunteers in 1989. The refuge is converting many old fields in this area to native vegetation that will provide additional food and shelter to the birds, Ocelots, and other wildlife that depend on brushland. The road leads to the parking area for **Osprey Overlook** on the east shore of Laguna Atascosa. The lake is filled with ducks and geese during the winter months. Eighty percent of the entire North American population of Redheads winters here. Shorebirds and waders use the shoreline, in case you missed them elsewhere. The surrounding fields to the north or south hold large flocks of wintering Sandhill Cranes and Snow, Canada, Ross's, and Greater White-fronted Geese. You may walk along the service roads behind the barriers. In winter you may be able to find a Sprague's Pipit or a Le Conte's Sparrow. A short walking-trail follows the shoreline to the north. It can be very good for buntings, grosbeaks, and other migrants in spring and for Greater Roadrunner, Groove-billed Ani, and other residents in summer. A side road to the north just before you reach the parking area follows the lake for approximately one mile to a locked gate. You may park here and walk in along the service roads that surround the lake; however, they are not marked, and there is no shade. *Do not cross into private property in this area.*

As you leave the refuge, check the entrance road for any of the birds that you may have missed. In the fall you may also encounter Mountain Plover in appropriate habitat. Harris's Hawks, Crested Caracaras, and vultures will perch in large trees or on the telephone poles.

Nearby camping facilities are available at the north end of the Refuge in Adolph Thomae, Jr., County Park on Farm Road 1847 (telephone: 210/748-2044) or at Isla Blanca Park on South Padre Island (telephone: 210/761-5493) for those wishing to get an early start.

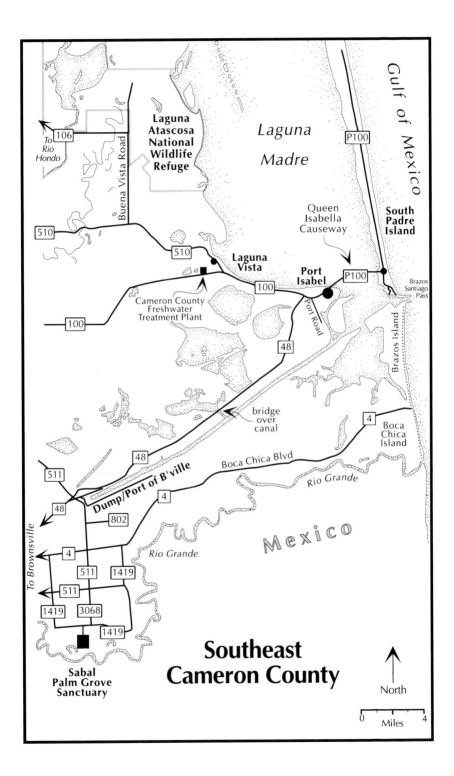

CHAPTER 16:
SOUTHEAST
CAMERON COUNTY

We are coming close to the end of the Texas Coast, but there are still a few good places to bird in the vicinity of Brownsville. Here the visiting birder gets a taste of the basically Mexican birdlife of the Lower Rio Grande Valley. Many birds that occur along the valley are essentially found nowhere else in the United States.

PORT ISABEL

To continue down the coast, go south on Buena Vista Road from the Laguna Atascosa National Wildlife Refuge Visitor Center to Farm Road 510 (7.2). Turn left through Laguna Vista to Highway 100 (5.3). The Cameron County Freshwater Treatment Plant is located down this road to your right (west)(1.5). It is good in winter for ducks. An Oldsquaw was found here several years ago. Lately, however, entry has been restricted. Return to Highway 100 and continue east toward **Port Isabel**. Go past Highway 48 (4.0) and turn right onto Port Road (0.5). A short way down this road is an area of mesquite that can be good for migrants. It is particularly good along the little side road leading to the Big Heart Pipe Line Corporation and the city dump. Return to Highway 100 and continue through Port Isabel to **South Padre Island** (4.0). This growing resort has beautiful beaches, campgrounds, motels, restaurants, stores, and hordes of college students during spring break. The best birding spots are usually along the Queen Isabella Causeway leading to the island, at the jetty on the south end, and north up the beach 12 miles past the end of the road. If your time is limited, after you exit the causeway go north to the first stop-light, turn eastward to the beach access (where, in winter, you can scan for Northern Gannet) or westward to check the mudflats (Black Skimmer, Gull-billed Tern, American Oystercatcher, and a variety or shorebirds).

If you are interested in a general birding boat trip of four hours up the Laguna Madre, try the *Duchess*, located just south of the Causeway at the Sea

Ranch Restaurant and Marina (telephone: 210/761-7646). The catamaran leaves at 8am and must have a minimum of 8 people per trip. These trips travel as far north as the Arroyo Colorado, known as the Harlingen Ship Channel where it empties into the Laguna Madre. (See the map for the previous chapter.) Look for a variety of herons, egrets, cormorants, gulls, terns, and shorebirds.

Retrace your route through Port Isabel, and turn left onto Highway 48 toward Brownsville. At the bridge over the canal (11.1) check for Black-crowned and Yellow-crowned Night-Herons on your right (winter). Exit right at the top of an overpass and turn left onto Farm Road 511 (8.5); go one block, and turn left toward the Port of Brownsville.

Brownsville City Dump   Paul J. Baicich

BROWNSVILLE SANITARY LANDFILL

An important stop is the **City Dump**. You will soon reach the Port guardhouse (0.5), where you bear right. Follow the road past the water tower on the right until you see the landfill entrance. The ever-changing entrance to the dump is currently 1.2 miles past the guardhouse. At the check-station, hold up your binoculars and tell them that you are looking for birds. (The dump, however, is closed on Sundays.) Proceed to where the trucks are dumping their garbage. It may be as much as two miles from the check-station.

Like dumps everywhere, this one attracts numerous birds. Gulls are usually plentiful. Franklin's Gull may be abundant during migration.

Glaucous Gull, Lesser Black-backed Gull, and an amazing Slaty-backed Gull have been recorded in the dump in the past few years. However, the big thing to look for here is the Mexican Crow, which closely resembles a Fish Crow.

The Mexican Crow was first recorded in the United States in 1968, but it is now usually abundant at the dump from November through February. There have even been a few recorded nestings in the area. It frequents the dump whenever the garbage trucks arrive, usually between 9am and 4pm. Its numbers vary, but sometimes it is the most numerous crow-like bird at the dump. You should have little difficulty in finding it among the numerous Great-tailed Grackles and Chihuahuan Ravens. Check comparative sizes, bills, and tail lengths, and listen for the frog-like croak of the Mexican Crow.

The dump has become so well-known as *the* place to find Mexican Crow that even the Brownsville Convention and Visitors' Bureau calls the dump "Brownsville's Famous Mexican Crow Park"! (The Bureau also puts out a little *Birder's Guide* that might interest you. You can contact them at 650 FM 802, Brownsville, Texas 78520; telephone: 800/626-2639.)

Return to Farm Road 511 and turn left. If you were not able to get into the dump at the port, turn left at Farm Road 802 (0.9), which leads to the back side of the dump. The crow can sometimes be seen here. Return to FM 511, turn left, and proceed to Highway 4 (Boca Chica Boulevard) (1.5).

BOCA CHICA

Highway 4 goes 16 miles to the Gulf. In years of good rains, or after a hurricane, which the area gets from time to time, you will find numerous mudflats along the way to check for shorebirds, Roseate Spoonbills, and White Ibises. Watch the power-lines for Harris's Hawks. During migration check the Black Mangrove and Ebony Trees for passerines.

At the Gulf, you can drive on the **damp** sand at low tide for miles. Up the beach to the north is the undeveloped Brazos Island State Recreation Area. Brazos Island is not an island at all, but a peninsula beach. The jetties at Brazos Santiago Pass (about 5 miles north) are a good spot for Brown Pelican. Down the **Boca Chica Beach** to the south is the mouth of the Rio Grande (2.5). Here, just behind the sand dunes, is a good stand of Black Mangrove which has been great for migrants over the years. The beaches are good for shorebirds such as Ruddy Turnstone, Sanderling, Black-bellied, Snowy, and Piping Plovers, and gulls. In summer you may find Wilson's Plover, and Least, Sandwich, Royal, and Caspian Terns. Migration time also brings a good flight of hawks, including Broad-winged and Swainson's, a few Merlins, and Peregrine Falcons, which you may see sitting on top of the higher sand dunes. Out in the waves of the Gulf watch for Brown Pelican and perhaps a Northern Gannet.

Golden-fronted Woodpecker
F.P. Bennett

F.P. BENNETT

SABAL PALM GROVE SANCTUARY

To reach this National Audubon Society sanctuary from Boca Chica, go west on Highway 4 (Boca Chica Boulevard) to FM 511 (16.0); turn south on FM 511 to FM 3068 (2.0) and proceed straight ahead (FM 511 turns west) until you reach Farm Road 1419 (1.4). Turn right (west) and watch for a dirt road and sign (0.7) on the left. The gate to the sanctuary is 0.8 mile along the road by the old Rabb Plantation House. The Rabb Plantation, established in 1876, originally occupied more than 20,000 acres. The Sabal Palm Grove Sanctuary is a fee area. Hours are 8am-5pm, seven days a week, year-round (PO Box 5052, Brownsville, Texas 78523; telephone: 210/541-8034).

The 172-acre sanctuary was acquired by the National Audubon Society in 1971, and it preserves the largest remaining stand of the native Texas Sabal Palm. Some 32 acres are palm forest and are home to many tropical plants and animals. Reportedly, the lush site was once used for an old Tarzan movie. This tract is about all that is left of the dense palm forest that inspired early Spanish explorers to call the lower Rio Grande *El Rio de las Palmas*. Although only 32 acres of original palm forest survive, extensive reforestation is occurring on almost 500 acres of old farm fields adjacent to the sanctuary.

The beautiful 32-acre grove is a great place for finding several notable bird species, some of which barely range north of the Rio Grande. Look for Plain

Chachalaca, Pauraque, White-winged and White-tipped Doves, Common Ground-Dove, Groove-billed Ani, Buff-bellied Hummingbird (year-round), Golden-fronted Woodpecker, Brown-crested Flycatcher (summer), Great Kiskadee, Green Jay, Tropical Parula (winter), Olive Sparrow, and Altamira Oriole. Recent winter sightings of such rarities as Clay-colored Robin, Gray-crowned Yellowthroat, Golden-crowned Warbler, Crimson-collared Grosbeak, and Blue Bunting have been recorded. During migration, warblers are often common in early morning or late afternoon. Also watch for the tropical butterflies, such as the very striking Zebra Longwing, and the Speckled Racer, a rare snake found at the sanctuary.

BROWNSVILLE

Continue west on Farm Road 1419 until it meets Highway 4 (5.7), then turn left to Brownsville (0.9). In wintertime you should be able to find small flocks of Red-crowned Parrots; Green Parakeets can also be found in Brownsville. How many of these birds are escapes and how many are truly wild birds from Mexico is debatable, though the Red-crowned Parrot's legitimacy seems more secure. Some individuals of both species apparently nest in the area now. In any case, Red-crowned Parrots can usually be found in the northwest section of the city in the area on both sides of Central Boulevard from Boca Chica Boulevard to and beyond Los Ebanos Boulevard. Late afternoon roosting-time is when they are usually the most obvious; listen for their raucous calls as they fly from large tree to large tree, for evening perching or for feeding. (Two vantage points to try might be Russell Street at Los Ebanos, and just west of there on Los Ebanos near the railroad tracks.) Green Parakeets are often more easily found on the side streets southeast of Central and Boca Chica Boulevards, especially east of the resaca.

Occasionally, a Clay-colored Robin or a Golden-crowned Warbler from Mexico may show up in winter somewhere in the city. The local recorded Rare Bird Alert can fill you in with the latest sightings for Brownsville and the entire Lower Rio Grande Valley.

Throughout Brownsville watch for signs which designate areas to be new Wildlife Habitat Areas. This sign will show a nesting Altamira Oriole. These areas are being developed as funds allow.

This is a fine way to finish your trip down the Texas Coast and to put you in a good mood for an exciting start up the Rio Grande. Remember, the Mexican flavor of the Lower Rio Grande Valley influences its birdlife as well as its culture. You will surely want to visit Santa Ana National Wildlife Refuge, Bentsen-Rio Grande State Park, Falcon Dam, and other spots for the Rio Grande specialties. For that you will want a copy of **A Birder's Guide to the Rio Grande Valley of Texas**.

SPECIALTIES OF THE
TEXAS COAST

Listed on the following pages are a number of species that may be of particular interest to birders visiting the Texas Coast. Some are Mexican species that barely range into the United States. Other are eastern species that may be of interest to western birders, or western species of interest to eastern birders. Specific locations where they may be found are given when possible, as well as other helpful information. Occasionally some identification hints are given, though this information is not meant to substitute for your field guide. For some complex identification questions (e.g. *Empidonax* flycatchers, some sandpipers and sparrows) you might want to refer to a specialized book, such as Kenn Kaufman's excellent *Advanced Birding*.

Least Grebe—Fairly common but sporadic resident of fresh-water ponds in the Lower Rio Grande Valley. The abundance of this bird (and of many other basically Mexican species) may be dependent upon the amount of rainfall in northeastern Mexico. In wet years, when there are numerous rain pools in Mexico, it may be more common in Texas; in dry years, less common. It is most abundant in summer and somewhat upriver of this book's coverage in the Lower Rio Grande Valley. The species becomes less common northward, but a few are found as far north as the Aransas National Wildlife Refuge, and even sometimes a bit farther. A good place to look for it is at Laguna Atascosa National Wildlife Refuge, but it has been found at Goose Island State Park, Ingleside, Flour Bluff, Pollywog Pond, Lake Corpus Christi, and along Highway 77 south of Kingsville, also.

pelagic birds—Much more needs to be learned about pelagic birds off the Texas Coast. For example, Cory's Shearwater was thought to be rare or casual off Texas; recent studies suggest that it may actually be of regular occurrence. Audubon's Shearwater is regular in the open Gulf; Sooty Shearwater, probably less so. There are also a handful of records for Greater Shearwater. Band-rumped Storm-Petrel probably occurs regularly in the open Gulf, and there are some records for Wilson's and Leach's Storm-Petrels. Among the boobies, the Masked is fairly common in the open Gulf, and is sometimes seen from shore—in winter and in late March. There are a smattering of spring and fall records for Brown Booby. Northern Gannets are regularly observed from shore in winter, with some spring and fall records for the Upper Texas Coast. Bridled Terns are occasionally found offshore in the fall. For **Magnificent Frigatebird**, the **jaegers**, and **Sooty Tern**, see their individual treatments on the pages which follow.

Neotropic Cormorant—Common regular summer visitor along the entire coast. Some winter, particularly southward. This is usually the only cormorant along the coast in summer, but the **Double-crested Cormorant** is far more common in winter. The white edging of the Neotropic's throat pouch is not as visible in winter when you need it most; however, this bird can still be identified by its smaller size, bill shape, proportionally longer tail, and more rapid wingbeat in flight. In summer look for it at Holly Beach, Anahuac National Wildlife Refuge, Big Reef at Galveston Island, Flour Bluff, and Lake Corpus Christi.

Anhinga—Fairly common summer resident of fresh-water swamps, rivers, and tree-lined lakes in East Texas and near the Upper Coast. Some winter, particularly southward. Migrant along entire coast. In summer look for it along the cypress-lined rivers of the Big Thicket, Brazos Bend State Park, Buckhorn Lake, Lake Charlotte, and along the Trinity River. In mild winters some remain in these areas and at Lake Corpus Christi.

Magnificent Frigatebird—Uncommon transient along entire coast, usually in late summer, particularly in August when juveniles move northward. Most often seen flying along the Gulf beaches, or perched on pilings in the bays, such as Galveston Bay, Lavaca Bay, or Corpus Christi Bay. When driving along the beach, scan the sky occasionally. This bird often flies very high. Often seen from the Bolivar Ferry or from the bridge over San Luis Pass.

Little Blue Heron—Fairly common permanent resident. It nests in inland areas of fresh water, so in summer it is more common in rice fields and swamps, or about tree-lined lakes. Try Buckhorn Lake, Rockport, Brazos Bend State Park, or Laguna Atascosa National Wildlife Refuge. Widely scattered in winter, but more common about the lagoons and marshes along the entire coast.

Tricolored Heron—Common permanent resident. Nests on islands in the bays and feeds in swamps, marshes, rice fields, lagoons, and on the beaches along the entire coast. Should be no problem to find. In fact, you will soon be saying, "It's just another Tricolored."

Reddish Egret—Uncommon permanent resident of salt-water areas. Nests on islands in the bays and feeds in shallow lagoons or along the Gulf beaches. Although uncommon, it is easily found, because it feeds in conspicuous places. Look for it along any of the beaches and in such areas as Bolivar Flats, Galveston Island, Rockport Beach, Dale Miller Causeway, Kennedy Causeway, Cayo del Oso, Laguna Atascosa National Wildlife Refuge, and Queen Isabella Causeway. The largest breeding colony—protected by the National Audubon Society—is on the southern end of Laguna Madre. Look for both color phases; there are about seven reddish individuals to every white one.

Yellow-crowned Night-Heron—Uncommon permanent resident. It nests singly or in small groups in wet, wooded areas throughout the eastern part of the state and may not be difficult to find at that time of year. In migration, and less commonly in winter, it may gather in flocks in the marshes along the coast. It can be found at nearly any time at Lake Charlotte, White Memorial Park, and the Trinity River delta. In winter it may be difficult to find on the Upper Texas Coast, although it can be found more easily as you move south. In winter try Anahuac National Wildlife Refuge, the Oryx Oil Field on Bolivar Peninsula, Freeport, Pollywog Pond, and along Highway 48 at the ship channel south of Port Isabel.

White Ibis—Uncommon permanent resident throughout. Nests in colonies with herons and egrets, and feeds in rice fields, marshes, and swamps. It has a tendency to feed in thickly vegetated parts of the marsh or field with only its head visible, so scan likely areas with your binoculars. Can usually be found at Sabine Marsh, Anahuac National Wildlife Refuge, Lake Charlotte, Galveston Island, San Bernard National Wildlife Refuge, Aransas National Wildlife Refuge, Cayo del Oso, and Laguna Atascosa National Wildlife Refuge. Also look in the rice fields of the Upper Texas Coast in spring. Flocks of hundreds can be found there feeding on crayfish.

White-faced Ibis—Uncommon permanent resident of rice fields, marshes, and wet pastures throughout. Nests on low, grassy islands such as South Deer in Galveston Bay. It is fairly easy to find in such places as Sabine Marsh, Anahuac National Wildlife Refuge, Galveston Island, San Bernard National Wildlife Refuge, Aransas National Wildlife Refuge, Matagorda Bay, and Laguna Atascosa National Wildlife Refuge.

Glossy Ibis—Spring visitor. This ibis is now of annual occurrence in the spring along the Upper Texas Coast. Watch for it.

Roseate Spoonbill—Fairly common summer resident near the coast, uncommon in winter. Nests in colonies on islands in the bays, and feeds in marshes, shallow lagoons, and on mudflats. It is fairly easy to find in summer, but in winter it may be hard to come by except in the river deltas at the upper end of the larger bays such as in Trinity Bay near Baytown and at White's Point in Corpus Christi Bay. The deltas are the principal spawning areas for shrimp, and the spoonbills may spend the winter feeding on baby shrimp. (Don't mention this to the shrimp fishermen.) In summer look for them at Sabine Marsh, Anahuac National Wildlife Refuge, Rollover Pass, Oryx Oil Field on Bolivar Peninsula, Galveston Island, San Bernard National Wildlife Refuge, Aransas National Wildlife Refuge, Cayo del Oso, Tule Lake, and Laguna Atascosa National Wildlife Refuge.

Wood Stork—Fairly common late-summer visitor throughout. Most often seen in rice fields, marshes, shallow lagoons, or circling overhead, but roosts in trees in unlikely places. Has been seen at Sabine Marsh, Anahuac National Wildlife Refuge, rice fields west of Houston, Cypress Creek south of Hockley, Aransas National Wildlife Refuge, White Point on Corpus Christi Bay, Tule Lake, and Laguna Atascosa National Wildlife Refuge. Large numbers can also be found feeding in crayfish farms along Interstate 10 between Winnie and Beaumont.

Fulvous Whistling-Duck—Common summer resident of the rice fields along the Upper Coast and occasionally in the marshes southward. A few winter along the coast, particularly in South Texas. It nests on the ground. Most commonly seen on the rice fields in spring migration, or when it gathers on the lakes before moving south in November. In fall look for it at Anahuac National Wildlife Refuge, Corpus Christi area, and Wright Ranch. In summer, after the rice is taller and the birds have dispersed, it may still be found by driving through the ricelands at dawn or in the evening, when the birds often fly around. The overpasses along Interstate 10 west of Katy often make good observation posts.

Black-bellied Whistling-Duck—Fairly common summer resident in fresh-water areas from the Lower Rio Grande Valley to Corpus Christi, and in the rice fields of the Upper Texas Coast. Some winter throughout. It normally nests in holes in trees, but has increased considerably since adapting to ground-nesting in rice fields. Look for it at Laguna Atascosa National Wildlife Refuge, Lake Corpus Christi, Wright Ranch, roadside ponds in South Texas, and in the rice fields around Katy.

Ross's Goose—Rare but regular winter visitor. Local birders estimate that its ratio to Snow Geese is about 1 to 1,000. Carefully scan every flock of Snow Geese until you find one. It is usually easier to find after the fields have been plowed and leveled near the end of the goose season. Look for it at Anahuac and San Bernard National Wildlife Refuges and at Katy Farms.

Mottled Duck—Common permanent resident of marshes, ponds, sloughs, lagoons, and rice fields throughout. Should not be hard to find. As pointed out by Charlie Clark in a recent article in *Birding*, the race of Mottled Duck occurring in Texas has a yellowish-olive bill, unlike that of the Florida race, which has a bright yellow bill.

Cinnamon Teal—Uncommon winter visitor to marshes, rice fields, and ponds throughout. More common southward and in fall. Look for it with other teal in such places as Anahuac National Wildlife Refuge, Lake Corpus Christi, and Laguna Atascosa National Wildlife Refuge.

Masked Duck—Very rare. The recorded occurrences of this bird are too few to establish a pattern of seasonal or regional distribution. It may very well get to Texas only when there is ample early-summer rain in Mexico to form a series of ponds up the coast. This in turn may depend upon the number of hurricanes or tropical storms. From the few records available, it would appear that it may arrive in late July or August, nest some years in September and October, and linger in Central and South Texas (perhaps in post-nesting family flocks) from November to March. The nesting records are for Shoveler Pond at Anahuac National Wildlife Refuge, near Falfurrias, and at Welder Wildlife Refuge. Some of the winter sightings were at Aransas National Wildlife Refuge, Brazoria National Wildlife Refuge, Brazos Bend State Park, Welder Wildlife Refuge, Rockport, Flour Bluff, Seadrift, and Willacy County. This bird is shy and can easily go unnoticed, but many birders now make the extra effort. They check all the likely spots where an ideal habitat of grass-lined fresh water ponds with emerging vegetation is present. They also take a second look at every female Ruddy Duck. The Masked can easily be passed off as a female Ruddy or even as an immature Pied-billed Grebe. In fact, most of the males found in Texas during the nesting season have either not attained adult plumage or are in eclipse plumage. Thus, both birds of nesting pairs may look like females.

Black Vulture—Common permanent resident of prairies and fields where there are some trees available for roosting. Occurs throughout, but is more common southward. Should not be hard to find in South Texas. In North Texas it is more common in wooded areas.

American Swallow-tailed Kite—Rare nester and uncommon migrant. Although there are no documented nestings since the early 1900s, American Swallow-tailed Kites probably nested for a few years recently at Taylor's Bayou. They may yet be discovered breeding on the Upper Texas Coast. Otherwise, they may be encountered as occasional migrants, usually in April and May. There are also fall records, usually from mid-August to early October.

Black-shouldered Kite—Uncommon, localized, permanent resident of the coastal prairie from Brownsville to Galveston. The main population is found in the Lower Rio Grande Valley; however, there appears to be a northward, post-breeding movement into the northern areas. It can often be seen hovering Kestrel-fashion over a pasture, or perched in the top of a nearby tree. Look for it near Brownsville, Laguna Atascosa National

Wildlife Refuge, and Kingsville, and, in winter, northward to Houston and Galveston. Has recently nested in the northern sector near Hitchcock, Freeport, Houston, and particularly on Galveston Island.

Bald Eagle—Uncommon winter visitor to the rice fields and lakes throughout. A few still nest in the area. Apparently, many eagles follow flocks of ducks and feed on the birds crippled by hunters. This would explain their presence in the rice fields, where hunting is common and injured birds numerous. Look for it near Winnie, west of Houston, Warren Lake, Brazos Bend State Park, and Aransas National Wildlife Refuge.

Harris's Hawk—Common permanent resident of the mesquite belt of South Texas, northward to about Rockport.

White-tailed Hawk—Fairly common permanent resident of coastal prairies from Brownsville to Aransas National Wildlife Refuge, then sparingly northward to Houston. The center of population is near Kingsville and south of Victoria. It is sometimes easier to find near Victoria; there are fewer Red-tails and Harris's Hawks to sort through in that area. Areas along Highway 77 south of Kingsville and particularly the chicken ranches south of Kingsville are good spots for this raptor. It has also occurred at Laguna Atascosa National Wildlife Refuge, Aransas National Wildlife Refuge, near Ellington Airport south of Houston, and in the Katy area.

Crested Caracara—Uncommon permanent resident of the prairies and farmlands from Brownsville to Victoria, then less common north to Houston. Look for it at Aransas National Wildlife Refuge, west side of Lake Corpus Christi, west of Riviera, near Alice, and Laguna Atascosa National Wildlife Refuge. Close studies are possible in the Kingsville area, especially at the "chicken factories." It can be distinguished at a distance by its low, direct flight with constant, rapid beats and almost no gliding. Most active at dawn.

Plain Chachalaca—Fairly common permanent resident in protected woodlands and thickets of the Lower Rio Grande Valley. Can usually be found at the start of the Gunnery Range Tour at Laguna Atascosa National Wildlife Refuge and at the Sabal Palm Grove Sanctuary.

Greater Prairie-Chicken—Rare and increasingly endangered permanent resident of the coastal prairies from Aransas National Wildlife Refuge to Victoria and Eagle Lake. The coastal populations are often hard hit by flooding during hurricanes, but are more threatened by loss of habitat. The Texas Parks and Wildlife Department has had some success in raising the Lesser Prairie-Chicken in captivity for later release, but the Greater does not respond to captivity. It is very wild and explodes into a frenzy whenever its cage is approached. Apparently, the only hope of saving the Attwater Prairie-Chicken, as this sub-species is called, is in establishing sanctuaries. You can occasionally see one feeding along the road like a

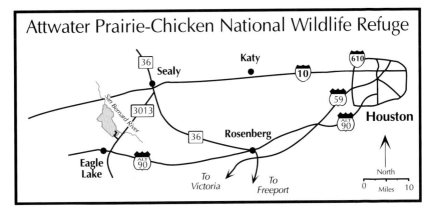

chicken, but normally it is much harder to find. At daybreak, you may see one flying around from roosting to feeding areas, but for the rest of the day it stays concealed in the tall grass. Your best bet is to be here between December and May when the males are booming. At that time they gather in open fields; however, you still have to get out at dawn to see them. The most popular places with local birders for finding the chickens are near Tivoli and at the **Attwater Prairie-Chicken National Wildlife Refuge**, located 7 miles northeast of Eagle Lake, off FM 3013, or south from Sealy on Highway 36 to FM 3013 and traveling west for 10 miles. This refuge is just beyond the regular coverage of this book but is included here nonetheless. Headquarters is reached by driving 2 miles west of the main entrance on FM 3013. The refuge is open 7 days a week from sunrise to sunset, except during the booming season (February 1 through April). Refuge hours during the booming season are 9am to 5pm. The refuge provides tours to the booming grounds (leks) during this time. Tours are by reservation only and begin at 7am. Headquarters hours are 7:30am to 4pm, Monday through Friday. Once numbering over a million individuals, the Attwater race of the Greater Prairie-Chicken has been reduced to fewer than 500 individuals. For additional information and reservations (February 1 through April) write to: Refuge Manager, Attwater Prairie-Chicken National Wildlife Refuge, PO Box 518, Eagle Lake, Texas 77434, or telephone 409/234-3021.

Yellow Rail—Fairly common winter visitor in the *Spartina* marshes and tall-grass pastures along the coast, and in the rice fields farther inland. It is so seldom seen, however, that little is known of its distribution. It can be coaxed into view by using a tape-recording of its call. This method is most effective at night. This rail is found at Anahuac National Wildlife Refuge, Sabine Marsh, Galveston Island, Freeport, San Bernard National

Wildlife Refuge, Aransas National Wildlife Refuge, and occasionally farther south. A good method of seeing the bird in the fall is to watch for rice field harvesting, and wait for the birds to be flushed by the combines.

Black Rail—Rare, or at least seldom seen. Little is known of the seasonal or regional distribution of this bird, but it has been found at all seasons in the marshes along the coast. Most of the recent sightings have been at Anahuac National Wildlife Refuge during spring migration. A number of nests were found after a fire at Brazoria National Wildlife Refuge. Your chances of seeing it are poor, but it will respond to taped calls, particularly at night. You might try this method—and never play the tapes excessively—at Sabine Marsh, Sea Rim State Park, the oil fields around High Island, Galveston Island, Rockport, Corpus Christi, and elsewhere.

Clapper and **King Rails**—It is not as hard to find these birds as it is to tell them apart. For the most part, the King Rail is more common in winter and in fresh-water marshes, while the Clapper is a permanent resident and stays in the salt marshes. However, they overlap in brackish areas and in migration. Look for the Clapper at Sabine Marsh, Anahuac National Wildlife Refuge, the "Rail Road" on Galveston Island, Galveston Island State Park, Freeport, Matagorda, and Laguna Atascosa National Wildlife Refuge. Try for the King in the rice fields near Winnie, Katy, Indianola, and Victoria.

Purple Gallinule—Fairly common summer resident in fresh-water marshes throughout; a few winter. Many inexperienced birders pass the young birds off as Common Moorhens. Study any large flock of moorhens/gallinules in summer, and you should be able to pick out a Purple Gallinule. Try Sabine Marsh, Sea Rim State Park, Anahuac National Wildlife Refuge, Galveston Island, Freeport, Aransas National Wildlife Refuge, Lake Corpus Christi, and Pollywog Pond.

Sandhill Crane—Fairly common winter visitor to pastures, stubble fields, rice fields, and marshes along the entire coast. If you are here at the right season, it is usually easy to find. Look for it in the rice fields near Winnie, Katy Farms, Eagle Lake, Port O'Connor, and Victoria, or in the pastures on West Galveston Island, Freeport, Aransas National Wildlife Refuge, FM 881 west of Rockport, and Laguna Atascosa National Wildlife Refuge.

Whooping Crane—Rare and endangered winter visitor to the Aransas National Wildlife Refuge. From a low of about 15 birds in 1941, their numbers have generally increased. In the winter of 1992-1993 there were 136 birds. While they may occasionally be seen from the road, or more commonly from the lookout tower on the refuge, the surest way to see them is by boat. Most popular are the few large group boats which anchor at the Sandollar Pavillion, Rockport Harbor, and Port Aransas. Party boats for six or more can also be rented at Rockport Harbor, Fulton Beach, or the Sea-Gun Resort. These small boats are often able to get rather close to the cranes. When you get close you may see that most of the cranes have colored bands on their legs (such as the young bird shown on the cover of this book). Many of the cranes have these bands so that the bird's individual movements, behavior, and pairing can be monitored.

Snowy Plover—Uncommon permanent resident of beaches and sandflats along the entire coast, locally common in some areas. Nests on oyster-shell bars or in dry sand. When feeding along the bays, it seems to prefer tidal flats that are on the lee side of an island or peninsula. Look for it along the Gulf beaches and at Bolivar Flats, San Luis Pass, Bryan Beach, Dale Miller Causeway, Kennedy Causeway, along Highway 181 on the Nueces Bay Causeway, Tule Lake, Cayo del Oso, Laguna Atascosa National Wildlife Refuge, and Queen Isabella Causeway.

Wilson's Plover—Fairly common summer resident of salt flats, tidal flats, and beaches along the entire coast. A few winter. Look for it at Bolivar Flats, San Luis Pass, West Galveston Island, Pelican Island, Matagorda, No Man's Land, the oil fields off Farm Road 1781 near Rockport, Rockport Beach, Fulton Beach, Cayo del Oso, Dale Miller Causeway, Kennedy Causeway, Tule Lake, Laguna Atascosa National Wildlife Refuge, and Queen Isabella Causeway.

Piping Plover—Fairly common winter visitor to beaches and tidal flats along the entire coast. Numbers wintering on the Texas Coast may disguise its "threatened" status. That is because half of the world's population winters (August-April) along the Texas Coast. A few will summer. You should have little trouble finding this bird except in midsummer, although you may have trouble separating it from the Semipalmated Plover, which is found in the same areas at the same time.

Mountain Plover—Rare and sporadic migrant through South Texas. It is easily overlooked. It blends well with the barren fields that it frequents. Check for it in newly-plowed fields that are free of clods, and in over-grazed pasturage. The rather smooth fields that are prepared for vegetables or rice are ideal. Be sure to use your binoculars. It usually stays on the back side as far as possible from the road. It seems to be most common in spring migration. Inexperienced birders sometimes mistake winter-plumaged Lesser Golden-Plovers for this bird.

American Oystercatcher—Uncommon permanent resident of beaches, tidal flats, and shell banks along the entire coast. Most often seen on islands in the bays or feeding on shell bars at low tide. It is found in such places as Bolivar Flats, Rollover Pass, the "Rail Road" on Galveston Island, Austwell, Rattlesnake Point and Oystercatcher Point at Rockport, Dale Miller Causeway, Kennedy Causeway, and Queen Isabella Causeway.

Black-necked Stilt—Common summer resident on rice fields, grassy marshes, and ponds throughout. A few winter, particularly on the Lower Coast. Look for it in the rice fields west of Houston and near Winnie, at Anahuac National Wildlife Refuge, Oryx Oil Field on Bolivar Peninsula, Bolivar Flats, Galveston Island, Freeport, Aransas National Wildlife Refuge, Rockport, Cayo del Oso, Pollywog Pond, and Laguna Atascosa National Wildlife Refuge.

American Avocet—Fairly common winter visitor to tidal flats, shallow lagoons, and rain pools throughout. Some nest on the Central Coast. Most common in migration. Look for it at Anahuac National Wildlife Refuge, Bolivar Flats, San Luis Pass, Indianola, Cayo del Oso, Mustang Island, Laguna Atascosa National Wildlife Refuge, and Queen Isabella Causeway.

Northern Jacana—Rare and sporadic. To find this bird, you can always ask the local birders as to its current status. It is not a shy bird, so after one is found it can usually be seen by a number of people. It is most often found around ponds overgrown with water-hyacinths.

This species has been found at a number of places, such as Falfurrias, Kingsville, Seadrift, and Brazoria National Wildlife Refuge. For many years (1967-1977) there was a colony of the birds in Brazoria County at Manor Lake. The colony grew to several dozen birds, but the hard freeze of 1977 wiped them out.

Local birders fumble over the pronunciation of Jacana too. Most of them pronounce the J as a J, and the word comes out Jah-CAH-nah. Those who speak Spanish give the J an H sound, and it becomes Hah-CAH-nah. The local people who are not birders say JACK-a-nah. Some authorities claim that it is a Portugese/Brazilian word, derived from a native South American language, and should be pronounced SHAW-sa-NAH. The author of a book on the birds of the world says that it should be YAH-say-NAH. However, if you use either of the latter pronunciations in Texas, everyone will give you a blank look. The easiest way out of the dilemma is to ask the other person first how he pronounces it. Chances are that he will not know either, so from then on he will not object, no matter how you slaughter the word.

Upland Sandpiper—Fairly common migrant through the prairies, fields, and pastures throughout. Most common in late March and early April. Look for it near Winnie, west of Houston, Oryx Oil Field on Bolivar Peninsula, West Galveston Island, near Port O'Connor, Corpus Christi Airport, and Laguna Atascosa National Wildlife Refuge. This species can often be heard passing overhead on spring nights.

Eskimo Curlew—No well-substantiated sightings in the last quarter-century, but lots of dubious reports. (There was a possible sighting in the spring of

1981 of an astounding 23 birds on Atkinson Island in Galveston Bay. The sighting was by two experienced observers from a boat within 50 meters of the birds.) Most sightings have been between March 22 and April 15, with most of these occurring in the first week of April. The bird prefers overgrazed pastures, and is usually in the company of Lesser Golden-Plovers and similar grassland-loving shorebirds. Reliable sightings have been from West Galveston and Rockport, but it would be best to be aware of the possibility of a sighting anywhere from the Corpus Christi area northward along the coast. Historically, Eskimo Curlews were found in pastures inland from the coast, though not in the last 80 or so years. If you think that you have carefully observed an Eskimo Curlew, write up the sighting, get supporting photographs, and round up corroborating observers. Also contact without delay the U.S. Fish and Wildlife Service, which is coordinating the international Eskimo Curlew Advisory Group (USFWS, 203 West Second Street, Grand Island, Nebraska 68801; telephone: 308/382-6468.)

Hudsonian Godwit—Uncommon late spring migrant on wet pastures, flooded fields, rice fields, and grassy marshes. Most common between May 1st and 15th, and inland from the coast, although it has been found on Mustang and Padre Islands. Look for it in the rice fields near High Island, Winnie, Katy, and Victoria, and in flooded fields west of Rockport, around Ingleside, south and west of Corpus Christi, and along Highway 77.

Marbled Godwit—Uncommon winter visitor to tidal flats, marshes, and sometimes rice fields throughout. More common in spring. Look for it in such areas as Anahuac National Wildlife Refuge, Bolivar Flats, San Luis Pass, West Galveston Island, Aransas National Wildlife Refuge, Rockport Beach, Cayo del Oso, Dale Miller Causeway, Kennedy Causeway, Laguna Atascosa National Wildlife Refuge, and Queen Isabella Causeway.

Semipalmated and **Western Sandpipers**—Fairly common migrants to tidal flats and beaches throughout, but sometimes hard to tell apart. Western Sandpipers are found in both saline and fresh-water habitats, although predominately in salt water. The Semipalmated Sandpiper is primarily a fresh-water species. Most guides stress the longer bill of the Western, but there is a sexual difference in the size of the bill of this species, with the female having the longer bill. Any peep of this type with a long drooping bill is probably a Western, but one with a short bill is not necessarily a Semipalmated. The Western is often browner on the back and may show a touch of rusty brown at the scapulars, crown, and ear-patch. There are probably no acceptable winter records for Semipalmated Sandpiper on the Texas Coast, so great care must be taken in calling a Semipalmated in this season.

White-rumped Sandpiper—Fairly common spring migrant in wet pastures and rice fields, and rare on tidal flats and beaches. Rare in fall. Most common in May and early June, and fairly easy to find if you know how to identify it. Look for its elongated profile (wingtips extended beyond the tail), "chevrons" on the flanks (in breeding plumage), and, of course, its white rump. It is found in many places, such as Anahuac National Wildlife Refuge, the rice fields near Winnie, Katy, and Victoria, West Galveston Island, Port O'Connor, Tule Lake, Cayo del Oso, Mustang Island, and Laguna Atascosa National Wildlife Refuge.

Baird's Sandpiper—Uncommon spring and fall migrant about rain pools, rice fields, tidal flats, and also over-grazed pastures. Apparently, more common in the central part of the state than on the coast. Look for it wherever you find other sandpipers, particularly in areas of fresh water and wet pastures. Its slim, long form (with wingtips extending beyond the tail) can help to pick it out when it is with other peeps. The scaly back (especially in juveniles), and the distinctive breast coloration (like a Pectoral Sandpiper) are also helpful. Baird's Sandpiper is found in just about the same locations as White-rumped Sandpiper, though it usually prefers drier ground.

Stilt Sandpiper—Uncommon migrant in April and early May and in August and September in the rice fields, wet pastures, and tidal flats. A few winter. Look for it in the same areas as the White-rumped Sandpiper.

Buff-breasted Sandpiper—Uncommon spring migrant on the short-grass prairies, golf courses, and rice fields throughout. A few occur in August and early September, particularly along the Central and Lower Coasts. Most often found on over-grazed pastures and plowed rice fields. Look for it at the Katy rice fields, West Galveston Island, rice fields near Winnie and Katy, Aransas National Wildlife Refuge, Rockport, near Corpus Christi, and at Laguna Atascosa National Wildlife Refuge. Most of the guide books fail to mention that in the fall and winter plumage this bird may not have a rich buffy breast. Most of those arriving early on the Texas Coast, in the last part of March and the first week of April, have only a faint wash of buff across the breast. At that time it is best to separate them by leg-color—yellow in the Buff-breasted and black in the Baird's. In this plumage, the Buff-breasted might also be mistaken for a Reeve, since both have yellowish legs.

Short-billed and **Long-billed Dowitchers**—Common migrant and winter visitors to rice fields, wet pastures, tidal flats, and beaches throughout. It is not hard to find these birds, but it is frustrating to try to tell them apart. As a rule, the Short-billed prefers salt-water areas, and the Long-billed, fresh water. However, there is always one dowitcher in every flock that didn't quite get the word.

At close range and in good light, breeding-plumaged Short-billed Dowitcher may show some white on the lower belly and vent. (Unfortunately, the *hendersoni* sub-species of Short-billed Dowitcher found on the Texas Coast can be almost as reddish below as Long-billed Dowitcher.) The *hendersoni* Short-billed Dowitcher usually has lightly spotted undertail coverts. In all races of Short-billed, the light bars on the tail are usualy as wide—or wider than—the dark bars. The juvenile is rather bright, especially the rusty-orange edged and striped tertials and scapulars. Grayish winter birds are whitish below. The call is a soft *tu-tu-tu*.

In breeding-plumaged Long-billed Dowitcher the throat and upper breast are darker and more heavily spotted, and the spotting changes to barring on the lower sides. The light bars on the tail are not as wide as the dark bars. Narrow bars usually mark the undertail coverts. The juvenile Long-billed has a darker back than the Short-billed, and its dark gray tertials and greater wing coverts will have narrow reddish edgings. In winter it is darker-breasted than the Short-billed. The call is a thin *keek*.

American Woodcock—Uncommon and sporadic winter visitor in moist woodlands and thickets from East Texas south sparingly to about Corpus Christi. Some years it is fairly common, but in most years can be hard to find. It may occur in the Big Thicket, High Island, Eisenhower Park, Memorial Park in Houston, Brazos Bend State Park, near the tower in Aransas National Wildlife Refuge, and sometimes Hazel Bazemore County Park.

jaegers—Two species, the **Pomarine** and **Parasitic Jaegers**, are uncommon winter visitors offshore. Most often seen from boats in the Gulf, but occasionally one will chase a gull or a tern toward shore. The best places from which to watch for them are the ends of the jetties, such as at Galveston, Freeport, or Port Aransas. Watch for Parasitic Jaegers harassing the gulls following shrimp boats—often off Highway 87—in March and April. There are still only a handful of records for **Long-tailed Jaeger** on the Texas Coast. As a rule, the Pomarine is the most common jaeger in Texas.

Lesser Black-backed Gull—Rare winter visitor to coastal areas, though now found almost yearly. Has been observed on the Texas City Dike, San Luis Pass, Aransas National Wildlife Refuge, Mustang Island, and the Brownsville Dump, to name a few places.

Gull-billed Tern—Fairly common resident of bays, salt flats, and fields throughout. Less common in winter. Most often seen hawking for insects over a field or pond, often quite far inland. Fairly easy to find in summer in such areas as the Bolivar Peninsula, South Jetty in Galveston, West Galveston Island, Freeport, Aransas National Wildlife Refuge, Rockport, Cayo del Oso, Tule Lake, and Laguna Atascosa National Wildlife Refuge.

Sandwich Tern—Fairly common summer resident along the Gulf. Some winter. Not particularly hard to find, but it may be hard to see the yellow tip on the bill. Some good places to study them closely are the Bolivar Flats, Rollover Pass, Bolivar Ferry, Rockport Beach, and from the jetties at Galveston, Freeport, and Port Aransas.

Sooty Tern—Very rare, but breeds annually with a few nesting pairs in colonies of Royal and Gull-billed Terns near Corpus Christi and Rockport. Can sometimes be seen along the Dale Miller Causeway to Port Aransas in summer. There are also a few isolated nests at the southern end of the Laguna Madre, near the outflow of the Harlingen Ship Channel. To visit this area—some of the islands are leased and patrolled by the National Audubon Society—you can hire Walt Kittelberger, a commercial guide (PO Box 153, Port Mansfield, Texas 78598; telephone: 210/944-2387). You may not land on the islands or disturb nesting birds (thousands of terns, skimmers, herons, and egrets). You can spend anywhere from an hour to several hours before seeing a Sooty Tern fly over the islands. Sooty Terns have also been observed offshore on pelagic trips, usually May through August.

Black Skimmer—Common summer resident along the beaches and bays. Less common in winter. Easy to see feeding along beaches, particularly at dusk.

Inca Dove—Fairly common resident in urban areas or about farm buildings in South Texas. Has spread northward to encompass the entire coastal area. This dove likes the city life, while the Common Ground-Dove prefers the country. They are sometimes found in the same areas, but it is usually the Inca Dove that has moved to the suburbs rather than the Common Ground-Dove to the city. Usually easiest to find in city parks such as Kempner Park in Galveston or Blucher and South Bluff Parks in Corpus Christi.

Common Ground-Dove—Common resident of South Texas farms, fields, and natural areas. Rare north of Rockport. You should have no trouble finding this bird in the Lower Rio Grande Valley.

White-tipped Dove—Uncommon resident of woodlands and thickets in the Lower Rio Grande Valley. Rare resident farther north into the lower Coastal Bend. Found at Laguna Atascosa National Wildlife Refuge (often near the Visitor Center), and at the Sabal Palm Grove Sanctuary, though more commonly seen upriver.

Groove-billed Ani—Uncommon permanent resident of brushlands in South Texas and northward sparingly to Louisiana. In South Texas it is more common in summer. However, on the Upper Coast or the Coastal Bend it is recorded more often in winter. There seems to be a northward, post-nesting dispersal, which would account for these winter sightings.

Look for the ani in thickets in the Lower Rio Grande Valley, Laguna Atascosa National Wildlife Refuge, Kingsville, along Up River Road in Corpus Christi, and Aransas National Wildlife Refuge.

Ferruginous Pygmy-Owl—Uncommon resident. It used to be found rarely along the rest stops on Highway 77, especially around Sarita and Norias. Now it is known to inhabit mesquite and live-oak groves on the King Ranch in some numbers. The only reliable way of seeing it is on a specific, organized VENT tour on the ranch's Norias division.

Burrowing Owl—Uncommon winter visitor to open country, mostly in South Texas. Usually hard to find in this area, but may sometimes be located by driving back roads through the farm lands at night and checking near culverts and irrigation standpipes. It has been found at Katy Farms and among the boulders at the base of the bridge across San Luis Pass.

Barred Owl—Common permanent resident of dense woodlands south to about Corpus Christi. Not hard to hear at night. It is rather noisy. Just before dark, it often comes out and sits on a fence post. Look, or rather listen, for it along river bottoms and other woodlands in such areas as the Big Thicket, White Memorial Park, Eisenhower Park, Memorial Park in Houston, Armand Bayou, Aransas National Wildlife Refuge, Hazel Bazemore County Park, and below Lake Corpus Christi dam.

Pauraque—Fairly common permanent resident of woodlands, thickets, and brushlands of the Lower Rio Grande Valley northward to about Rockport. Easy to hear on warm nights, but in winter, when not calling, it often goes unnoticed. By checking the underbrush at the start of the Bayside Tour at Laguna Atascosa National Wildlife Refuge or at the Sabal Palm Grove Sanctuary you might find one.

Chuck-will's-widow—Fairly common migrant, but seldom seen. Nests in East and Central Texas, but not near the coast. In migration, look for it in trees or thickets in such areas as High Island, Aransas National Wildlife Refuge, Blucher Park in Corpus Christi, Hazel Bazemore County Park, and Laguna Atascosa National Wildlife Refuge.

Chimney Swift—Abundant migrant along the entire coast, and common summer resident south to about Corpus Christi and occasionally farther. Hard to miss.

Buff-bellied Hummingbird—Locally common resident in the Lower Rio Grande Valley, becoming an uncommon breeder in the lower Coastal Bend, and downright rare or irregular in winter on the Upper Texas Coast. The Sabal Palm Grove Sanctuary is usually a reliable place for this bird year-round. At Aransas National Wildlife Refuge check stands of Turk's-cap Lilies in summer. Try any hummingbird feeders in between. Sooner or later you will see this bird.

kingfishers—The only kingfisher to expect on the Texas Coast is the **Belted Kingfisher**. In the Lower Rio Grande Valley and the Coastal Bend, the Belted is not to be expected during the breeding season. The **Green Kingfisher** and **Ringed Kingfisher** are found uncommonly in the Lower Rio Grande Valley, around ponds and resacas. The Green becomes irregular northward into the Coastal Bend area.

Red-headed Woodpecker—Uncommon and declining permanent resident. Hard to find in winter. Usually found about farms and cities, particularly in areas with standing dead trees. Look for it around the new lake developments where the rising water has killed numerous trees, and in summer at Beaumont, near Anahuac, and in Alexander Deussen Park.

Golden-fronted Woodpecker—Common permanent resident of the Lower Rio Grande Valley northward sparingly to Victoria. Not hard to find, for instance, at Lake Corpus Christi State Park, Pernitas Point, Kingsville, Highway 77, Laguna Atascosa National Wildlife Refuge, and in the Brownsville area.

Red-bellied Woodpecker—Common permanent resident of woodlands and towns of the Upper Coast, south sparingly to the Guadalupe River near Victoria. It is the most common woodpecker on the Upper Coast and is hard to miss.

Ladder-backed Woodpecker—Fairly common permanent resident of arid brushlands and river-bottoms in the Lower Rio Grande Valley northward to Aransas National Wildlife Refuge and sometimes farther. If this bird is needed for your life list, it can be frustratingly hard to find; then it seems to be everywhere. Look for it at Laguna Atascosa National Wildlife Refuge, the Kingsville area, Lipantitlan State Park, Lake Corpus Christi, and Aransas National Wildlife Refuge.

Red-cockaded Woodpecker—Rare and endangered permanent resident in localized areas of the pine woods of East Texas. Between 3,000 and 10,000 are believed to exist in the entire United States. Prefers open stands of pines with reduced understory. For a woodpecker, it is rather sociable and quite noisy, particularly early in the morning. At times five or six birds may be seen at once or heard conversing back and forth in voices that sound somewhat like those of Brown-headed Nuthatches or young European Starlings. The birds even nest in loose colonies. The nesting hole is made in a living pine, but usually one that is infected with red-heart disease. Such nesting-trees are easily found, because the holes are surrounded by conspicuous patches of oozing pitch. These patches decrease predation from ants and flying squirrels. It has been found in some numbers in the Angelina National Forest (north of the Big Thicket area and just beyond the coverage of this book), but the spots most recommended by local birders are Fire Tower Road northwest of Silsbee and especially the W.G. Jones State Forest north of Houston. These spots are described elsewhere in the book.

Pileated Woodpecker—Fairly common permanent resident of woodlands along the Upper Coast, south sparingly to Guadalupe River near Victoria. Once the call is learned, these noisy birds are not hard to locate. Look for them in the Big Thicket, Beaumont, White Memorial Park, Armand Bayou, Eisenhower Park, Memorial Park in Houston, and near Freeport. The Freeport Christmas Count often leads the nation in the number of these birds found.

Ivory-billed Woodpecker—The controversy over the existence of this bird in Texas still rages. The last solid observation was probably in 1938. However, there are 20 or so people who claim to have seen the bird in East Texas much more recently, and many more people who hope that they are right. On the other hand, there are numerous doubters who say that the reported sightings were really of albinistic Pileated Woodpeckers or were made by inexperienced birders. (Aberrant Pileated Woodpeckers have been photographed in central Florida with white on their wings—looking not unlike Ivory-bills.) Some critics even go so far as to say that the flurry of East Texas sightings was a publicity stunt to promote the Big Thicket National Preserve. Perhaps the most interesting evidence was a possible recording of the Ivory-billed Woodpecker in 1968. The problem is that a Blue Jay mimic cannot be ruled out from the recording. If you want to try for yourself, find an area of mature hardwood forest and carry your good luck charm. The areas where Ivory-bills have been reported are: along the Trinity River in Anderson County near Tennessee Colony, between the Neches and Angelina Rivers north of the Dam B Reservoir near Jasper, the Alabama-Coushatta Indian Reservation east of Livingston, Hardin County between Village Mills and Farm Road 420, along the Neches River north of Evadale, southeast of Kountze, near Massey Lake south of Silsbee, along Pine Island Bayou north of Beaumont, and the Sam Houston National Forest.

Northern Beardless-Tyrannulet—Rare and local resident of thickets and mottes in the Lower Rio Grande Valley into the lower Coastal Bend. Rarely found at rest stops along Highway 77. Can usually been seen on the VENT tours to the King Ranch's Norias Division after late February. When present, this species can be located by its *ee ee ee ee* call.

Eastern Wood-Pewee—Fairly common summer resident of woodlands on the Upper Coast, south to about Victoria. Abundant in migration. Easy to find on the breeding grounds by its frequent calls. Look for it in the Big Thicket, Tyrrell Park, White Memorial Park, Eisenhower Park, and Memorial Park in Houston.

Empidonax flycatchers—During migration, these small flycatchers are abundant, but separating them is almost a hopeless task, particularly in the fall. The ones found here will be Yellow-bellied, Acadian, Alder, Willow, or Least. Most of these will usually appear at the very last days of April and will occur through most of May. The spring exceptions are breeding Acadian and a few early Leasts. Empids in the fall will start passing through in early August, peak at the beginning of September, and linger through most of October. The fall exception will be the Least, a few of which may actually linger into winter. Occasionally, an empid will call its own identifiable note or will be distinctly marked, so that even in migration you can pick out most of the various species. The **Acadian Flycatcher** is a fairly common summer resident in woodlands of East Texas, south to about Houston. Its distinctive song, a loud *pizza!*, is heard frequently from late April through the nesting season. Look for it in the Big Thicket, White Memorial Park, Eisenhower Park, and Memorial Park in Houston.

Eastern Phoebe—Fairly common winter visitor in woodlands and farms throughout. Usually near water. Should be no problem to find. Feeds from exposed twigs and fence lines.

Ash-throated Flycatcher—Fairly common summer resident in dry chaparral, thickets, and mesquite from the Lower Rio Grande Valley to the southern part of the Coastal Bend. Rare at other seasons, or elsewhere along the coast. Try areas around Lake Corpus Christi and along Highway 77.

Great Crested Flycatcher—Common migrant along the entire coast. Nests in woodlands and thickets of the Upper Coast, south sparingly to about Rockport. In summer look for it in the Big Thicket, High Island, White Memorial Park, Eisenhower Park, and Memorial Park in Houston.

Brown-crested Flycatcher—Common summer resident in woodlands and thickets of Lower Rio Grande Valley, northward to about Victoria. Like the Great Crested, it is heard more often than seen, but with a little searching you can find it around Lake Corpus Christi, Kingsville, Laguna Atascosa National Wildlife Refuge, and the Sabal Palm Grove Sanctuary.

Great Kiskadee—Fairly common resident of woodlands and thickets in Lower Rio Grande Valley, northward sparingly to Corpus Christi. It is usually found near water and often catches fish like a kingfisher. It is a noisy bird and easy to locate by its call, but not always easy to see.

Couch's Kingbird—Fairly common summer resident of woodlands, thickets, and farms of the Lower Rio Grande Valley, northward to about Corpus Christi. Some will winter. This is the common kingbird of the Lower Rio Grande Valley; it can be seen sitting in tree-tops and on telephone wires throughout that area. A bright yellow-bellied kingbird in south Texas in the winter will almost always be a Couch's Kingbird. However, several appearances of **Tropical Kingbird** in south Texas since 1988 make it useful to verify identifications by call. The Tropical Kingbird has a thin, distinctive twitter: *pip-pip-pip-pip-pip*. The usually more vocal Couch's Kingbird will give a sharp *kip* and also a rolling *breeeeer*, which can build into a rising *beer-beer-beer-BEE-ow*.

Don't expect Cassin's Kingbird—it's out of range—and don't count on Western Kingbird in the winter.

Scissor-tailed Flycatcher—Abundant summer resident of open country throughout. Hard to miss.

Cave Swallow—Common summer resident, nesting in area caves, culverts, and under bridges. Since the mid-1980s this once-uncommon species has been extending its range and numbers. It has been found nesting along the Coastal Bend at least as far north as Matagorda Island. You can also try Dick Kleberg Park and other locations around Kingsville, as well as bridges along Highway 77 from March into September. In recent years it has even nested on the Upper Texas Coast at Sea Rim State Park.

Blue Jay— Common permanent resident of woodlands and towns of East Texas, south to about Houston; then sparingly south to the big wooded area on the south side of Victoria. Hard to miss in East Texas.

Green Jay—Fairly common permanent resident of thickets and woodlands of the Lower Rio Grande Valley, northward to Kingsville, and sparingly through Corpus Christi. Also try at Laguna Atascosa National Wildlife Refuge and Sabal Palm Grove Sanctuary.

Mexican Crow—First recorded in the U.S. in 1968, but now a common winter resident near Brownsville. A few linger all year, and some have even nested. Unlike the Fish Crow, which it closely resembles, this bird does not prefer areas near water. It has a different call that some folks say sounds more like that of a Pinyon Jay than that of a Fish Crow. (Of course, if you are not familiar with the call of a Pinyon Jay or a Fish Crow, the hint doesn't help much.) Other birders just listen for a frog-like croak from the Mexican Crow. The very best place to look for it is at the Brownsville City Dump. On occasion Mexican Crow can also be found on the back road to the dump, on the north side of the ship channel, or in nearby livestock lots.

Fish Crow—Common permanent resident in Orange, Beaumont, and environs. In recent years it has gradually moved down the west side of the Beaumont/Port Arthur corridor to Sabine Pass, and for the last three or four years one pair has nested in the Sabine Woods Sanctuary. The best place to see it in Beaumont is the Sanitary Landfill at the end of Lafin Road. The grounds of the Beaumont Medical and Surgical Hospital is another reliable spot. In Texas it is rarely found along the open shores of the Gulf or bays, but frequents water-courses in wooded areas, especially areas with pines. It is almost never seen west of Jefferson County.

Carolina Chickadee—Common permanent resident of woodlands in East Texas, southward sparingly to just beyond Victoria. Not hard to find in the Big Thicket, Beaumont, White Memorial Park, Eisenhower Park, and Bear Creek Park.

Tufted Titmouse—Common permanent resident of woodlands in East Texas, south sparingly to Victoria, where it interbreeds with the Black-crested race. Conspicuous, noisy, and not hard to find in the Big Thicket, Tyrrell Park, High Island, White Memorial Park, and Brazos Bend State Park.

Tufted ("Black-crested") Titmouse—This race of the Tufted Titmouse is a common permanent resident of woodlands in the Lower Rio Grande Valley, northward to Victoria. Conspicuous, noisy, and easy to find at such places as Rockport, Goose Island State Park, Kingsville, Aransas National Wildlife Refuge, and Sabal Palm Grove Sanctuary. It was once considered a separate species from Tufted Titmouse, but was "lumped" years ago. There is some serious consideration to have it "split" again; watch your titmice carefully when in the field.

Brown-headed Nuthatch—Fairly common permanent resident of open pine woods in East Texas, south to about Houston. It travels in small, twittering flocks that fly from one pine to the next, so once the call is learned, it is easy to find. Look for it in the Sam Houston Forest, near Silsbee, W.G. Jones State Forest, and occasionally at White Memorial Park and Memorial Park in Houston. It occupies the same areas as the Red-cockaded Woodpecker and Bachman's Sparrow.

Carolina Wren—Common permanent resident of woodlands and moist thickets throughout. Loud and noisy, and not hard to find. Look for it in the Big Thicket, High Island, Eisenhower Park, Aransas National Wildlife Refuge, Rockport, and Hazel Bazemore County Park.

Sedge Wren—Fairly common winter visitor in grassy and sedge fields throughout. Squeak near any patch of bluestem or broomsedge in winter and it may pop into view. Look for it at Sabine Marsh, Sea Rim State Park, Anahuac National Wildlife Refuge, West Galveston Island, Freeport, San Bernard National Wildlife Refuge, Aransas National Wildlife Refuge, and Laguna Atascosa National Wildlife Refuge.

Clay-colored Robin—Uncommon visitor and rare nester in Lower Rio Grande Valley. Usually found in winter. There are records northward to Sarita, Kingsville, and Aransas National Wildlife Refuge.

Eastern Bluebird—Fairly common but decreasing permanent resident of open woodlands above the Upper Coast, south sparingly to about Corpus Christi. Most common and widespread in winter. Look for it in the pine woods north of Beaumont, White Memorial Park, Alexander Deussen Park, Buckhorn Lake, and Lipantitlan State Park.

Brown Thrasher—Common winter visitor to thickets and woodlands in East Texas, south to about Corpus Christi. Some nest in East Texas. Not hard to find in such areas as the Big Thicket, High Island, White Memorial Park, Eisenhower Park, Memorial Park in Houston, Aransas National Wildlife Refuge, and Rockport.

Long-billed Thrasher—Fairly common resident in the Lower Rio Grande Valley, north to Corpus Christi. Prefers dense brush, while the Curve-billed is more often found in open brush. This shy bird stays hidden and is difficult to find; however, it responds to squeaking. The best way to see it is to stand quietly by a path through dense brush and watch for it to come out and feed. Look for it at the start of the Bayside Tour at Laguna Atascosa National Wildlife Refuge, Lake Corpus Christi, under the bluff at Hazel Bazemore County Park, around Kingsville, and at Sabal Palm Grove Sanctuary.

Curve-billed Thrasher—Fairly common permanent resident of open, arid brushlands from the Lower Rio Grande Valley northward to about Indianola. Easy to find in the Kingsville area and at Laguna Atascosa National Wildlife Refuge, and becomes even more common as you go westward up the Rio Grande.

Sprague's Pipit—Uncommon winter visitor to grasslands throughout. It is not as rare as the literature would indicate, but you must make a special effort to find it. By walking back and forth over the right grassy field, you can usually flush one. It will usually fly rather high, then drop quickly to the ground like a falling stone. It seems to prefer areas where the grass is not over six inches high, or, if taller, spaced with open areas for running. Some places where it can usually be found are along the west side of Anahuac National Wildlife Refuge, along the levee at Texas City Dike, around the edges of the golf course on West Galveston Island, along the levee crossing Farm Road 332 near Freeport, along Farm Road 2004 east of Angleton, Katy Farms, near Port O'Connor, at the "pipit corner" near Kingsville, and occasionally at the north end of the Lakeside Tour at Laguna Atascosa National Wildlife Refuge.

White-eyed Vireo—Common migrant and fairly common summer resident in woodlands and thickets throughout. Some will winter. This is the most common vireo in the area, although in migration you will also find Yellow-throated, Solitary, Red-eyed, Philadelphia, Warbling, and, in the south, Bell's. The White-eyed Vireo may be hard to see, but it is often heard. Look for it north of Beaumont, Eisenhower Park, White Memorial Park, Aransas National Wildlife Refuge, Rockport, Hazel Bazemore

County Park, and at the start of the Bayside Tour at Laguna Atascosa National Wildlife Refuge.

Yellow-throated Vireo—Uncommon summer resident of woodlands above the Upper Coast. Migrant throughout. Look for it in the Big Thicket, White Memorial Park, Brazos Bend State Park, and Alexander Deussen Park.

Yellow-green Vireo—Rare migrant and nester. Has nested in recent years behind the visitor center at Laguna Atascosa National Wildlife Refuge.

Black-whiskered Vireo—Rare visitor. There are fewer than a dozen records for the coast, mostly in spring (April and early May), and mostly for the Upper Texas Coast. Check migrating Red-eyed Vireos carefully.

Tropical Parula—Uncommon breeder and possible resident. Sometimes observed at rest stops along Highway 77. The bird is actually more easily seen on specific bird tours after mid-March to the Norias section of the King Ranch. Also seen in the Lower Rio Grande Valley at such sites as the Sabal Palm Grove Sanctuary.

Yellow-throated Warbler—Most common as a migrant, but some nest in the woodlands of East Texas, south to about Houston. Some winter on the Lower Coast. During the nesting season, look for it in the Big Thicket, White Memorial Park, Lake Charlotte, Eisenhower Park, and at Buckhorn Lake.

Pine Warbler—Common permanent resident of the pine woods of East Texas, south to about Houston. More widespread in winter. From late February until it starts to feed young in late April, its loud trill is the most frequently heard song in the pine woods. Look for it north of Beaumont and in Tyrrell Park, Alexander Deussen Park, and White Memorial Park.

Prairie Warbler—Uncommon summer resident in the open pine woods of East Texas. It arrives on the breeding grounds in late April; look for it along Lookout Tower Road and Waluta Girls Camp Road north of Silsbee. Seldom found as a spring migrant along the coast, though somewhat more common in the fall, especially among Tamarisks (Salt-cedars).

Prothonotary Warbler—Uncommon summer resident in the cypress swamps of East Texas. Early migrant elsewhere. The bulk of its migration is across the Upper Coast, and, unless there is severe weather, it is not commonly seen on the Central and Lower Coasts. In summer look for it in the Big Thicket area, Lake Charlotte, Buckhorn Lake, Brazos Bend State Park, and Taylor's Bayou.

Swainson's Warbler—Uncommon summer resident in moist woodlands of East Texas, south to about Houston. Early migrant elsewhere. Because of its secretive habits and plain markings, it slips through almost unnoticed in migration. It is often easier to find on the nesting grounds, if you learn its song. During late April and early May, it sings frequently and is fairly easy to locate. It also responds to squeaking. The nest is usually located in a clump of cane, Yaupon, palmetto, or other tangle along a moist river bottom. Look for it in the Big Thicket, White Memorial Park, Eisenhower Park, Bear Creek Park, and Jesse H. Jones County Park north of Houston. In migration it is often found near the ground in the dense underbrush, such as at High Island.

Louisiana Waterthrush—Uncommon summer resident of wet tangles and woodlands along the watercourses of East Texas. Early migrant elsewhere. Hard to see, because it usually stays hidden in the thickets. Even in migration, it is hard to find, although this may be due in part to the fact that the bulk of the population moves through in late March and early April before most birders come out of winter hibernation. On the breeding grounds in April and May, it can often be located by its clear, musical song. It usually nests near a small creek, particularly one with a sandy or gravelly bottom. Some known nesting areas are: near the Big Creek Scenic Area in Sam Houston National Forest, the Angelina National Forest, and along Village Creek south of Silsbee.

Kentucky Warbler—Common migrant along the Upper Coast, but less common on the Lower Coast. Uncommon summer resident of moist woodlands of East Texas, south to about Houston. Normally found in a tangle near the ground. On the breeding grounds, it can be located by its loud, Carolina-Wren-like song. In summer look for it at the Big Thicket, White Memorial Park, Bear Creek Park, Lake Charlotte, and Eisenhower Park.

MacGillivray's Warbler—Rare but regular migrant along the Lower Coast. Females of this species are often passed off as Nashvilles, because their color combinations are very similar. It pays to check for the yellow throat on every Nashville, particularly if the bird looks larger than usual.

Hooded Warbler—Uncommon summer resident of moist woodlands of East Texas, south sparingly to around the San Jacinto River. Common migrant elsewhere along the coast. Occurs in about the same habitat as the Kentucky.

Pyrrhuloxia—Fairly common permanent resident of arid brushlands from the Lower Rio Grande Valley through the Coastal Bend area north to Rockport. It is common in the mesquite patches along the Rio Grande and becomes even more common as you go upriver toward West Texas. Look for it at Laguna Atascosa National Wildlife Refuge, the Kingsville area, Lake Corpus Christi State Park, and along Up River Road in Corpus Christi.

Varied Bunting—Very rare summer resident of mesquite thickets in the Lower Rio Grande Valley. Has been found near the start of the Bayside Tour at Laguna Atascosa National Wildlife Refuge. A few records for Aransas National Wildlife Refuge (April) and elsewhere.

Painted Bunting—Common summer resident of brushlands and hedgerows of the coast. Easy to find in summer in South Texas. On the Upper Coast try such places as Bear Creek Park, High Island, and near Vidor east of Beaumont. Look for it at Laguna Atascosa National Wildlife Refuge, Kingsville area, Lipantitlan State Park, Lake Corpus Christi State Park, and the Aransas National Wildlife Refuge.

Dickcissel—Fairly common migrant in fields and pastures throughout and a common summer resident along the Upper Coast, south to about Corpus Christi. Look for it in fallow rice fields west of Houston (Katy Farms), and at Winnie, and at Anahuac National Wildlife Refuge.

Olive Sparrow—Fairly common permanent resident of thick brushlands in Lower Rio Grande Valley, northward sparingly to Corpus Christi. It is a shy bird that is usually located by its loud, distinctive song. Responds to squeaking. Look for it at the start of the Bayside Tour at Laguna Atascosa National Wildlife Refuge, in Lake Corpus Christi State Park, the Kingsville area, and sometimes at Hazel Bazemore County Park.

Bachman's Sparrow—Uncommon and local permanent resident in grassy areas of the open pine woods of East Texas. Often found in the same areas as the Red-cockaded Woodpecker. Prefers spots beneath open pines where the grass is thick and about a foot high. In winter it is not easily found, because it becomes very secretive. When flushed, it flies rapidly to a bush and disappears, but it will respond to a taped recording of its song. In the spring and summer, it and the Chipping Sparrow are the only sparrows around, and the males sit boldly on a twig and sing their beautiful song. Look for it along Fire Tower Road and at the Big Creek Scenic Area of Sam Houston Forest.

Botteri's Sparrow—Uncommon and usually hard-to-find summer resident in grasslands with scattered bushes in the Lower Rio Grande Valley north rarely to Kingsville. Some may winter. It can be flushed by walking across grassy pastures. Hard to separate from the Cassin's Sparrow, which occurs in the same areas. The Botteri's is usually browner, especially on the tail. It is easy to tell them apart in the spring and summer when they are singing, because their songs are quite different. Look for this sparrow along the Bayside Tour at Laguna Atascosa National Wildlife Refuge, near the intersection of Highway 4 and Farm Road 1419 east of Brownsville, at the Brownsville Dump, and along Farm Road 497 near Port Mansfield.

Cassin's Sparrow—Common summer resident of grasslands in the Lower Rio Grande Valley, northward to Rockport. Some winter. Easier to find than to identify, because it sits on fence lines and bare bushes. In the spring and summer it is easy to locate by its song, which is delivered while skylarking, and it may sing 24 hours a day. Look for it at Bayside, Farm Road 881 at Rockport, west of Lake Corpus Christi, Laguna Atascosa

National Wildlife Refuge, along Highway 4 east of Brownsville, and throughout the chaparral belt in the inland part of South Texas.

Clay-colored Sparrow—An often abundant migrant in South Texas in April. A few winter in the grassy fields of the Lower Rio Grande Valley, as at Laguna Atascosa National Wildlife Refuge.

Field Sparrow—Uncommon winter visitor to brushy pastures and open woodlands throughout, but less common southward. More common inland than near the coast. Look for it near Silsbee, Bear Creek Park, hedgerows west of Houston, and sometimes at Aransas National Wildlife Refuge.

Black-throated Sparrow—Fairly common permanent resident of arid brushlands in the Lower Rio Grande Valley, sparingly northward to Corpus Christi. Less common in winter. Easy to find when present. It is not a shy bird, and it prefers areas where the brush is fairly low and open. Common at Laguna Atascosa National Wildlife Refuge and farther west along the Rio Grande. Also found at Dinero west of Lake Corpus Christi and sometimes along Highway 881 at Rockport.

Henslow's Sparrow—Rare, or at least rarely seen, winter visitor to weedy fields and grasslands on the Upper Coast and in East Texas. It apparently likes about the same habitat as the Le Conte's Sparrow, but is much rarer. As a rule, it stays in the area only from about the first of December to March. However, it has nested in southeast Houston, Deer Park, and College Station in the recent past. Check with local birders for its current status. There are recent winter records from near Silsbee, Baytown, the San Jacinto Monument, Freeport, west of Houston, and Smith Point.

Le Conte's Sparrow—Uncommon winter visitor throughout, less common southward. It is shy, and you will have to kick it out of the weedy fields and grasslands. The best way to find it is to walk across a grassy field with scattered bushes. When flushed, it will fly into a bush, and you can walk around the clump until you find it. Sometimes responds to squeaking. Look for it near Anahuac National Wildlife Refuge, Angleton, and west of Houston.

Sharp-tailed Sparrow—Fairly common, but not often seen, winter visitor to the salt marshes of the Upper and Central Coast, south to about Aransas National Wildlife Refuge. It can be lured into view at dawn or dusk by squeaking. Try along the edge of the numerous little canals that meander through the salt marshes. The bird will often run back and forth over the open mud between the water's edge and the vegetation. Look for it at Anahuac National Wildlife Refuge, Bolivar Flats, the "Rail Road" on Galveston Island, South Jetty at Galveston, Freeport, and Aransas National Wildlife Refuge.

Seaside Sparrow—Common permanent resident of salt marshes from the Upper Coast to about Corpus Christi, farther south in winter. Singing males can be readily seen in April and May. Responds well to squeaking at other seasons. Not hard to find if you search the *Spartina* marshes at Sabine, Sea Rim State Park, Anahuac National Wildlife Refuge, Bolivar Flats, the "Rail Road" on Galveston Island, County Road 242 at Freeport, and San Bernard National Wildlife Refuge.

Swamp Sparrow—Fairly common winter visitor to fresh-water marshes, wet tangles, and drainage ditches throughout. Occurs in the same areas as the Song Sparrow, for which it is often mistaken. This bird is shy and sometimes hard to see, but it responds well to squeaking. The best way to study it is to sit quietly by a ditch and wait for it to come out. Look for it in the roadside ditches near the rice fields at Winnie and Katy, Anahuac National Wildlife Refuge, among the Tamarisks that overgrow the ditches on West Galveston Island, Aransas National Wildlife Refuge, Pollywog Pond, below Lake Corpus Christi, Hazel Bazemore County Park, and Laguna Atascosa National Wildlife Refuge.

White-throated Sparrow—Fairly common winter visitor to moist undergrowth and thickets throughout, but less common southward. Prefers wetter and denser growth than does the White-crowned Sparrow. Look for it in the Big Thicket, Tyrrell Park, High Island, White Memorial Park, Eisenhower Park, Memorial Park in Houston, Freeport, and Aransas National Wildlife Refuge.

Harris's Sparrow—Uncommon and sporadic winter visitor to the open woodlands, brushlands, and hedgerows inland from the Upper Coast. Prefers the drier brushlands rather than wet tangles. Look for it near Silsbee and in the hedgerows west of Houston.

Rusty Blackbird—Uncommon winter visitor to the woodlands of the Upper Coast, occasionally as far south as the Aransas National Wildlife Refuge and Corpus Christi. This is a bird of the swamps and woodlands. It is seldom found in the fields as is the Brewer's, nor is it often found in mixed flocks with other blackbirds. Look for it in the Big Thicket, Tyrrell Park, White Memorial Park, Eisenhower Park, and along Cemetery Road near Angleton.

Great-tailed and **Boat-tailed Grackles**—The Upper Texas Coast provides just about the only opportunity to compare these two species side-by-side. These birds differ in several ways—coloration, size, voice, and habitat. After studying them a few times, it is easy to tell them apart. <u>Coloration</u>: The most noticeable difference is in the color of the eye. Both male and female Boat-tailed Grackles have dark eyes. (You may have trouble with the male Boat-tailed at close range, for its eye may reflect a yellow-brown hue. Some others just seem to be dull-yellow eyes.) However, both male and female Great-taileds have bright yellow eyes. Immature Great-tailed Grackles may, nonetheless, have dark eyes until some time in the fall. The light eye of the female Great-tailed is not always as bright as that of the male, and the color may be indiscernible except at close range. Size: The Boat-tailed is a smaller bird. The tail of the male is shorter and less bulky. The overall size is intermediate between that of the Common Grackle and the Great-tailed. The Boat-tailed Grackle has a more rounded head. Voice: One vocalization of the Boat-tailed resembles somewhat that of the Red-winged Blackbird. It has a soft, pleasing bubbling sound that is quite unlike the harsh, raucous calls of the Great-tailed. Other Boat-tailed calls include squeaks, rattles, and chattering. The Great-tailed Grackle seems more vocal, not only in the loudness of its call, but also in its variety. Listen for a series of *clacks*. It often ends its chattering with a loud, rising *wheeeee*, which is never given by the Boat-tailed. Habitat: The Boat-tailed prefers areas near coastal waters and marshes, rice fields, and lakes, although it will resort to nearby trees for roosting and nesting. It is not common in urban areas. On the other hand, the Great-tailed seems able to adapt to almost any habitat. It is found on beaches, tidal flats, salt marshes, fresh marshes, dry fields, woodlands, lakes, and about cities. In Texas the Boat-tailed Grackle is an uncommon permanent resident along the Upper Coast, south sparingly to the Guadalupe River near Victoria. The Great-tailed is abundant throughout and impossible to miss. Some areas where the Boat-tailed has been found are the San Bernard National Wildlife Refuge, Anahuac National Wildlife Refuge, by the Intracoastal Canal on Highway 124 north of High Island, and Sea Rim State Park.

Common Grackle—Fairly common permanent resident in woodlands, farms, and cities of East Texas, south to about Houston and west to Austin. More common and widespread in winter. Often found in urban yards and in areas of large oak trees. Look for it in Beaumont, Fort Anahuac Park, Rice University and Memorial Park in Houston, and Alexander Deussen Park.

Bronzed Cowbird—Fairly common summer resident of farms, brushlands, and feed lots from Lower Rio Grande Valley to Corpus Christi, sparingly northward to Freeport. Many winter. Not hard to find in South Texas, especially near feed lots.

Altamira Oriole—Fairly common resident of the Lower Rio Grande Valley, found at such places as Sabal Palm Grove Sanctuary and around Brownsville. Rarely nests farther northward.

Audubon's Oriole—Rare to uncommon in the Lower Rio Grande Valley, they are rather common nesters on parts of the King Ranch, though frustratingly in areas away from public access. With luck they may be found around Kingsville, along "Hawk Alley" east of Falfurrias, and in ranch country northwest of Corpus Christi.

Lesser Goldfinch—Rare to uncommon in the Coastal Bend area. During some years it can be found in fields and sunflowers in the Kingsville area and along Highway 77.

BIRDS FOUND ALONG THE TEXAS COAST

Listed in the bar-graphs which follow are the birds regularly found within this book's geographic coverage. The bar-graphs are designed to show the probability of seeing the birds rather than their actual abundance. For example, a large bird such as the Red-tailed Hawk may be shown as *hard to miss* while a shy, hard-to-identify bird such as the Botteri's Sparrow may occur in greater numbers, but be shown as *lucky to find.*

Hard to Miss	▬▬▬▬▬▬▬▬
Should See	▬▬▬▬▬▬▬▬
May See	══════
Lucky to Find	─────
How Lucky Can You Get	────────

Many local birders were consulted in determining the status of each species. Since these people are familiar with the birds and their habitats, they are good at finding the more elusive ones. On your first trip, you may think that some of the birds are harder to find than is indicated. However, if you are in the right area and the right habitat at the proper season, you should find the *hard to miss* birds on nearly every trip afield, the *should see* on over 50% of the trips, the *may see* on about 25%, and the *lucky to find* on 10% or fewer. The *how lucky can you get* species occur at very infrequent intervals or take an expert to identify.

When inquiring about the very rare species, you will probably be told to forget it, but do not stop looking. Adding one of these birds to your list is what puts the topping on the trip. If you are positive of your identification, take careful notes and report your observation to the regional editors of *American Birds*: Greg W. Lasley, 305 Loganberry Ct., Austin, Texas 78745 and Chuck Sexton, 101 E. 54th Street, Austin, Texas 78751. A report should also be sent to the Texas Birds Records Committee (TBRC); a sample report form is included toward the back of this book.

The first four columns in the bar-graphs indicate four geographic regions covered in this book. The Lower Coast extends northward from the Rio Grande to Baffin Bay south of Corpus Christi. The Central Coast extends from Baffin Bay to Port O'Connor, and the Upper Coast from Port O'Connor to the Sabine River on the Louisiana border. There is another sector called East Texas, which takes in the heavily wooded areas north of Houston and Beaumont.

This is not truly a part of the coastal region, but was added to give a clearer picture of the birdlife near the Upper Coast.

✓	East Texas	Upper Coast	Central Coast	Lower Coast		January	February	March	April	May	June	July	August	September	October	November	December
☐ Pacific Loon		▬				▬											
☐ Common Loon		▬▬				▬▬▬		▬								▬	
☐ Least Grebe		▬															
☐ Pied-billed Grebe	▬	▬▬▬				▬▬▬									▬▬		
☐ Horned Grebe		▬				▬▬		▬									
☐ Eared Grebe		▬				▬▬										▬	
☐ Western Grebe		▬													▬		
☐ Masked Booby											▬						
☐ Northern Gannet		▬				▬									▬		
☐ American White Pelican		▬▬▬				▬▬▬									▬▬		
☐ Brown Pelican		▬ ▬															
☐ Double-crested Cormorant	▬	▬▬▬				▬▬▬									▬▬▬		
☐ Neotropic Cormorant		▬							▬▬▬								
☐ Anhinga " "	▬	▬▬▬							▬▬▬		▬▬						
☐ Magnificent Frigatebird		▬									▬						
☐ American Bittern		▬							▬						▬▬		
☐ Least Bittern		▬				▬											
☐ Great Blue Heron	▬▬▬	▬▬▬▬				▬▬▬▬			▬▬▬					▬▬▬▬			
☐ Great Egret	▬	▬▬▬				▬▬▬▬▬▬▬▬▬▬▬▬											
☐ Snowy Egret	▬	▬▬▬				▬▬▬▬▬▬▬▬▬▬▬▬											
☐ Little Blue Heron		▬▬▬				▬▬▬▬			▬▬▬								
☐ Tricolored Heron		▬▬▬				▬▬▬▬▬▬▬▬▬▬▬▬											
☐ Reddish Egret		▬				▬▬▬▬▬▬▬▬▬▬▬▬											
☐ Cattle Egret	▬▬▬	▬▬▬				▬				▬▬▬▬▬▬				▬			
☐ Green-backed Heron	▬▬	▬▬				▬			▬▬▬▬▬▬				▬				
☐ Black-crowned Night-Heron	▬	▬				▬▬▬▬▬▬▬▬▬▬▬▬											
☐ Yellow-crowned Night-Heron	▬	▬						▬	▬▬▬▬				▬				
☐ White Ibis	▬	▬							▬▬▬▬▬				▬				
☐ Glossy Ibis		▬ ▬				▬											

✓	East Texas	Upper Coast	Central Coast	Lower Coast		January	February	March	April	May	June	July	August	September	October	November	December
White-faced Ibis																	
Roseate Spoonbill																	
Wood Stork																	
Fulvous Whistling-Duck																	
Black-bellied Whistling-Duck																	
Greater White-fronted Goose																	
Snow Goose																	
Ross's Goose																	
Canada Goose																	
Wood Duck																	
Green-winged Teal																	
Mottled Duck																	
Mallard																	
Northern Pintail																	
Blue-winged Teal																	
Cinnamon Teal																	
Northern Shoveler																	
Gadwall																	
American Wigeon																	
Canvasback																	
Redhead																	
Ring-necked Duck																	
Greater Scaup																	
Lesser Scaup																	
Oldsquaw																	
Surf Scoter																	
White-winged Scoter																	
Common Goldeneye																	
Bufflehead																	
Hooded Merganser																	

✓	East Texas	Upper Coast	Central Coast	Lower Coast	January	February	March	April	May	June	July	August	September	October	November	December
Common Merganser																
Red-breasted Merganser																
Ruddy Duck																
Masked Duck																
Black Vulture																
Turkey Vulture																
Osprey																
American Swallow-tailed Kite																
Black-shouldered Kite																
Mississippi Kite																
Bald Eagle																
Northern Harrier																
Sharp-shinned Hawk																
Cooper's Hawk																
Harris's Hawk																
Red-shouldered Hawk																
Broad-winged Hawk																
Swainson's Hawk																
White-tailed Hawk																
Red-tailed Hawk																
Ferruginous Hawk																
Rough-legged Hawk																
Golden Eagle																
Crested Caracara																
American Kestrel																
Merlin																
Peregrine Falcon																
Prairie Falcon																
Plain Chachalaca																
Greater Prairie-Chicken																

✓		East Texas	Upper Coast	Central Coast	Lower Coast	January	February	March	April	May	June	July	August	September	October	November	December
☐	Wild Turkey																
☐	Northern Bobwhite																
☐	Scaled Quail																
☐	Yellow Rail																
☐	Black Rail																
☐	Clapper Rail																
☐	King Rail																
☐	Virginia Rail																
☐	Sora																
☐	Purple Gallinule																
☐	Common Moorhen																
☐	American Coot																
☐	Sandhill Crane																
☐	Whooping Crane																
☐	Black-bellied Plover																
☐	Lesser Golden-Plover																
☐	Snowy Plover																
☐	Wilson's Plover																
☐	Semipalmated Plover																
☐	Piping Plover																
☐	Killdeer																
☐	Mountain Plover																
☐	American Oystercatcher																
☐	Black-necked Stilt																
☐	American Avocet																
	" "																
☐	Northern Jacana																
☐	Greater Yellowlegs																
☐	Lesser Yellowlegs																
☐	Solitary Sandpiper																

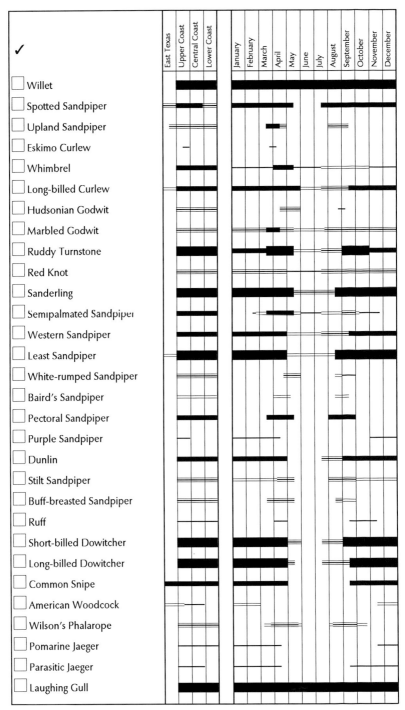

✓	East Texas	Upper Coast	Central Coast	Lower Coast		January	February	March	April	May	June	July	August	September	October	November	December
Willet																	
Spotted Sandpiper																	
Upland Sandpiper																	
Eskimo Curlew																	
Whimbrel																	
Long-billed Curlew																	
Hudsonian Godwit																	
Marbled Godwit																	
Ruddy Turnstone																	
Red Knot																	
Sanderling																	
Semipalmated Sandpiper																	
Western Sandpiper																	
Least Sandpiper																	
White-rumped Sandpiper																	
Baird's Sandpiper																	
Pectoral Sandpiper																	
Purple Sandpiper																	
Dunlin																	
Stilt Sandpiper																	
Buff-breasted Sandpiper																	
Ruff																	
Short-billed Dowitcher																	
Long-billed Dowitcher																	
Common Snipe																	
American Woodcock																	
Wilson's Phalarope																	
Pomarine Jaeger																	
Parasitic Jaeger																	
Laughing Gull																	

✓		East Texas	Upper Coast	Central Coast	Lower Coast	January	February	March	April	May	June	July	August	September	October	November	December
☐	Franklin's Gull																
☐	Bonaparte's Gull																
☐	Ring-billed Gull																
☐	California Gull																
☐	Herring Gull																
☐	Lesser Black-backed Gull																
☐	Glaucous Gull																
☐	Gull-billed Tern																
☐	Caspian Tern																
☐	Royal Tern																
☐	Sandwich Tern																
☐	Common Tern																
☐	Forster's Tern																
☐	Least Tern																
☐	Sooty Tern																
☐	Black Tern																
☐	Black Skimmer																
☐	Rock Dove																
☐	Red-billed Pigeon																
☐	White-winged Dove																
☐	Mourning Dove																
☐	Inca Dove																
☐	Common Ground-Dove																
☐	White-tipped Dove																
☐	Red-crowned Parrot																
☐	Black-billed Cuckoo																
☐	Yellow-billed Cuckoo																
☐	Greater Roadrunner																
☐	Groove-billed Ani																
☐	Barn Owl																

✓	East Texas	Upper Coast	Central Coast	Lower Coast		January	February	March	April	May	June	July	August	September	October	November	December
☐ Eastern Screech-Owl																	
☐ Great Horned Owl																	
☐ Ferruginous Pygmy-Owl																	
☐ Burrowing Owl																	
☐ Barred Owl																	
☐ Short-eared Owl																	
☐ Lesser Nighthawk																	
☐ Common Nighthawk																	
☐ Pauraque																	
☐ Chuck-will's-widow																	
☐ Whip-poor-will																	
☐ Chimney Swift																	
" "																	
☐ Buff-bellied Hummingbird																	
☐ Ruby-throated Hummingbird																	
" "																	
☐ Black-chinned Hummingbird																	
☐ Rufous Hummingbird																	
☐ Ringed Kingfisher																	
☐ Belted Kingfisher																	
" "																	
☐ Green Kingfisher																	
☐ Red-headed Woodpecker																	
☐ Golden-fronted Woodpecker																	
☐ Red-bellied Woodpecker																	
☐ Yellow-bellied Sapsucker																	
☐ Ladder-backed Woodpecker																	
☐ Downy Woodpecker																	
☐ Hairy Woodpecker																	
☐ Red-cockaded Woodpecker																	

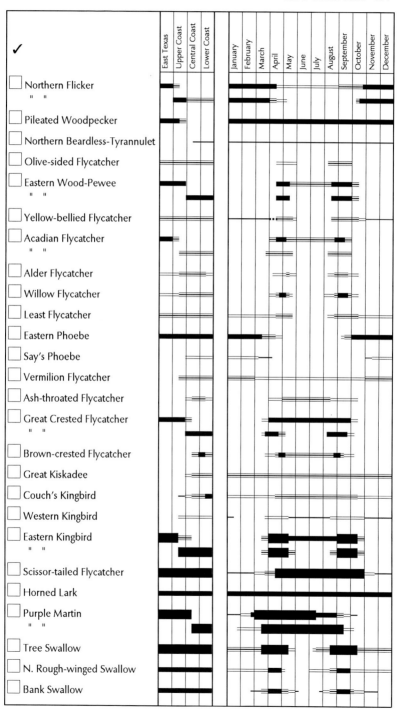

✓	East Texas	Upper Coast	Central Coast	Lower Coast		January	February	March	April	May	June	July	August	September	October	November	December
Northern Flicker																	
" "																	
Pileated Woodpecker																	
Northern Beardless-Tyrannulet																	
Olive-sided Flycatcher																	
Eastern Wood-Pewee																	
" "																	
Yellow-bellied Flycatcher																	
Acadian Flycatcher																	
" "																	
Alder Flycatcher																	
Willow Flycatcher																	
Least Flycatcher																	
Eastern Phoebe																	
Say's Phoebe																	
Vermilion Flycatcher																	
Ash-throated Flycatcher																	
Great Crested Flycatcher																	
" "																	
Brown-crested Flycatcher																	
Great Kiskadee																	
Couch's Kingbird																	
Western Kingbird																	
Eastern Kingbird																	
" "																	
Scissor-tailed Flycatcher																	
Horned Lark																	
Purple Martin																	
" "																	
Tree Swallow																	
N. Rough-winged Swallow																	
Bank Swallow																	

✓	East Texas	Upper Coast	Central Coast	Lower Coast		January	February	March	April	May	June	July	August	September	October	November	December
Cliff Swallow																	
" "																	
Cave Swallow																	
Barn Swallow																	
Blue Jay																	
Green Jay																	
American Crow																	
Mexican Crow																	
Fish Crow																	
Chihuahuan Raven																	
Carolina Chickadee																	
Tufted Titmouse																	
Tufted "Blk-crested" Titmouse																	
Verdin																	
Red-breasted Nuthatch																	
White-breasted Nuthatch																	
Brown-headed Nuthatch																	
Brown Creeper																	
Cactus Wren																	
Carolina Wren																	
Bewick's Wren																	
House Wren																	
Winter Wren																	
Sedge Wren																	
Marsh Wren																	
" "																	
Golden-crowned Kinglet																	
Ruby-crowned Kinglet																	
Blue-gray Gnatcatcher																	
Eastern Bluebird																	

✓		East Texas	Upper Coast	Central Coast	Lower Coast	January	February	March	April	May	June	July	August	September	October	November	December
☐	Mountain Bluebird																
☐	Veery																
☐	Gray-cheeked Thrush																
☐	Swainson's Thrush																
☐	Hermit Thrush																
☐	Wood Thrush																
	" "																
☐	Clay-colored Robin																
☐	American Robin																
☐	Gray Catbird																
☐	Northern Mockingbird																
☐	Sage Thrasher																
☐	Brown Thrasher																
☐	Long-billed Thrasher																
☐	Curve-billed Thrasher																
☐	American Pipit																
☐	Sprague's Pipit																
☐	Cedar Waxwing																
☐	Loggerhead Shrike																
	" "																
☐	European Starling																
☐	White-eyed Vireo																
☐	Bell's Vireo																
☐	Solitary Vireo																
☐	Yellow-throated Vireo																
	" "																
☐	Warbling Vireo																
☐	Philadelphia Vireo																
☐	Red-eyed Vireo																
	" "																
☐	Yellow-green Vireo																

✓	East Texas	Upper Coast	Central Coast	Lower Coast		January	February	March	April	May	June	July	August	September	October	November	December
☐ Blue-winged Warbler																	
☐ Golden-winged Warbler																	
☐ Tennessee Warbler																	
☐ Orange-crowned Warbler																	
☐ Nashville Warbler																	
☐ Northern Parula																	
" "																	
☐ Tropical Parula																	
☐ Yellow Warbler																	
☐ Chestnut-sided Warbler																	
☐ Magnolia Warbler																	
☐ Cape May Warbler																	
☐ Black-throated Blue Warbler																	
☐ Yellow-rumped Warbler																	
☐ Black-throated Gray Warbler																	
☐ Hermit Warbler																	
☐ Black-throated Green Warbler																	
☐ Blackburnian Warbler																	
☐ Yellow-throated Warbler																	
" "																	
☐ Pine Warbler																	
" "																	
☐ Prairie Warbler																	
" "																	
☐ Palm Warbler																	
☐ Bay-breasted Warbler																	
☐ Blackpoll Warbler																	
☐ Cerulean Warbler																	
☐ Black-and-white Warbler																	
" "																	
☐ American Redstart																	

✓	East Texas	Upper Coast	Central Coast	Lower Coast		January	February	March	April	May	June	July	August	September	October	November	December
☐ Prothonotary Warbler																	
" "																	
☐ Worm-eating Warbler																	
☐ Swainson's Warbler																	
" "																	
☐ Ovenbird																	
☐ Northern Waterthrush																	
☐ Louisiana Waterthrush																	
" "																	
☐ Kentucky Warbler																	
" "																	
☐ Connecticut Warbler																	
☐ Mourning Warbler																	
☐ MacGillivray's Warbler																	
☐ Common Yellowthroat																	
☐ Hooded Warbler																	
" "																	
☐ Wilson's Warbler																	
☐ Canada Warbler																	
☐ Yellow-breasted Chat																	
☐ Summer Tanager																	
☐ Scarlet Tanager																	
☐ Western Tanager																	
☐ Northern Cardinal																	
☐ Pyrrhuloxia																	
☐ Rose-breasted Grosbeak																	
☐ Black-headed Grosbeak																	
☐ Blue Grosbeak																	
☐ Indigo Bunting																	
☐ Varied Bunting																	
☐ Painted Bunting																	

✔	East Texas	Upper Coast	Central Coast	Lower Coast		January	February	March	April	May	June	July	August	September	October	November	December
☐ Dickcissel																	
☐ Olive Sparrow																	
☐ Green-tailed Towhee																	
☐ Rufous-sided Towhee																	
☐ Bachman's Sparrow																	
☐ Botteri's Sparrow																	
☐ Cassin's Sparrow																	
☐ Chipping Sparrow																	
☐ Clay-colored Sparrow																	
☐ Field Sparrow																	
" "																	
☐ Vesper Sparrow																	
☐ Lark Sparrow																	
☐ Black-throated Sparrow																	
☐ Lark Bunting																	
☐ Savannah Sparrow																	
☐ Grasshopper Sparrow																	
☐ Henslow's Sparrow																	
☐ Le Conte's Sparrow																	
☐ Sharp-tailed Sparrow																	
☐ Seaside Sparrow																	
☐ Fox Sparrow																	
☐ Song Sparrow																	
☐ Lincoln's Sparrow																	
☐ Swamp Sparrow																	
☐ White-throated Sparrow																	
☐ White-crowned Sparrow																	
☐ Harris's Sparrow																	
☐ Dark-eyed Junco																	
☐ Lapland Longspur																	

✓	East Texas	Upper Coast	Central Coast	Lower Coast		January	February	March	April	May	June	July	August	September	October	November	December
☐ Bobolink																	
☐ Red-winged Blackbird																	
☐ Eastern Meadowlark																	
☐ Western Meadowlark																	
☐ Yellow-headed Blackbird																	
☐ Rusty Blackbird																	
☐ Brewer's Blackbird																	
☐ Great-tailed Grackle																	
☐ Boat-tailed Grackle																	
☐ Common Grackle																	
☐ Bronzed Cowbird																	
☐ Brown-headed Cowbird																	
☐ Orchard Oriole																	
☐ Hooded Oriole																	
☐ Altamira Oriole																	
☐ Audubon's Oriole																	
☐ Northern Oriole																	
☐ Purple Finch																	
☐ House Finch																	
☐ Pine Siskin																	
☐ Lesser Goldfinch																	
☐ American Goldfinch																	
☐ Evening Grosbeak																	
☐ House Sparrow																	

SELDOM SEEN BUT POSSIBLE

Red-throated Loon
Sooty Shearwater
Cory's Shearwater
Audubon's Shearwater
Wilson's Storm-Petrel
Leach's Storm-Petrel
Band-rumped Storm-Petrel
Brown Booby
Tundra Swan
Brant
Eurasian Wigeon
Black Scoter
Hook-billed Kite
Common Black-Hawk
Gray Hawk
Ring-necked Pheasant
Red-necked Phalarope
Thayer's Gull
Great Black-backed Gull
Black-legged Kittiwake
Sabine's Gull
Bridled Tern
Elf Owl
Long-eared Owl
Common Poorwill
White-throated Swift
Blue-throated Hummingbird
Anna's Hummingbird
Broad-tailed Hummingbird
Allen's Hummingbird
Black Phoebe
Tropical Kingbird
Violet-green Swallow
Rock Wren
Black-tailed Gnatcatcher
Varied Thrush
Phainopepla

Townsend's Warbler
Lazuli Bunting
Baird's Sparrow
Chestnut-collared Longspur
McCown's Longspur
Red Crossbill

ACCIDENTALS

Red-necked Grebe
Yellow-nosed Albatross *(2 records)*
Greater Shearwater
Manx Shearwater
Red-billed Tropicbird
Blue-footed Booby *(1 record)*
Red-footed Booby *(1 record)*
Jabiru *(3 records)*
Greater Flamingo
American Black Duck
Trumpeter Swan
White-cheeked Pintail *(1 record)*
Garganey *(1 record)*
Harlequin Duck *(1 record)*
Barrow's Goldeneye *(3 records)*
Snail Kite
Northern Goshawk
Roadside Hawk *(1 record)*
Aplomado Falcon
Double-striped Thick-knee
    (1 record)
Wandering Tattler *(1 record)*
Surfbird *(3 records)*
Curlew Sandpiper
Red Phalarope
Long-tailed Jaeger
Little Gull *(4 records)*
Heermann's Gull *(1 record)*
Slaty-backed Gull *(1 record)*
Elegant Tern *(1 record)*
Brown Noddy *(3 records)*
Black Noddy *(1 record)*
Band-tailed Pigeon
Mangrove Cuckoo
Flammulated Owl
Snowy Owl
Northern Saw-whet Owl
White-collared Swift *(3 records)*
Green Violet-ear *(5 records)*

Broad-billed Hummingbird
    (2 records)
Lucifer Hummingbird
Costa's Hummingbird *(1 record)*
Acorn Woodpecker
Williamson's Sapsucker
Greenish Elaenia *(1 record)*
Sulphur-bellied Flycatcher
    (4 records)
Gray Kingbird *(3 records)*
Fork-tailed Flycatcher *(5 records)*
Rose-throated Becard *(1 record)*
Clark's Nutcracker
Western Bluebird
White-necked Robin *(1 record)*
Aztec Thrush *(1 record)*
Gray Silky-flycatcher *(1 record)*
Northern Shrike
Yucatan Vireo *(1 record)*
Virginia's Warbler
Golden-cheeked Warbler
Connecticut Warbler *(2 records)*
Gray-crowned Yellowthroat
    (3 recent records)
Painted Redstart
Golden-crowned Warbler
    (6 records)
Hepatic Tanager
Crimson-collared Grosbeak
    (3 records)
Blue Bunting *(3 records)*
Rufous-crowned Sparrow
American Tree Sparrow
Brewer's Sparrow
Sage Sparrow
Smith's Longspur
Black-vented Oriole *(1 record)*
Common Redpoll

Other Vertebrates of the Texas Coast
Exclusive of Fish
Compiled by Alan H. Chaney

The names, order, abbreviated status, and ranges used in this list of vertebrates are generally based on those used in the works of Chaney, Dixon, and Schmidley listed in the references. There are numerous subspecies listed; these are given because they are often quite distinctive in range, form, or color.

Mammals of the Texas Coast

Opossum—*Common*; woodlands and farms throughout.

Desert Shrew—*Uncommon*; occurs in many habitats, but only in the arid parts of South Texas and westward.

Least Shrew—*Common*; grasslands throughout; active in daytime.

Southern Short-tailed Shrew—*Uncommon*; moist soils in wooded areas from East Texas to Aransas National Wildlife Refuge.

Eastern Mole—*Common*; in sandy soils throughout.

Eastern Pipistrelle—*Uncommon*; occurs in buildings, caves, and hollow trees throughout. Often seen flying about watercourses before dark. Flight is slow, erratic, moth-like.

Big Brown Bat—*Fairly common*; pine forests of Upper Coast; feeds about the tree-tops.

Red Bat—*Common*; in summer in wooded areas throughout. Solitary, roosts in trees, and feeds low to the ground under trees.

Seminole Bat—*Rare*; forested areas of East Texas.

Hoary Bat—*Rare migrant*; coastal prairie and forests.

Northern Yellow Bat—*Uncommon*; throughout in Spanish Moss; summer only.

Evening Bat—*Fairly common*; in woodlands and along watercourses throughout.

Brazilian Free-tailed (Guano) Bat—*Common;* in buildings in South Texas. This species also makes up the famous bat flights of Carlsbad Caverns, New Mexico, and the caves of Central Texas. Most leave Texas in winter.

Raccoon—*Common*; throughout.

White-nosed Coati—*Rare* visitor to extreme South Texas.

Long-tailed Weasel—*Uncommon*; in many habitats throughout.

Mink—*Uncommon*; along waterways of East Texas and the Upper Coast.

River Otter—*Rare*; along waterways of East Texas and the Upper Coast.

Badger—*Uncommon*; on prairies and arid brushland of South Texas.

Eastern Spotted Skunk—*Uncommon*; in wooded and grassy areas throughout.

Striped Skunk—*Common*; in woodlands and brushlands throughout.

Eastern Hog-nosed Skunk—*Uncommon*; in brushlands of South Texas and occasionally in the Big Thicket of East Texas.

Coyote—*Common;* in many habitats throughout, more so in South Texas.

Red Wolf—*Extirpated.*

Gray Fox—*Fairly common;* in wooded areas throughout.

Ocelot—*Rare and endangered*; in the brushlands of South Texas.

Jaguarundi—*Rare and endangered*; in the brushlands of South Texas.

Bobcat—*Uncommon east, common south;* in forest and brushlands.

Mexican Ground-Squirrel—*Common;* prairies and brushland of South Texas.

Spotted Ground-Squirrel—*Uncommon*; prairies of South Texas. More common farther west.

Eastern Gray Squirrel—*Common*; dense hardwood forests of East Texas.

Fox Squirrel—*Common*; woodlands of Upper and Central Coasts and extending its range into South Texas.

Southern Flying-Squirrel—*Fairly common* but rarely seen in forests of East Texas; nocturnal.

Baird's Pocket Gopher—*Abundant*; in sandy soils in East Texas and the Upper Coast.

Attwater's Pocket Gopher—*Common*; sandy soils of Central Coast.

Texas Pocket Gopher—*Abundant*; sandy soils of South Texas.

Mexican Spiny Pocket Mouse—*Uncommon*; dense thickets of South Texas.

Silky Pocket Mouse—*Common*; brushland of South Texas.

Hispid Pocket Mouse—*Common;* sand or loose soil of thickets throughout.

Ord Kangaroo Rat—*Common*; sandy, barren areas of South Texas.

Padre Island Kangaroo Rat—*Common*; on Padre and Mustang islands and mainland sand sheets. Separated from Ord Kangaroo Rat.

Beaver—*Uncommon*; along wooded watercourses throughout.

Eastern Harvest Mouse—*Uncommon*; grasslands of Upper Coast.

Fulvous Harvest Mouse—*Common*; grassy areas throughout.

Deer Mouse—*Common*; brushlands and prairies of East Texas.

White-footed Mouse—*Abundant*; woodlands throughout.

Cotton Mouse—*Common;* woodlands of East Texas.

Golden Mouse—*Uncommon*; woodlands of East Texas.

Pygmy Mouse—*Common*; pastures and weedy fields throughout.

Northern Grasshopper Mouse—*Uncommon*; sandy soil in grasslands of South Texas.

Eastern Woodrat—*Common*; woodlands of Upper Coast.

Southern Plains Woodrat—*Common*; brushlands of South Texas.

Marsh Rice Rat—*Common*; marshes of Upper and Central Coasts.

Cove's Rice Rat—*Uncommon*; extreme South Texas.

Hispid Cotton Rat—*Common*; tall grass throughout.

Prairie Vole—*Extinct.*

Muskrat—*Common;* marshes of Upper Coast.

Norway Rat—*Common*; cities throughout.

Black Rat—*Common*; cities throughout.

House Mouse—*Common*; cities throughout.

Nutria—*Common* and frequently seen in marshes and streams throughout.

Black-tailed Jackrabbit—*Common*; brushlands and prairies of South Texas, *uncommon* on Upper Coast.

Eastern Cottontail—*Common*; brushlands and forest edges throughout.

Swamp Rabbit—*Common*; marshes and bottomlands of Upper and Central Coasts.

Collared Peccary (Javelina)—*Fairly common*; brushlands of South Texas.

White-tailed Deer—*Common*; woodlands and brushlands throughout.

Nine-banded Armadillo—*Common* and often seen in areas with sandy or alluvial soils throughout.

Spotted Dolphin—*Rare* inshore; found offshore.

Atlantic Bottle-nosed Dolphin—*Fairly common* in the Gulf and larger bays throughout.

Common Blackfish (Pilot Whale)—*Uncommon* in the Gulf.

Whales—Several species of whales occur in the Gulf and are occasionally seen in coastal waters or found washed ashore on Texas beaches. Records include Gervais Beaked, Sperm, Pygmy Sperm, Finback, Blue, and Atlantic Right Whales.

AMPHIBIANS AND REPTILES OF THE TEXAS COAST

American Alligator—*Uncommon* but increasing in protected freshwater marshes and ponds throughout.

Common Snapping Turtle—*Common*; permanent ponds and streams of the Upper and Central Coasts.

Alligator Snapping Turtle—*Uncommon*; permanent ponds and streams of extreme East Texas.

Stinkpot—*Common*; permanent ponds of East and Central Texas.

Razor-backed Musk Turtle—*Uncommon*; streams and bayous of East Texas.

Yellow Mud Turtle—*Common*; wet areas and muddy-bottomed ponds in South Texas.

Mississippi Mud Turtle—*Common*; bayous and swamps of East Texas.

Three-toed Box Turtle—*Common*; woodlands and thickets of East Texas.

Ornate Box Turtle—*Common*; prairies and fields throughout.

Texas Diamond-backed Terrapin—*Uncommon*; salt-water bays and marshes North and Central.

Mississippi Map Turtle—*Fairly common*; larger rivers and lakes of East Texas.

Sabine Map Turtle—*Fairly common*; Sabine River drainage.

Red-eared Slider—*Abundant*; most fresh-water habitats throughout. Easily identified by bright red ear-patch.

Texas River Cooter—*Uncommon*; central rivers.

Metter's River Cooter—*Uncommon*; ponds and rivers of East Texas.

Western Chicken Turtle—*Uncommon*; still-water ponds and ditches of East Texas.

Texas Tortoise—*Fairly common*; brushlands and prairies of South Texas.

Atlantic Green Turtle—*Common* in the Gulf.

Atlantic Loggerhead—*Fairly common* in the Gulf.

Atlantic Ridley—*Uncommon* in the Gulf.

Atlantic Leatherback—*Rare* in the Gulf.

Smooth Soft-shelled Turtle—*Uncommon*; rivers of East Texas.

Spiny Soft-shelled Turtle—*Common*; permanent streams throughout.

Green Anole—*Common*; gardens and woodlands throughout. Commensal with Man.

Spot-tailed Earless Lizard—*Uncommon* inland and *rare* near the coast in arid areas of mesquite on the Central Coast.

Keeled Earless Lizard—*Common*; coastal and inland sand dunes of South Texas.

Rose-bellied Lizard—*Uncommon*; arid areas of South Texas.

Mesquite Lizard—*Uncommon*; mesquite trees in cities of South Texas.

Texas Spiny Lizard—*Fairly common*; trees and buildings of Lower and Central Coasts. A large, very spiny lizard found in a tree in South Texas would be of this species.

Fence Lizard—*Abundant*; trees, buildings, and fences throughout.

Texas Horned Lizard—*Fairly common*; arid, barren areas and coastal prairies throughout.

Mediterranean Gecko—*Fairly common*; gardens and fields of all coastal cities. Has spread north and inland.

Prairie-lined Racerunner—*Fairly common*; open areas with loose and sandy soil throughout.

Spotted Whiptail—*Common*; arid, open country of South and Central Texas.

Ground Skink—*Common*; gardens and woodlands throughout.

Five-lined Skink—*Common*; dead stumps and fallen logs in woodlands of East Texas and the Upper Coast.

Broad-headed Skink—*Uncommon* but often identified because of its massive red head. Occurs in woodlands in East Texas.

Great Plains Skink—*Common*; soft soils and prairies of South Texas.

Four-lined Skink—*Common*; woodlands and gardens of the Lower Valley.

Prairie Skink—*Uncommon*; prickly-pear and brush of Central Coast.

Slender Glass Lizard—*Fairly common*; sandy grasslands and open woods throughout.

Texas Blind Snake—*Uncommon*; moist areas in prairies, cities, and brushlands of South Texas. Smallest U.S. snake.

Green Water Snake—*Fairly common*; marshes, rice fields, and ponds of Upper Coast.

Diamond-backed Water Snake—*Common*; most fresh-water areas throughout.

Yellow-belly Water Snake—*Fairly common*; most fresh-water habitats on the Upper Coast.

Blotched Water Snake—*Fairly common*; fresh-water habitats on the Central and Lower Coasts.

Broad-banded Water Snake—*Fairly common*; most fresh-water habitats on Upper Coast.

Gulf Salt Marsh Water Snake—*Uncommon*; salt marshes of the Upper and Central Coasts.

Graham's Water Snake—*Fairly common*; still water in East and Central Texas.

Gulf Crayfish Snake—*Rare*; most fresh-water habitats of East Texas.

Texas Brown Snake—*Common* but secretive in gardens, woodlands, thickets, and marshes throughout.

Eastern Checkered Garter Snake—*Fairly common*; near water in Central and South Texas.

Eastern Garter Snake—*Common*; almost any moist habitat in East Texas.

Gulf Coast Ribbon Snake—*Common*; most semi-aquatic habitats throughout.

Rough Earth Snake—*Common* but secretive in woodlands and trash piles throughout.

Eastern Hog-nosed Snake—*Fairly common*; sandy soils in many habitats throughout.

Western Hog-nosed Snakes (2 subspecies)—*Fairly common*; sandy soils in prairies throughout.

Mississippi Ring-necked Snake—*Common*; woodland stumps of East Texas.

Mud Snake—*Rare*; swamps and lowlands of East Texas.

Black-striped Snake—*Uncommon*; woodlands, gardens, and trash heaps in Lower Valley.

Racer—*Fairly common*; many habitats throughout; there are four subspecies.

Eastern Coachwhip—*Fairly common*; many habitats on Upper Coast.

Western Coachwhip—*Fairly common*; many habitats on the Central and Lower Coasts.

Whipsnakes (2 subspecies)—*Fairly common*; arid brushlands of South Texas.

Rough Green Snake—*Common;* woodlands and thickets near water throughout.

Smooth Green Snake—*Rare*; Eastern coastal wet grassy areas.

Speckled Racer—*Rare;* dense vegetation near water in the Lower Valley.

Texas Indigo Snake—*Fairly common*; unsettled areas of brush or open woodlands in South Texas. Largest U.S. snake.

Texas Patch-nosed Snake—*Common*; prairies and brushlands of South Texas.

Great Plains Rat Snake—*Common*; open woodlands and rocky brushlands of Central and South Texas.

Corn Snake—*Uncommon*; woodlands of East Texas.

Texas Rat Snake—*Fairly common*; woodlands and swamps throughout.

Texas Glossy Snake—*Fairly common*; sandy areas of brushlands and prairies of South Texas.

Bullsnake—*Common*; brushlands and prairies of South Texas.

Louisiana Pine Snake—*Uncommon*; pinelands of East Texas.

Speckled Kingsnake—*Fairly common*; many habitats on Upper Coast.

Desert Kingsnake—*Fairly common*; many habitats on Lower Coast.

Louisiana Milk Snake—*Uncommon*; many habitats on Upper and Central Coasts.

Mexican Milk Snake—*Uncommon*; many habitats on Lower Coast.

Prairie Kingsnake—*Fairly common*; grasslands and open woodlands of Upper and Central Coasts.

Scarlet Snakes (2 subspecies)—*Rare*; burrows in sandy or loamy soils in scattered colonies along the Central and Southern Coasts.

Texas Long-nose Snake—*Uncommon*; arid brushlands and prairies of South Texas.

South Texas Ground Snake—*Common;* rocky areas and trash piles in South Texas.

Mexican Hook-nose Snake—*Uncommon*; loose soil near water in Lower Valley.

Texas Night Snake—*Fairly common*; arid regions of South Texas.

Northern Cat-eyed Snake—*Rare*; along streams in Lower Valley.

Flat-headed Snake—*Common*; areas under logs, rocks, and debris on Lower and Central Coasts.

Plains Black-head Snake—*Uncommon*; under rocks and debris in arid areas of South Texas.

Texas Black-head Snake—*Uncommon*; under rocks and debris in arid areas of South Texas.

Texas Coral Snake—*Fairly common*; wooded areas and other habitats throughout.

Copperhead (**Southern** and **Broad-banded**)—The Southern subspecies is fairly common in woodlands of the Upper and Central Coasts. The Broad-banded occurs less commonly on the Central Coast.

Western Cottonmouth—*Common*; lowlands near water on the Upper and Central Coasts.

Massasauga (**Desert** and **Western**)—*Fairly common*; wet grasslands and moist woodlands throughout.

Western Pigmy Rattlesnake—*Uncommon*; wet grasslands, floodplains, and marshes of Upper and Central Coasts.

Canebrake Rattlesnake—*Uncommon*; canebrakes, thickets, and moist woodlands of Upper and Central Coasts.

Western Diamond-backed Rattlesnake—*Common*; many habitats in arid areas throughout. Often found on sand dunes along the Gulf.

Gulf Coast Waterdog—*Fairly common*; sandy-bottomed streams of East Texas. Sold as bait to fishermen.

Lesser Siren (**Western** and **Rio Grande**)—*Fairly common*; shallow ponds and ditches with muddy bottoms throughout.

Three-toed Amphiuma—*Fairly common*; rice fields, marshes, ponds, and swamps of East Texas.

Small-mouthed Salamander—*Common*; moist woodlands, ponds, and swamps of East and Central Coasts.

Marbled Salamander—*Common*; many habitats of East Texas.

Tiger Salamander (**Eastern** and **Barred**)—*Fairly common*; ponds and moist habitats throughout.

Central Newt—*Fairly common*; river bottoms and in and near ponds and ditches of the Upper Coast.

Black-spotted Newt—*Uncommon*; in and near ponds of Lower Valley.

Southern Dusky Salamander—*Common*; ponds, marshes, and swamps in East Texas.

Dwarf Salamander—*Common*; pinelands of East Texas.

Hurter's Spadefoot Toad—*Common* after heavy rains in woodlands and prairies throughout.

Couch's Spadefoot Toad—*Common* after heavy rains in South Texas.

Plains Spadefoot Toad—*Uncommon* after heavy rains in the prairies of the Lower Coast.

White-lipped Frog—*Uncommon*; wet pastures and ponds of the Lower Valley.

Rio Grande Chirping Frog—*Fairly common*; gardens and ditches of Lower Valley.

Houston Toad—*Rare*; indigenous to ditches and marshes near Houston.

Woodhouse Toad (**Woodhouse's** and **East Texas**)—*Common* after rains in many habitats throughout. Subspecies overlap in their ranges.

Gulf Coast Toad—Most *common* toad along the coast, found in many habitats throughout.

Texas Toad—*Fairly common;* ponds and ditches of Lower and Central Coasts.

Giant Toad—*Uncommon*; ponds and wet thickets of Lower Valley.

Eastern Green Toad—*Uncommon* after rains in arid areas of South Texas.

Cricket Frogs (3 subspecies)—*Common*; around lakes, streams, and ponds throughout.

Northern Spring Peeper—*Fairly common*; woodlands of East Texas.

Green Treefrog—*Common*; moist areas throughout.

Squirrel Treefrog—*Common*; woodlands and marshes of Upper and Central Coasts.

Gray Treefrogs (2 species identical in color)—*Common;* thickets near water on the Upper and Central Coasts.

Mexican Treefrog—*Uncommon;* moist thickets and woodlands of Lower Valley.

Upland Chorus Frog—*Common*; marshes and woodlands of East Texas and the Central and Upper Coasts.

Spotted Chorus Frog—*Common* after rains on prairies of Lower and Central Coast.

Strecker's Chorus Frog—*Rare*; moist habitats near the Central and South Coasts.

Eastern Narrow-mouthed Toad—*Fairly common* after rains in moist habitats in East Texas.

Great Plains Narrow-mouthed Toad—*Common* after rains in grasslands and open woodlands throughout.

Sheep Frog—*Uncommon* after rains in South Texas.

Bullfrog—*Common*; about ponds and rivers throughout.

Pig Frog—*Uncommon*; about ponds and lakes in East Texas.

Bronze Frog—*Uncommon*; moist woodlands and swamps of East Texas.

Leopard Frogs (2 species)—*Common*; wet meadows and ponds throughout.

Pickerel Frog—*Uncommon;* meadows and thickets of East Texas.

Southern Crayfish Frog—*Uncommon*; in old crawfish holes in East Texas.

REFERENCES

Ajilvsgi, Geyata **Wild Flowers of the Big Thicket** (1979) Texas A&M University Press, College Station.

Andrews, Jean **Shells and Shores of Texas** (1977) University of Texas Press, Austin.

Arnold, Keith A. **T.O.S. Checklist of Birds of Texas** (1984) Texas Ornithological Society

Brown, C. A. **Wildflowers of Louisiana and Adjoining States** (1972) Louisiana State University Press, Baton Rouge.

Chaney, Alan H. **Keys to the Vertebrates of Texas** (1990) Texas A&I University

Davis, W. B. **The Mammals of Texas** (1974) Texas Parks and Wildlife Department, Austin.

Dixon, J. R. **Amphibians and Reptiles of Texas** (1987) Texas A&M University Press

Edwards, E. P. **A Field Guide to the Birds of Mexico** (1972) Sweet Briar, Virginia

Graham, Gary L. **Texas Wildlife Viewing Guide** (1992) Falcon Press, Helena, Montana

Gollop, J. B., Barry T. W., and Iversen E. H. **Eskimo Curlew: A vanishing species?** (1986) Saskatchewan Natural History Society

Irwin and Wells **Roadside Flowers of Texas** (1961) Univ. of Texas Press, Austin

Jones, Barry **Birder's Guide to Aransas National Wildlife Refuge** (1992) Southwest Natural and Cultural Heritage Association

Jones, E. B. **Flora of the Texas Coastal Bend** (1975) Welder Wildlife Refuge, Sinton, Texas.

Kaufman, Kenn **Advanced Birding** (1990) Houghton Mifflin, Boston

Kutac, E. A. **Birder's Guide to Texas** (1989) Gulf Publishing Co.

Lowery, G. H., Jr. **The Mammals of Louisiana and its Adjacent Waters** (1974) LSU Press, Baton Rouge.

Matthews, W. H., III **Texas Fossils: An Amateur Collector's Handbook** (1960) Bureau of Economic Geology, Univ. of Texas, Austin.

McAlister, Wayne H. and Martha K. **Guidebook to the Aransas National Wildlife Refuge** (1987) Mince Country Press, Victoria

Mueller-Wille, Christopher (ed.) **The Roads of Texas** (1988) Shearer Publishing

Oberholser, et al **Birds of Texas** (1974) Two volumes, University of Texas Press, Austin.

Peterson, R. T. **A Field Guide to the Birds of Texas** (1960) Houghton Mifflin, Boston.

Peterson, R. T. and Chalif, E. L. **A Field Guide to Mexican Birds** (1973) Houghton Mifflin, Boston.

Rappole, John H. and Blacklock, Gene W. **Birds of the Texas Coastal Bend** (1985) Texas A&M Press

Raun, G. G. **A Guide to Texas Snakes** (1965) Texas Memorial Museum, Austin.

Rickett, H. W. **Wild Flowers of the United States**, Volume III, Texas (1970) McGraw-Hill, New York.

Schmidly, David J. **Texas Mammals East of the Balcones Fault Zone** Photographs by J.L.Tveten (1983) Texas A&M University Press, College Station.

Simpson, B. W. **Gem Trails of Texas: A Field Guide for Collectors** (1967) Gem Trails Publishing Company, P.O. Box 828, Bowie, Texas 76230.

Texas Forest Service **Forest Trees of Texas: How to Know Them** (1963) Texas Forest Service, College Station.

Tveten, J. L. **Coastal Texas: Water, Land, and Wildlife** (1982) Texas A&M University Press, College Station.

Vines, R.A. **Trees, Shrubs, and Woody Vines of the Southwest** (1960) University of Texas Press, Austin.

THE GREAT TEXAS COASTAL BIRDING TRAIL

(Comments for the second printing of the fourth edition of this guide)

When Jim Lane (1926-1987) wrote the first edition of *A Birder's Guide to the Texas Coast* it was back in 1973. The original book, 108 pages long, was loaded with the kind of information that makes birders want to pack their binoculars and run off into the field. Jim probably couldn't have imagined the many changes that have taken place along the Texas Coast since that time, both good and bad.

Among the very best things to happen to Texas birding has been the recent development of the **Great Texas Coastal Birding Trail**. The brainchild of Ted Eubanks in tandem with folks at the Texas Parks and Wildlife Department (TPWD) Nongame and Urban Program, and sponsored by the Texas Department of Transportation's (TX DOT) local highway districts with funds from the Statewide Transportation Enhancement Program, this Trail could revolutionize birding in Texas and elsewhere.

The Trail was unveiled in September 1995, when officials dedicated its Central section. Bird author, photographer, and artist, the late Roger Tory Peterson declared at the Connie Hagar Cottage Sanctuary in Rockport, that the Great Coastal Birding Trail would be "a model for other states." In fact, Texas has now become the first state in the nation to promote an organized, multi-site birding trail, and to market it to a small army of traveling birders.

In 1993, Ted Eubanks and Madge Lindsay, trail coordinator for Texas Parks and Wildlife, began to chart the possibilities. Linking farm-to-market roads and state and U.S. highways, from birding site to birding site, the Trail began to take form. With state support, federal money, and the backing of hundreds of people from public and private groups alike, the Trail came together so that the beginnings were announced for the Central section in 1995.

This Trail, when completed, will consist of numbered and signed birding sites nominated by coastal communities. Its design runs the length of the coast from Beaumont to Brownsville (the same as this book), and, when finished, may feature over 200 sites along that 500-mile route. Here is a creative use of federal highway dollars to enhance bird habitat, avitourism, and the promotion of birding. The Trail is funded mainly with federal highway dollars (Intermodal Surface Transportation Efficiency Act—ISTEA). The source of the funding is 80% federal and 20% local.

The entire Trail parallels the Texas coast, with several loops extending into the interior. These loops lead through nearby birding sites that contain a variety of habitats and different species that might not otherwise be found along the immediate coast. Nowhere along the Trail, however, is a site more that a half-hour from the next site.

Coastal communities are excited about the Trail because they are learning that birders coming to the Texas Coast spend millions of dollars on food, lodging, and amenities. What's more, as the state found out, birders spend *more* money and impact the communities *less* than almost any other tourists. Birders do not require large capital "improvements" to lure them in. All they basically want is birds and access to see them! Local communities in Texas are beginning to understand that keeping plenty of good habitat available is ultimately good for business.

The birds—especially Texas specialties such as Least Grebe, Masked Duck, White-tailed Hawk, Whooping Crane, Buff-bellied Hummingbird, Great Kiskadee, Couch's Kingbird, Green Jay, Olive Sparrow, and Altamira Oriole—give the Trail its allure. The individually marked sites make these same birds accessible. The sites are to be marked with distinctive signs, each with a Black Skimmer logo. Each site will also be clearly designated and described on the official Trail map.

The Trail will develop in three sections, each with dozens of individual sites. The three sections, with some characteristic sites for each, are as follows:

Upper Texas Coast

Big Thicket National Preserve
Taylor Bayou
Sabine Woods
Sea Rim State Park
High Island
Anahuac National Wildlife Refuge
Sheldon Wildlife Management Area
Rollover Pass
Bolivar Flats
Galveston Island State Park
Brazoria National Wildlife Refuge

Central Texas Coast

Big Boggy National Wildlife Refuge
Lake Texana State Park
Bennett Park
Port Lavaca Bird Sanctuary
Port O'Conner/Matagorda Island
Aransas National Wildlife Refuge
Fennessey Ranch
Welder Park
Goose Island State Park
Connie Hagar Bird Sanctuary
Port Aransas Jetty
Packery Channel
Padre Island National Seashore
Hans Suter Park
Santa Gertrudis Creek

Lower Texas Coast

Sarita/Falfurrias Roadside Parks
Port Mansfield
Laguna Atascosa National Wildlife Refuge
Boca Chica/South Bay
Sabal Palm Grove Sanctuary
Santa Ana National Wildlife Refuge
Bentsen-Rio Grande Valley State Park
Kiskadee Wildlife Management Area

Best of all, free materials will be made available to help the birder follow the Trail. You can get a newsletter, accommodations guide, discount promotions, and maps from the Great Texas Coastal Birding Trail, c/o Texas Parks and Wildlife Department, Nongame and Urban Program, 4200 Smith School Road, Austin, TX 78744. When the Trail is finished there will probably be a detailed Trail Guide. (The Trail Guide and some other materials will have a modest cost. The proceeds from these materials will go toward maintaining the Trail and will help sustain coastal bird conservation.)

When the next edition of this birdfinding guide is prepared, I hope its text will be fully integrated with the sites and attractions around the Great Texas Coastal Birding Trail. This will make the wonders of Texas Coast birding accessible to even more appreciative birders.

April 1997

OTHER ABA BIRDFINDING GUIDES

These books specialize in accurate, detailed instructions for finding birds in North America's most productive locations. For a current listing of ABA and *ABA/Lane Birdfinding Guides* and their prices, contact American Birding Association Sales.

Phone

800/634-7736
or **719/578-0607**

Fax

800/590-2473
or **719/578-9705**

e-mail

abasales@abasales.com

ABA Sales, the largest birding supply business of its kind in North America, also carries a full line of optics, books, checklists, and other birding supplies and equipment. Call for a free 96-page catalog.

A BIRDER'S GUIDE TO VIRGINIA
David W. Johnston
April 1997

A BIRDER'S GUIDE TO COLORADO
Harold R. Holt
February 1997

A BIRDER'S GUIDE TO FLORIDA
Bill Pranty
May 1996

A BIRDER'S GUIDE TO
NEW HAMPSHIRE
Alan Delorey
January 1996

BIRDFINDER: A BIRDER'S GUIDE TO
PLANNING NORTH AMERICAN TRIPS
Jerry A. Cooper
November 1995

A BIRDER'S GUIDE TO
SOUTHEASTERN ARIZONA
Rick Taylor
August 1995

A BIRDER'S GUIDE TO ARKANSAS
Mel White
May 1995

A BIRDER'S GUIDE TO
EASTERN MASSACHUSETTS
Bird Observer
August 1994

A BIRDER'S GUIDE TO CHURCHILL
Bonnie Chartier
January 1994

A BIRDER'S GUIDE TO WYOMING
Oliver K. Scott
February 1993

A BIRDER'S GUIDE TO
THE RIO GRANDE VALLEY OF TEXAS
Harold R. Holt
January 1992

A BIRDER'S GUIDE TO
SOUTHERN CALIFORNIA
Harold R. Holt
December 1990

TEXAS ORNITHOLOGICAL SOCIETY
Texas Bird Records Committee
Report Form

This form is intended as a convenience in reporting observations of rare or unusual birds. It may be used flexibly and need not be used at all except as a guideline. Attach additional sheets as necessary. PLEASE PRINT IN BLACK INK OR TYPE. Attach original field notes, drawings, photos, etc., if possible. When complete, mail to: Greg W. Lasley, Secretary, Texas Bird Records Committee, 305 Loganberry Court, Austin, Texas 78745-6527. Thank you!

1. Common and scientific name: _____

2. Number of individuals, sexes, ages, general plumage (e.g., 2 adults in breeding plumage):

    _____

3. Location: _____ County, Texas; specifically:

    _____

4. Date and time observed: _____

5. Reporting observer and address: _____

    _____

    _____

6. Other observers: _____

7. Light conditions: _____

8. Optical equipment: _____

9. Distance to bird: _____

10. Duration of observation: _____

11. Habitat (be specific): _____

    _____

12. Description: (Include only what was actually seen, not what "should" have been seen. Include, if possible, size and shape of the bird, the bill, the eye color, other characters. Include plumage patterns and colors. Try to describe voice, behavior, or anything else that might help to confirm the identification.) _____

    _____

    _____

(Description, continued) _____

_____

_____

_____

_____

_____

_____

_____

_____

_____

13. How were similar species eliminated? _____

_____

_____

14. Was it photographed? By whom? Attached? _____

_____

15. Previous experience with this and similar species: _____

_____

16. List any books or references used in identification:

    a. at time of observation_____

    b. after observation _____

17. This description was written from:_____ notes made during observation;

    _____ notes made after observation; _____ memory.

18. Are you positive of your identification?_____If not, explain: _____

_____

19. Signature of reporter along with date and time of writing this account:

_____

(please attach additional sheets if necessary)

American Birding Association

ABA is the organization of North American birders, and its mission is to bring all the excitement, challenge, and wonder of birds and birding to you. As an ABA member you will get the information which you need to increase your birding skills so that you can make the most of your time in the field.

ABA supports the interests of birders of all ages and experiences. The organization promotes birding publications, projects, and partnerships. It focuses on bird identification and birdfinding skills and the development and dissemination of information on bird conservation. ABA also champions ethical birding practices.

Each year members receive six issues of ABAs award-winning magazine **Birding** and twelve issues of **Winging It**, a big monthly newsletter. ABA conducts regular conferences and biennial conventions in the continents best birding locations, publishes a yearly **Membership Directory/Yellow Pages** to help you keep in touch, offers discount prices for many of the bird books, optical gear, and other birding equipment through ABA Sales, and compiles an annual **Directory of Volunteer Opportunities** for birders. The organization's **ABA/Lane Birdfinding Guide Series** sets the standard for accuracy and excellence in its field.

ABA is engaged in bird conservation through such institutions and activities as Partners in Flight and the American Bird Conservancy. ABA also actively promotes the economic and environmental values of birding.

ABA encourages birding among young people through sponsoring birding camps and other activities, and publishes **A Birds-Eye View**, a newsletter by and for its younger members.

In short, the American Birding Association works to insure that birds and birding have the healthy future that they deserve. In the words of the late, great Roger Tory Peterson, ABA is the best value in the birding community today.

The American Birding Association gives active birders what they want. Consider joining today! You will find a membership form on the other side of this page.

American Birding Association
PO Box 6599
Colorado Springs, Colorado 80934-6599

ABA Membership Services
telephone 800/850-2473
fax 719/578-1480
e-mail: member@aba.org

AMERICAN BIRDING ASSOCIATION
Membership Application

All memberships include six issues of **Birding** magazine, monthly issues of **Winging It** newsletter, member discounts offered by ABA Sales, and full rights of participation in all ABA activities.

Membership classes and dues

❏ Individual - US $40 / yr   ❏ Family - US $47 / yr

❏ Individual - Canada $50 / yr*   ❏ Family - Canada $58 / yr*

❏ Individual - Int'l $50 / yr   ❏ Family - Int'l $58 / yr

❏ Century Club $140 / yr, US   ❏ Student newsletter $6 / yr
                     $150/yr, Canada
                     & international

All membership dues include $30 for *Birding* magazine and $10 for *Winging It* newsletter   * includes GST

Application Type

❏ New Membership   ❏ Renewal

Name _____

Address _____

_____

_____

Phone _____

Payment Information

❏ Check or Money Order enclosed (US funds only)

❏ Charge to VISA / MasterCard (circle one)

Account Number _____

Exp Date _____

Signature _____

Sent this completed form with payment to: **ABA Membership**
                                           PO Box 6599
                                         Colorado Springs, CO 80934

TC 2/99

INDEX

H